T0301575

A Research Agenda for Trust

Elgar Research Agendas outline the future of research in a given area. Leading scholars are given the space to explore their subject in provocative ways, and map out the potential directions of travel. They are relevant but also visionary. Forward-looking and innovative, Elgar Research Agendas are an essential resource for PhD students, scholars and anybody who wants to be at the forefront of research.

For a full list of Edward Elgar published titles, including the titles in this series, visit our website at www.e-elgar.com.

A Research Agenda for Trust

Interdisciplinary Perspectives

Edited by

ROGER C. MAYER

Professor of Leadership, Department of Management, Innovation, and Entrepreneurship, Poole College of Management, North Carolina State University, USA

BARBARA M. MAYER

Development Consultant, USA

Elgar Research Agendas

Edward Elgar
PUBLISHING

Cheltenham, UK • Northampton, MA, USA

Published by
Edward Elgar Publishing Limited
The Lypiatts
15 Lansdown Road
Cheltenham
Glos GL50 2JA
UK

Edward Elgar Publishing, Inc.
William Pratt House
9 Dewey Court
Northampton
Massachusetts 01060
USA

A catalogue record for this book
is available from the British Library

Library of Congress Control Number: 2023948504

This book is available electronically in the **Elgar**online
Business subject collection
http://dx.doi.org/10.4337/9781802200942

ISBN 978 1 80220 093 5 (cased)
ISBN 978 1 80220 094 2 (eBook)

Printed and bound in Great Britain by
TJ Books Limited, Padstow, Cornwall

This book is for Kian, Sydney, and Freya, whose trust is tangible and invaluable to the two of us. We leave in your hands to build a more trustworthy world than you found.

Contents

Figures

About the editors

Dr. Roger C. Mayer is a Professor of Leadership in the department of Management, Innovation & Entrepreneurship at the Poole College of Management, NC State University. He received a Ph.D. from the Krannert School of Management at Purdue University. A leading scholar on trust in organizations, his research has been published in many premiere scholarly journals. He serves on the editorial boards of *Journal of Management*, *Journal of Managerial Psychology*, and *Journal of Trust Research*.

Barbara M. Mayer is the Development Director for St. Emma's Monastery in Greensburg, PA. She received an MSHR from the Krannert School of Management at Purdue University, and after several years as a compensation manager, she shifted to focus on in-home management of four little human resources. Currently she is a self-employed consultant and an ad hoc caretaker for her and Roger's three grandchildren in WA and OH. Her experience with the topic of trust spans over 30 years as she has been a sounding board and editor for many trust papers written by Roger.

Contributors

Dr. Philip Bobko (B.S., MIT; M.S., Bucknell; Ph.D., Cornell) is Professor Emeritus at Gettysburg College. His research interests include personnel selection, test fairness and validation, regression analysis, suspicion, and trust in automation. He has been Scientific Advisor or Principal Scientist on several government contracts and is currently chair of the US Space Force's Talent Management Advisory Group. He served as Consulting Editor for the *Academy of Management Journal* and Editor of the *Journal of Applied Psychology*.

William A. Boettcher III is an Associate Professor of Political Science at North Carolina State University. His research focuses on nuclear nonproliferation and safeguards, foreign policy decision-making, sensemaking in intelligence, and wartime public opinion. He has published multiple articles in the *Journal of Conflict Resolution*, *Journal of Applied Social Psychology*, *Political Psychology*, and *Energy Research & Social Science*, and is the author of *Presidential Risk Behavior in Foreign Policy: Prudence or Peril*.

Dr. Gene A. Brewer is a Professor of Psychology at Arizona State University who studies how people coordinate their memory and attention in service of goal-pursuit.

Rainer Bromme is a Senior Professor at the Department of Psychology, University of Münster. His research addresses the public's trust in science, science communication, learning in formal and informal learning contexts, and the communication among experts and laypersons. His most recent research is about trust in science in the context of the COVID-19 pandemic.

Xavier Celaya is a Ph.D. student at Arizona State University whose research looks at how acute and chronic drug use affects cognition, specifically memory and attention.

Jasmine Cervantes received her B.Sc. in Psychology at Arizona State University where she studied the interplay between trust and Catholicism. After graduating, she developed a love for social services after working with people battling addiction and mental illness. Jasmine followed her newfound passion and is currently pursuing her Master's in social work to advocate for disadvantaged populations and promote socioeconomic change through policy and direct practice.

Adam B. Cohen is a Professor of Psychology at Arizona State University. As a social and cultural psychologist, he is interested in religion, morality, virtues, flourishing, and trust. His research has been honored with awards from the American Psychological Association and the International Association for the Psychology of Religion. His research has been funded by the National Science Foundation, the Templeton Foundation, the Air Force Office of Scientific Research, and the Army Research Institute.

Karen S. Cook is the Ray Lyman Wilbur Professor of Sociology at the Department of Sociology, Stanford University, the founding Director of the Institute for Research in the Social Sciences (IRiSS) at Stanford, and a trustee of the Russell Sage Foundation. She was elected to the American Academy of Arts and Sciences in 1996, to the National Academy of Sciences in 2007, and a fellow of the American Philosophical Society in 2018. Professor Cook has a long-standing interest in social exchange, social networks, social justice, and trust in social relations.

Arvin Damodaran is a physician and clinical teacher based in Sydney, Australia. He is a consultant rheumatologist at Prince of Wales Hospital, Randwick and is the Director of Teaching for the School of Clinical Medicine, Faculty of Medicine and Health, UNSW Sydney. His areas of research include medical education, particularly workplace-based learning and assessment, and in musculoskeletal medicine.

James H. Davis is the Buehler Endowed Professor of Management, Chairman of the Marketing and Strategy Department, and Executive Board Member of the Stephan R. Covey Leadership Center in the Huntsman School of Business at Utah State University. He was the John F. O'Shaughnessy Professor of Family Enterprises and Professor of Strategic Management in the Mendoza College of Business at the University of Notre Dame for over 25 years. His research focuses upon strategy, stewardship, corporate governance, trust, and family business.

Lucca Eloy is a Ph.D. candidate in Computer Science at the University of Colorado Boulder, where he studies the social, cognitive, and affective processes involved in human–agent teaming. He specializes in applying nonlinear methods to functional near-infrared spectroscopy (fNIRS) sensor data to obtain real-time measurements of user trust, cognitive load, and affect in naturalistic task settings. His research efforts focus on using interpersonal and team-level measures to build trust-sensitive adaptive systems that improve the quality of human–agent teaming.

Nicole Gillespie is the KPMG Chair in Organizational Trust and Professor of Management at the University of Queensland Business School, and an International Research Fellow at the Centre for Corporate Reputation, Oxford University. Trained as an organizational psychologist, Nicole's research focuses on trust development and repair in organizational contexts, and in contexts where trust is challenged (e.g., after a trust failure, in complex stakeholder environments, during organizational transformation and digital disruption, in emerging technologies and virtual healthcare, in cross-cultural relations).

Friederike Hendriks is Leader of the Junior Research Group *Communicating Scientists: Challenges, Competencies, Contexts (fourC)*, at Technische Universität Braunschweig, Germany. Her research interests include people's perceptions of science communication, especially their trust in science and scientists, as well as studying and training researchers who engage in science communication.

Leanne Hirshfield is an Associate Research Professor in the Institute of Cognitive Science at the University of Colorado, Boulder. She directs the System Human Interaction with NIRS and EEG (SHINE) Lab at the University of Colorado, and is on the leadership team for the NSF funded Institute on Student AI Teaming (iSAT). Hirshfield's research explores the use of non-invasive brain measurement to passively classify users' social, cognitive, and affective states in order to enhance usability testing and adaptive system design.

Sarah A. Jessup is a Consortium Doctoral Research Fellow in the Collaborative Teaming Section within the 711th Human Performance Wing at Wright-Patterson AFB, Ohio. She earned a B.Sc. in Psychology and M.Sc. in Human Factors and Industrial/Organizational Psychology from Wright State University in 2015 and 2018, respectively. She is currently pursuing a Ph.D. in Human Factors and Industrial/Organizational Psychology at the same university. Her research interests include human–robot interaction, social robots, attitudes towards technology, trust, individual differences, emotions, and psychophysiology.

Frank Krueger is a Full Professor of Systems Social Neuroscience at the School of Systems Biology at George Mason University, VA, USA. After receiving a Master's degree in Psychology and Physics, he obtained a Ph.D. in Cognitive Psychology from Humboldt University Berlin in Germany. By combining paradigms from social psychology and experimental economics with methods from social and computational neuroscience, Frank leads the Social Cognition and Functional Imaging (SCI:FI) lab aiming at studying the underlying psychoneurobiological signatures of human–human and human–machine trust.

Dr. Steve Lockey is a Postdoctoral Research Fellow at The University of Queensland. His primary research focus is on the development, and repair, of trust in organizational contexts. He also examines attitudes and expectations about the use of emerging technology in the workplace and in society. Steve has published in journals such as *Business Ethics Quarterly, Computer in Human Behavior, AI & Ethics,* and *The International Journal of Medical Informatics.* His work has been cited by the UK and Australian governments.

Chris P. Long is the Paul Naughton Associate Professor of Management at the Peter J. Tobin College of Business, St. John's University in New York City. He researches how leaders balance their efforts to apply controls, demonstrate trustworthiness, and promote fairness as well as how these actions jointly and independently influence the cognitions, emotions, and behaviors of other stakeholders. He holds a Ph.D. in Management from Duke University.

Joseph B. Lyons is a Principal Research Psychologist within the 711th Human Performance Wing at Wright-Patterson AFB, OH. Dr. Lyons received his Ph.D. in Industrial/Organizational Psychology from Wright State University in Dayton, OH, in 2005. Some of Dr. Lyons' research interests include human–machine trust, interpersonal trust, human factors, and influence. Dr. Lyons is an AFRL Fellow, a Fellow of the American Psychological Association, and a Fellow of the Society for Military Psychologists.

Jordan W. Moon is a Research Fellow at the Institute for Advanced Study in Toulouse, France. Before moving to France, he received his Ph.D. in Social Psychology from Arizona State University. His work on religion, morality, and social perception has been published in leading psychology and interdisciplinary journals, and his work is currently funded by the Templeton World Charity Foundation, Inc.

Scott M. Mourtgos is a Ph.D. candidate in the Department of Political Science at the University of Utah. He is a National Institute of Justice LEADS Scholar and studies policing and criminal justice policy.

Dr. Holly P. O'Rourke is an Assistant Professor of Quantitative Methodology at the T. Denny Sanford School of Social and Family Dynamics, as well as a Core Scientist with the Human Behavior Decision Making initiative, at Arizona State University. Her work focuses on the statistical underpinnings and applications of quantitative methods in the social sciences. She is an expert in statistical models for examining change over time, specifically the methodological areas of mediation analysis and longitudinal structural equation modeling.

Dr. Margarida Pitaes is a Mental Health Therapist at a dual-diagnoses treatment center. She works directly with patients who struggle with addiction and mental health problems. Dr. Pitaes' research interests revolve around understanding how early experiences in life affect how people make trustworthiness judgments.

Martin Reimann is an Associate Professor of Marketing at the Eller College of Management at the University of Arizona, with appointments as associate professor in the Department of Psychology, the College of Veterinary Medicine, and the Cognitive Science Graduate Interdisciplinary Program. His research investigates how people form, maintain, and dissolve social relations with other humans, products, and pets. His work has been honored by several awards, including the Society for Consumer Research's Young Contributor Award and the International Social Cognition Network's Best Paper of the Year Award.

Matthias Scheutz received a Ph.D. degree in Philosophy from the University of Vienna and a joint Ph.D. in Cognitive Science and Computer Science from Indiana University. He is the Karol Family Applied Technology Professor of Computer and Cognitive Science in the Department of Computer Science at Tufts University in the School of Engineering, and Director of the Human–Robot Interaction (HRI) Laboratory and the HRI Masters and Ph.D. programs. He has over 400 peer-reviewed publications in artificial intelligence, artificial life, agent-based computing, natural language understanding, cognitive modeling, robotics, human–robot interaction, and foundations of cognitive science. His current research focuses on complex ethical cognitive robots with natural language interaction, problem-solving, and instruction-based learning capabilities in open worlds.

Oliver Schilke is an Associate Professor of Management and Organizations at the University of Arizona, where he also has a courtesy appointment with the School of Sociology and serves as the Director of the Center for Trust Studies. His research interests include collaboration, trust, organizational routines/capabilities, and micro-institutional processes. He received a CAREER Award from the National Science Foundation and an Emerging Scholar Award from the Strategic Management Society, among other recognitions.

Boaz Shulruf (Ph.D., MPH) is Professor in Medical Education at the University of New South Wales, Sydney, Australia. His main research interest is in the areas of psycho-educational assessment and measurement in education, particularly within the context of Medical and Health Sciences Education.

Munindar P. Singh is a Professor in Computer Science at NC State University. His interests include sociotechnical systems and the uses of AI in society. Munindar is a Fellow of AAAI (Association for the Advancement of Artificial Intelligence), AAAS (American Association for the Advancement of Science), ACM (Association for Computing Machinery), and IEEE, and foreign member (*honoris causa*) of Academia Europaea. His recognitions include the ACM SIGAI Autonomous Agents Research Award. He has graduated 30 Ph.D. and 40 M.Sc students.

Sim B. Sitkin is Michael W. Krzyzewski University Distinguished Professor of Leadership and Professor of Management and Public Policy at Duke University and a Fellow of the Academy of Management, Society for Organizational Behavior, Society for Organizational Learning, and International Network for Trust Research. He studies the effects of leadership and organizational control on trust, risk-taking, experimentation, learning, and innovation. His most recent books are *Organizational Control, The Six Domains of Leadership,* and *The Routledge Companion to Trust.*

Alexis Torres is a Ph.D. student at Arizona State University who studies behavioral and psychophysiological factors that contribute to individual differences in sustained attention.

Sydney Tran is a social Psychology Ph.D. student at the University of California, Los Angeles. Her research interests revolve around studying religious and racial identities and ameliorating conflict in real-world instances such as the workforce, politics, and education. Her work has been published in interdisciplinary social science journals.

Alan R. Wagner is an Associate Professor of Aerospace Engineering and a Senior Research Associate with the Rock Ethics Institute at The Pennsylvania State University. His research interests include human–robot trust, developing evacuation robots, and machine ethics. He received his Ph.D. in Computer Science from Georgia Institute of Technology. He also holds a Master's degree in Computer Science from Boston University and a bachelor's degree in Psychology from Northwestern University.

Dr. Kimberly M. Wingert is currently a Research Associate at the Portland office of RMC Research Corporation. She received her Ph.D. in Cognitive Science from Arizona State University, where she studied emotion (including motivation), memory, attention, and intelligence. Dr. Wingert completed her first postdoctoral position at the University of Southern California examining the impact of delivering an intervention with fidelity on student outcomes. Her second postdoctoral position was a fellowship with the Consortium of Universities of the Washington Metropolitan Area.

Richard A. Wise is an Associate Professor of Psychology at the University of North Dakota. He practiced law for many years including in the Legal and Regulatory Department of the American Psychological Association, as an associate in a law firm, as an assistant county prosecutor, and an attorney-law clerk to an appellate judge. He has a Ph.D. in Clinical Psychology, completed a postdoctoral fellowship in forensic psychology, and is a licensed psychologist. His primary research area is psychology and law.

Alexandra S. Wormley is a Ph.D. student at Arizona State University studying the relationships between ecology, culture, and belief systems. Her work has been published in *Perspectives on Psychological Science* and *Current Research in Ecological and Social Psychology*. She is also a recipient of the National Science Foundation's Graduate Student Fellowship and an adjunct professor at Glendale Community College.

Yan Wu is Full Professor of Decision Neuroscience at the Department of Psychology of the Hangzhou Normal University (HZNU). After studying Psychology and Neuroscience, she obtained a Ph.D. in Learning Science at Southeast University in 2010 and has been working at HZNU since then. In her research, Yan investigates how people make social decisions with the aim to reveal the brain mechanisms by which social decision-making operates and to explain social behavior across many diverse contexts.

Acknowledgments

We wish to thank Dr. Cecily Cooper and Dr. Ed Tomlinson for supporting our efforts as independent reviewers. We also wish to thank these organizations for encouraging and supporting interdisciplinary academic research, without which this book would not have been written: the Laboratory for Analytic Sciences (LAS) at NC State University; the Trust & Influence Program of the Air Force Office of Scientific Research (AFOSR); the Research Training Group—Trust and Communication in a Digitized World, at the University of Münster in Germany. Their commitment to bringing together diverse approaches to science was invaluable—both to our thinking, and to this book.

1 Towards interdisciplinary scholarship in trust: the *needs*, some *leads*, and a *seed*

Roger C. Mayer and Barbara M. Mayer

The big context of this book: our changing world

Roger's grandfather Clyde J. Mayer lived 1894–1990. Our lives thankfully overlapped by decades, as he was still working full-time into his nineties; both editors knew him well. Our generation of family members learned much from his wisdom, including gaining a perspective on change from him. Consider his experience: he could recall life before running water and toilets were common in U.S. homes, radio and telephone did not exist, nor did electricity in homes, let alone television, telecommunications, heavier than air flight, humans on the moon, the space shuttle. Readers are encouraged to pause a moment and reflect on this: after *millennia* of gazing at the moon in wonder, in Clyde's lifetime humans went from not having heavier than air flight (they had balloons) to walking on the moon. The world's technology is increasing at a growing pace, providing the ability to solve complex problems much faster (e.g., a COVID-19 vaccine was produced within one year of its initial detection).

Unfortunately, complex problems themselves seem to be proliferating at an increasing rate as well. The editors of this book were born into a world of about three billion people—almost twice that of when Clyde was born. While growth has slowed, the current population estimate is nearly eight billion. Global warming is top of mind to many, yet a global study by Pew Research (2019a) found that nearly a third of those surveyed worldwide did not think it was more than a minor threat to their country. In the U.S.A., Pew Research Center (2019b) also found that two-thirds of adults believe the federal government is doing too little to deal with climate change—meaning one-third believe it is doing enough or too much. Recent years have seen at least two countries threaten global stability via development of their nuclear weapons programs, and the struggle to prevent their proliferation. We suggest that such issues are both complex and serious for us all. Solutions for such complex problems are often beyond the reach of any single field of study's capability to fully understand—let alone to solve.

Key to repairing any problem is understanding it. Bromme and Hendriks' chapter (4) considers why so many people do not trust scientific evidence regarding such issues as global warming or the effect that humans can have on slowing it. Trust in science is critical to building consensus to combat this and many other problems, like eradicating the spread of deadly diseases such as COVID-19. Boettcher's chapter (11) explains where we are with nuclear proliferation, and the history of how we arrived at this point. These represent just two of the potentially most devastating trust-related situations worldwide: the possibility that in the reader's lifetime the world's weather will increasingly devastate the planet and humankind's ability to sustain itself, or that a single leader could trigger a nuclear holocaust that changes life as we know it within a matter of minutes. Such thoughts range from depressing to shocking.

Such problems have given rise to many calls by universities and those in the "real" world that researchers should work in interdisciplinary teams towards solving "grand challenges" of the world's population (Weiss & Khademian, 2019). For many new and even established researchers this may sound intriguing in the abstract, but for many it also seems almost unapproachable or even intimidating. A specific field of study shares terminology, often methodology, and often a shared mindset about what a problem is and what its important dimensions are. This is often not the case when looking across disciplines.

Purpose of this book

It seems to be a common theme that many research universities are asking faculty to tackle what some call Grand Challenges, or big problems that affect society in some major way or ways (Weiss & Khademian, 2019). Many of these problems are complex, and do not fit neatly into the disciplinary silos that have traditionally existed within most universities. As such, making progress towards solving them requires teams of researchers with skill sets and backgrounds that may have little overlap with one another, who often do not share common language, research methodologies, or goals.

This book is intended to help provide a remedy for this impediment, and to encourage more such grassroots facilitation of interdisciplinary research in other critical topics. When not necessarily looking, we found trust researchers in fields where we did not expect to find them. What's more, we found people who wanted to include trust in what they were studying but did not know where to start. We would be unsurprised to learn that if in search of trust researchers, those in other fields did not first look to a business school. For us, finding our way to those researchers in other fields was in no small part due to the interdisciplinary nature of several entities: the Laboratory for Analytic Sciences (LAS) at NC State University and the Trust & Influence Program at the Air Force Office of Scientific Research (AFOSR) are U.S. federally funded approaches to building interdisciplinary trust research for the purposes of supporting both basic science and defense. A third was the Research Training Group—Trust and Communication in a Digitized World at the University of Münster in Germany. There is a department with doctoral students who are all focused on conducting trust dissertations in multiple disciplines. We are very thankful to these organizations for putting us into the position to do this work. The majority of the chapters in this book came from connections we made directly or indirectly through association with these three organizations.

Most scholars do not have access to these or similar organizations. Our intention with this book is to highlight some of these diverse areas to scholars in other disciplines, with the hope of piquing interest in connecting with researchers who are more accessible to them—perhaps at their own university—who may be interested in conversations or projects in areas of mutual interdisciplinary interest. Furthermore, we hope that reading about trust research in dissimilar fields may help to encourage broader thinking on research methodology, such as the measurement of trust.

We approached scholars who we knew were doing research on trust or closely allied areas, and explained the focus of this book—90 percent of those invited agreed to contribute a chapter. We did not shy away from including chapters on controversial topics, like trust in the Catholic Church after the abuse scandal broke (Cervantes, Wormley, Moon, Tran, & Cohen, Chapter 16) or police–public trust (Wise, Mayer, Mourtgos, & O'Rourke, Chapter 12). To make this book as approachable as possible we asked that authors minimize the use of jargon, and to explain it when they did. We asked them to write at the level of an audience of college graduates (i.e., new graduate students) in fields other than their own. Each chapter had two blind reviews, generally one from a similar discipline and one from an outside discipline. We also asked that after reviewing preliminary abstracts of all the chapters, that they connect their own chapter with references to at least two others by discussing overlap or interesting interactions between topics or approaches. Other than that, we sought to empower our authors as much as possible to write what they wanted and how they wanted. Consequently, readers will find notable differences in the "feel" or "flavor" of the various chapters.

Since a number of the chapters were built on or referred to the Mayer, Davis, and Schoorman (1995) model of trust, we summarized it below to make it easier for the authors to meet their stringent manuscript length limits.

The Mayer, Davis, and Schoorman (1995) model of trust

Over 30 years ago, with colleagues Jim Davis and David Schoorman, we (i.e., both editors) became interested in why parties trust one another, launching us into a fascinating journey. Several years later we published a model of trust (Mayer, Davis, & Schoorman, 1995). There are of course a plethora of variables that could be considered within a single model of a trust relationship. Our intent was to produce a model that was as parsimonious as possible (i.e., the smallest number of boxes and arrows), while being applicable in as broad a range of situations as possible. As we were developing the model, we sought to make it applicable not only to interpersonal trust, but also to intergroup and interorganizational trust and across these levels (e.g., a person trusting an organization: Schoorman, Mayer, & Davis, 1996). We are pleased to report that it has not only found a great deal of empirical support where we originally intended the model to be applicable, but also that it has been found to be helpful in a wide variety of other fields of study. For the overall brevity of this book, below we reproduce the model in this chapter (with permission from the Academy of Management) and briefly describe its major features in order to save space for this book's authors, who each had to deal with space constraints. For a more detailed explanation, readers are referred to the original 1995 publication which both provides more in-depth explanations of the key issues and constructs, and also broaches numerous other closely related issues not discussed here (e.g., trust's relationships with cooperation, predictability, etc.).

Some of the earliest work in the organization sciences that considered trust was by Julian Rotter (1967). The focus of his interpersonal trust scale was on how much a person trusted other people in general. We termed this the *propensity to trust* (Mayer et al., 1995: 715), which we argue is a relatively stable within-trustor quality. A negative interaction with someone is likely to lead to less trust in that party, but (except in very extreme circumstances) is not likely to make the focal party less trusting of other people in general. Conversely, interactions with a single person who is found to be highly trustworthy is likely to engender internal attributions to the quality and trustworthiness of that person (Tomlinson & Mayer, 2009), but not to make the focal party more trusting of people in general.

As we read about trust in a variety of fields including management, psychology, sociology, law, philosophy, and so on, we found three characteristics, appearing by various names, to be qualities of another party that seemed to warrant thinking of that party as trustworthy: ability, benevolence, and integrity.

Ability is an assessment that the party can accomplish what is needed from them in the situation. For a supervisor to be trustworthy, this often includes such issues as knowledge of the process that needs to be completed, and influence within the organization to allow influence for the trustor (i.e., employee of the supervisor) to be recognized and promoted within the organization. The capacity to accomplish whatever the trustor deems is needed from a party in the role in question is included in the trustor's view of ability.

Benevolence captures the relationship the trustor (i.e., trusting party) perceives with the trustee (i.e., to be trusted party). Does the trustee really care about what is important to the trustor? Does the trustee want good things for the trustor? This is easiest to understand as being the trustor's perception that the trustee cares for the best interests of the trustor as an individual.

Integrity is the perception that the trustee will behave according to principles that the trustor finds acceptable. The principles may differ from the trustor's in some ways, but must align well enough to be palatable to the trustor. A judgment of high integrity involves not only a trustee espousing an acceptable set of values, but also following those values consistently. Either espousing an unacceptable set of values (e.g., "winner take all, I will crush you if I can" may well not be acceptable to the trustor) or failing to follow accepted values consistently (e.g., "we are all a team and are in this together," then behaving in a self-serving way that hurts other team members) will damage the perception of the trustee's integrity.

The perceptions of these three characteristics—sometimes referred to as ABI—comprise the trustworthiness of the party under consideration (Figure 1.1). There are times when more than one of them co-varies highly, but they have been found to be conceptually and empirically different enough across enough situations to warrant keeping them distinct (see Singh & Mayer, Chapter 8).

One's propensity to trust others as well as the perception of the trustee's trustworthiness both affect trust, which we defined as the *willingness to be vulnerable to another party who cannot be monitored or controlled.* Vulnerability

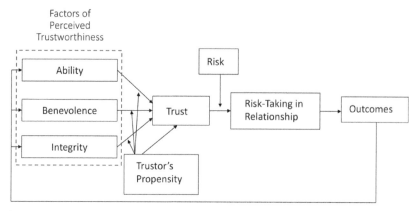

Source: The authors

Figure 1.1   Proposed model of trust

implies risk, and the potential for damage to be done to the trustor's interests if the trustee defects on the relationship or is unable to accomplish what the trustor needs done.

It is important to note that using this approach trust is a *willingness* to be vulnerable; it is *not actually taking actions that make the trustor vulnerable.* When the trustor actually takes a risk at the hands of the trustee, we refer to this as risk-taking in the relationship (RTR). One is more likely to engage in a risk-taking action if (1) they have more trust in the trustee and (2) the *risk inherent in the action* (regardless of who the trustee is) is lower.

For example, suppose that in order to seek developmental feedback, an employee was considering sharing with a supervisor a mistake the employee made. If the mistake were embarrassing, there is some risk of ridicule from peers if the information about the mistake gets out. If the mistake were major and the employee could be fired for it, then sharing it with *anyone* would involve higher risk. Damage to the employee's reputation, and perhaps employment, would be jeopardized—*regardless* of who shared the secret. If the employee had a low–moderate level of trust in the supervisor, they would likely share the embarrassing mistake but not the mistake for which they could be terminated. The trustor, trustee, and level of trust of the former in the latter are all consistent, but the difference in the perceived risk between the two possible revelations would lead the trustor to admit to the smaller mistake, but withhold sharing the latter.

Thus, in the model we separated risk from the trustworthiness of the party. We also separated risk, as well as trust itself, from the *observable behavior*, or RTR (in this case, *actually sharing the information*). This fundamentally differentiates this model from the approach of behavioral economics, which using the above language, ignores trust (willingness to be vulnerable) and treats the RTR as trust itself. Our concern with that is that there are other factors that influence whether someone engages in a given risk, such as a lack of perceived alternatives or a sense of obligation to behave in a certain way.

After a risk is taken with the trustee, there are some outcomes. Following the example above, the supervisor might help fix the employee's mistake and train the employee and their peers how to avoid making it in the future. This would be a good outcome from the employee's perspective. If the supervisor instead reported the mistake to upper management for punishment, or spread the word that the employee was incompetent, the employee would likely view this as a negative outcome of having taken the risk. In either case, at the next encounter with the supervisor, the employee would likely update their prior assessments of some combination of the supervisor's ABI. This is represented by the feedback loop on the model, which explains the evolution of the employee's trust in the supervisor over time.

Although the model was not designed to be used with inanimate objects like sensors, computers, robots, and artificial intelligence (AI), it has found its way into such areas as computer science and engineering. Some of the variables require adapting for this purpose, since such "trustees" as a computer do not really "care about" a trustor. Nevertheless, a trustor can make a decision about how willing they are to be vulnerable to a computer. The assessment of benevolence—or something like it—often still seems to be made in some fashion, even when one is evaluating how much to trust a robot (see the interplay between Singh & Mayer and Wingert & Mayer, Chapters 8 and 5, respectively, in this book).

Book structure

With so much diversity among the papers on so many dimensions, we avoided grouping the chapters thematically. Several chapters deal with trust in purely social relationships (e.g., Davis (17); Long & Sitkin (6); Schilke, Reimann, & Cook (9)), or between people and an organization (Cervantes, Wormley, Moon, Tran, & Cohen (16); Damodaran & Shulruf (15)), country, or even a system of government (e.g., Boettcher (11)). Some deal with intergroup conflicts (e.g., Wise, Mayer, Mourtgos, & O'Rourke (12)).

Some of the chapters deal with what is going on internal to a trustor during a situation requiring trust, or how to measure it (e.g., Brewer, Torres, Celeya, & Pitaes (7); Eloy, Bobko, & Hirshfield (3); Wu & Krueger (14)).

Several of the chapters deal with humans interacting with non-humans, including artificial intelligence (Lockey & Gillespie (2)), science (Bromme & Hendriks (4)), socio-technical systems that use AI (Singh & Mayer (8)), robots (Lyons, Scheutz, & Jessup (10); Wagner (13)) and autonomous machines like self-driving cars (Wingert & Mayer (5)).

While the above may be one way to group the chapters, there are multiple dimensions that cut across these. For example, one theme is identifying and being clear on the referent of trust. Cervantes et al. (Chapter 16) consider trust in the Catholic Church, and find differences depending on which referent within the church is examined. Both Singh and Mayer (Chapter 8) and Wingert and Mayer (Chapter 5) contrast with one another by either including or excluding relevant people with the technological artifacts as the referent. Clarity on the referent of trust is thus critical whether the trust relationship is purely social or some mix of social and technological entities.

As a means of promoting cross-disciplinary trust research, chapter authors were asked to link their chapter in some way(s) to a couple of other chapters. One of the hopes of this book's editors and authors is that it will intrigue someone interested in a particular chapter to look at another chapter (or more), particularly from a very different field of study. We hope that readers will take a little time to at least read the abstracts of all of the chapters—and then go where intellectual curiosity takes them.

Our hope is that the reader's thinking will go beyond the inter-chapter ties and questions to formulate other research questions. Looking forward not far into the future, we are struck by some of the simultaneous changes that are happening with both technology and the news. A few thoughts about this follow: How will perceived physical threats from other countries, or threats to the ego of a country's key decision-maker, affect brain physiology and trust? Can laboratory studies lend insight to this using the technology discussed by Eloy et al. (Chapter 3)? It is clear that robots and AI are likely to play an important role in the future of society, and both are currently in their infancy. As they each develop more, what overlap is there between understanding trust-related reactions to them and the rest of the topics of chapters in this book? How do the questions and issues discussed by Damodaran and Shulruf (Chapter 15) with respect to the healthcare system evolve when AI and robots grow more prominent in the mix of decisions and execution (e.g., diagnoses, billing, robots performing operations with decreasing human involvement)?

Conclusion

People trusting one another is difficult enough—now, as one might glean from this book, those difficulties seem to be finding new heights. Even with having a background in research in this space, it was challenging to review some of the chapters. If you find yourself likewise challenged, we encourage you to forge on because the very next one you read may be very different. Our hope is that this book will make that journey towards more interdisciplinary research a little easier and more inviting for those who follow.

We recently acknowledged that modern organizations ask many things of their employees, often without recognizing the strain it puts on them when the expectations are inconsistent or even conflicting. We coined the term organizational dissociative identity disorder (ODID: Mayer & Williams, 2021) for an employee's perception that dealing with their employer is *like dealing with a person who has "multiple personalities."* Perhaps the nature of universities allows them to easily fall prey to becoming ODID, and we empathize with any of our colleagues for whom this strikes a familiar note. To deal with this strain while considering research with multiple disciplines, we strongly encourage scholars to take the advice of a scholar who has been highly influential in our thinking as well as that of many colleagues. Per the chapter's title, we began by highlighting some *needs*, we offered some *leads*, and we conclude with this *seed*: "Do something that matters"—F. David Schoorman.

References

Mayer, R. C., Davis, J. H., & Schoorman, F. D. (1995). An integrative model of organizational trust. *Academy of Management Review*, 20, 709–34.

Mayer, R. C., & Williams, M. (2021). Trust across organizational levels: ODID you see we have a new vice-president? In Nicole Gillespie, Ashley Fulmer, & Roy Lewicki (eds.), *Multilevel Trust in Organizations*, pp. 256–76. Newcastle upon Tyne, UK: Sage.

Pew Research Center (2019a). A look at how people around the world view climate change. https:// www .pewresearch .org/ short -reads/ 2019/ 04/ 18/ a -look -at -how -people-around-the-world-view-climate-change/ (downloaded May 16, 2023).

Pew Research Center (2019b). U.S. public views on climate and energy. https://www .pewresearch .org/ science/ 2019/ 11/ 25/ u -s -public -views -on -climate -and -energy/ (downloaded May 16, 2023).

Rotter, J. B. 1967. A new scale for the measurement of interpersonal trust. *Journal of Personality*, 35, 651–665.

Schoorman, F. D., Mayer, R. C., & Davis, J. H. (1996). Organizational trust: philosophical perspectives and conceptual definitions. *Academy of Management Review*, 21, 337–40.

Tomlinson, E. C., & Mayer, R. C. (2009). The role of causal attribution dimensions in trust repair. *Academy of Management Review*, 34, 85–104.

Weiss, J. A., & Khademian, A. (2019). What universities get right—and wrong—about grand challenges. *Inside Higher Education*, September 3. https://www.insidehighered .com/ views/ 2019/ 09/ 03/ analysis -pros -and -cons -universities -grand -challenges -opinion (downloaded September 4, 2022).

2 Understanding trust in artificial intelligence: a research agenda

Steve Lockey and Nicole Gillespie

Artificial intelligence (AI) is an increasingly ubiquitous part of our everyday lives and is transforming the way people live and work, whether to navigate the most efficient travel route, optimize a website search, or connect on social media (Gillespie, Lockey & Curtis, 2021). Investment in and use of AI have increased dramatically in recent years, and its growth shows no signs of slowing (IDC, 2021). The potential benefits of AI are numerous, from helping people make better decisions to driving organizational efficiencies and supporting the fight against COVID-19. However, AI also poses unique risks and challenges, including infringement of human rights, the spread of misinformation, and the codification and exacerbation of unfair biases that disproportionally impact marginalized groups (Curtis, Gillespie & Lockey, 2023). These issues have led to questions about the trustworthiness of AI systems, and calls from policymakers to better understand how AI can be developed and deployed in a manner that promotes trust (OECD, 2019). This is in recognition that the widespread adoption and acceptance of AI, and the societal and economic benefits it can produce, will not be realized if AI systems do not prove to be trustworthy (AI HLEG, 2019).

Against this backdrop, scholarly interest in trust in AI is gaining momentum. However, we remain at an early stage of understanding the interplay between trust and AI. The aims of this chapter are to provide a high-level overview of the key limitations and empirical gaps in the literature examining trust in AI, and outline a future research agenda based on six research directions to advance a rigorous understanding of trust in AI systems.

Defining AI and trust

We adopt the OECD's definition of an AI system as "a machine-based system that can, for a given set of human-defined objectives, make predictions, recommendations, or decisions influencing real or virtual environments … AI systems are designed to operate with varying levels of autonomy" (OECD, 2019, pp. 23–4). Most notable advances in AI systems are driven by *machine learning*, which is characterized by the ability of a machine to keep improving its performance without the requirement of human input (Jordan & Mitchell, 2015). Advances in machine learning increase the functionality of AI systems, but they also create unique risks, trust challenges, and uncertainties compared to traditional technological artifacts that lack the capacity for autonomous learning (Lockey et al., 2021). For example, the opacity of machine learning algorithms makes them difficult to comprehend, and therefore more difficult to trust.

Trust is commonly defined as "the willingness of a party to be vulnerable to the actions of another party based on the expectation that the other party will perform a particular action important to the trustor, irrespective of the ability to monitor or control that other party" (Mayer, Davis & Schoorman,1995, p. 712; see also Mayer & Mayer, Chapter 1). Trust matters under conditions of risk and uncertainty, where misplaced trust results in loss or harm. Examples include relying on an autonomous vehicle to drive safely, or on the decision of an AI system to be accurate and unbiased. At the same time, there must be some expected utility to accept vulnerability to AI systems—that is, to have positive expectations that the system will be useful, reliable, and operate as intended (McKnight et al., 2011).

Trust in AI: insights, empirical gaps, and future research directions

There is a growing body of academic literature on trust in AI that spans multiple disciplines, including human factors, computer science, engineering, psychology, and management (Glikson & Woolley, 2020; Lockey et al., 2021). This fragmented literature includes investigation of the antecedents of trust, research on trustworthy AI, and the outcomes of trust in AI systems. From our review of this literature, we identify six critical empirical gaps and challenges that limit current understanding of trust in AI systems and warrant future research attention. For each research direction, we discuss high-level insights from prior research and how gaps and limitations can be addressed to advance a rigorous understanding of trust in AI.

1. Advancing a multistakeholder and multilevel approach to understanding trust in AI socio-technical systems

In a recent review of the literature, Lockey and colleagues (2021) highlighted that conceptual and empirical work on trust in AI largely relates to five key features of AI systems that pose trust challenges: (1) transparency and explainability, (2) accuracy and reliability, (3) anthropomorphism, (4) automation, and (5) mass data extraction. These features each create trust challenges that are unique to or exacerbated by AI. While the first three features can increase trust when present, and the last two features are necessary for AI development and use, they also pose risks and vulnerabilities to stakeholders that have not been adequately addressed to date. For instance, there is an entire field of study around explainable AI (XAI) in recognition that it is difficult to trust "black-box" systems, with research demonstrating that while explainability enhances trust, the provision of an explanation may lead users to trust a system even when that trust is not warranted (Weller, 2017). Equally, research suggests that anthropomorphizing an AI system can increase trust, but there is also the possibility that this can be manipulated to lead to overtrust (Culley & Madhavan, 2013). AI automation can threaten not only jobs and skills, but also the notion of human agency and control (Raisch & Krakowski, 2021), while mass data extraction raises concerns around privacy, meaningful consent, and acceptable data use and sharing (Zuboff, 2015).

While these risks and concerns have been raised conceptually, they have not yet been systematically examined empirically. Furthermore, we have limited understanding of how these risks and vulnerabilities may differ depending on the stakeholder group (e.g., the user or those affected by AI, developers, deploying organizations), and how these risks influence trust. To address this limitation, we call for research that examines how stakeholders experience the risks and vulnerabilities related to AI systems, and how this informs their trust in these systems. Such an understanding is foundational to understanding effective AI risk mitigation and how AI systems can be designed to be "worthy" of trust.

Relatedly, we call for future research that advances a multistakeholder understanding of trust in AI systems. To date, the empirical literature on trust in AI largely focuses on a single AI stakeholder or does not specify the stakeholder role of research subjects (Lockey et al., 2021). This may be because the literature primarily comprises experimental studies focused on understanding how specific characteristics of AI systems influence user trust. Experimental research enables the examination of causal relationships, but people often act differently in laboratory settings compared to naturalistic situations (Wagner, Chapter 13), where risks and vulnerabilities relative to the object of trust are contextual and dependent on stakeholder roles.

Due in part to the dependence on experiments and focus on micro-level trust cues (e.g., those arising from the AI system), research into how macro-level trust cues (e.g., those arising from the environment in which the AI operates) impact stakeholder trust remains underdeveloped (van der Werff, Blomqvist & Koskinen, 2021). To address this shortcoming, we recommend future work exploring trust in AI adopts a multilevel perspective that complements micro-level examination with a macro *institutional trust* lens. Institutional trust theory and research shows how trust in an object or party can be based on cues emanating from the broader environment, including contracts, regulations, guarantees, recommendations of third parties, and stable institutions and structures (e.g., Bachmann & Inkpen, 2011; Zucker, 1986). It has been argued that institutional trust may crowd out and substitute the need for an individual to trust specific others, because institutional assurances reduce uncertainty, making trust in specific others less relevant (Yamagishi & Yamagishi, 1994). However, considerable research shows that institutional trust can complement and promote trust by increasing feelings of security and expectation of trustworthy conduct, which in turn allows people to *accept* vulnerability and trust others (for a review, see Long & Sitkin, 2018; see also Spadaro et al., 2020; Weibel et al., 2016).

Recent research indicates that structural assurance, an operationalization of institutional trust based on the perceptions of the structures and safeguards surrounding a trust object, can positively influence trust in AI-enabled systems such as ridesharing platforms (Shao et al., 2020), and service robots (Park, 2020). However, this research is nascent, and further empirical work is required to determine if and how specific structural assurance mechanisms influence trust in AI systems, and how this may differ across stakeholder groups. The mapping of AI stakeholder vulnerabilities by Lockey and colleagues (2021) suggests that factors that enhance the trust of certain stakeholder groups may potentially challenge or undermine the trust of other stakeholder groups. For example, having privacy and data regulation laws in place may mitigate risks associated with AI use and assuage the concerns of users and regulators, while simultaneously augmenting trust-related challenges and risks for developers and the stakeholders responsible for governing data privacy and appropriate data use. This is a rich unchartered terrain for future research.

Trust in organizations and institutional systems can also transfer trust to a specific trust object (Stewart, 2003), with research indicating that trust in the technology provider is as important as trust in the technology itself when it comes to intention to use a technological system (Söllner, Hoffmann & Leimeister, 2016). This highlights the importance of researching trust and adoption of AI within holistic, naturalistic settings. Wingert and Mayer (Chapter 5) further explore the question of whether the relevant referent in trusting a technological artifact is the technology itself or the maker of the technology. Taken together, future research should examine trust in multiple referents, including the AI system itself, the developer(s) of the system, and other actors involved in making the system function. Another important line of future research is to examine how various types of stakeholders' experience trust cues and vulnerabilities in these different referents.

2.   Understanding "optimal" trust in AI systems

A dominant assumption in the literature on trust in AI is that increasing trust is a desirable end state. However, trust opens up vulnerability and potential for exploitation, and trusting is not always appropriate or beneficial to stakeholders—particularly if "trust" occurs without good reason (Lewis & Weigert, 1985). Indeed, a growing body of research indicates that certain AI system characteristics, such as explainability and anthropomorphism, tend to engender trust in users (de Visser et al., 2016; Glikson & Woolley, 2020; Lockey et al., 2021), yet these characteristics do not necessarily indicate that an AI system is *trustworthy*. Equally, there are times when people do not trust AI systems as much as reason would suggest they should (e.g., algorithm aversion, Dietvorst, Simmons & Massey, 2015). These problems result in *overtrust*, trusting an AI system more than is warranted by its capabilities, which can lead to complacency and misuse, and *undertrust*, causing inefficiencies, unrealized benefits, and ultimately, disuse (de Visser et al., 2020). While there is a large body of evidence from various disciplines to suggest that inappropriate or insufficient trust can have negative consequences, what enables and motivates stakeholders to appropriately calibrate trust in AI systems is not well understood and is an important avenue for future research.

Relatedly, it is important to explore whether there are occasions when, in contravention of the implicit notion inherent in many existing empirical studies that increasing trust in AI is a good thing, taking steps to dampen trust may be appropriate. Elish and Boyd (2018) assert that when AI proponents propagate the fantastical discourse that AI is a silver bullet, or that it works like magic, this undermines the potential of the systems they are building. Indeed, such a hype-driven ecosystem may encourage overconfidence in the implementation of "poorly constructed models produced through methodologically unsound practices" (Elish & Boyd, 2018, p. 74) increasing the risk of negative unintentional outcomes (Curtis et al., 2023).

3.   Understanding AI trust failures and repair

At the other end of the spectrum, errors, mismatched expectations, and other unintended consequences in the process of automation and AI development and deployment have been documented undermining trust, both in the systems and deploying agencies (e.g., Rinta-Kahila et al., 2021), triggering the question of how trust can be repaired. Preliminary evidence suggests that some trust repair methods proposed in the human–human literature are effective at buffering the effects of AI trust violations (Kim & Song, 2021; Kohn et al., 2018). Kim and Song (2021) found that apologies with internal attributions were most successful in repairing trust in human-like agents, but apologies with external attributions were most successful in repairing trust in machine-like agents. Apologies were more successful than explanations in repairing trust in autonomous vehicles, indicating that while explanations may be useful in developing trust in AI technologies, they may not be the most appropriate mechanism to repair trust (Kohn et al., 2018). Further investigation of the similarities and difference between human–machine and human–human trust repair is warranted, as is examination of steps other trust referents (such as deploying organizations) can take to repair trust after AI system failures.

4.   Closing the gap between the principles and practice of trustworthy AI

There has been a proliferation of frameworks related to trustworthy and ethical AI in recent years, with over 80 industry and government reports articulating principles for trustworthy AI development (Jobin, Ienca & Vayena, 2019). The European Commission's High-Level Expert Group on AI (AI HLEG, 2019) identified seven key principles for trustworthy AI systems: (1) human agency and oversight, (2) technical robustness and safety, (3) privacy and data governance, (4) transparency, (5) fairness, non-discrimination & diversity, (6) societal and environmental well-being, and (7) accountability.

Researchers have integrated these trustworthy AI principles with seminal theories of trust (e.g., Mayer et al., 1995) to propose trustworthy AI systems must be designed and operate with: (1) competence (i.e., perform reliably and produce accurate output), (2) integrity (i.e., by adhering to ethical principles and values such as fairness and honesty, operating within the law, and with transparency of function and limitations), and (3) benevolence (i.e., designed to achieve beneficial outcomes aligned with human interests, and at a minimum, not causing harm; Gillespie et al., 2020; Rieder, Simon & Wong, 2021; see also Wingert & Mayer, Chapter 5). However, scholars have noted that a shortcoming of trustworthy AI principles is that they do not prescribe or even indicate their normative implementation (Knowles & Richards, 2021), and argue there is an urgent need to move beyond abstract principles, whilst acknowledging the difficulty of translating these principles into practice (Mittelstadt, 2019).

Recent research has proposed individual, organizational, and institutional practices that can be undertaken to promote trustworthy AI development and deployment (e.g., Brundage et al., 2020; Gillespie et al., 2020), and these models now require empirical validation. Our recent survey of over 6,000 respondents across five countries codified practices underlying the trustworthy principles, with 95 percent of respondents indicating that each of the practices were important for trust in AI systems (Gillespie et al., 2021). While this provides strong evidence of public endorsement for the trustworthy AI principles, how trustworthy AI can be developed and deployed in practice, and the extent to which demonstration of these practices promotes the trust, acceptance, and adoption of AI envisioned by policymakers, is not well understood and an important area of future research. Currently there is a fundamental lack of understanding around the extent to which trustworthy AI principles are being employed in AI development and deployment—and where responsibility lies for their enactment. Furthering knowledge of how organizations can close the principle–practice gap is of paramount practical importance (Curtis et al., 2023; see also Singh & Mayer, Chapter 8). This is particularly urgent for organizations deploying AI, given principles-based requirements are included in the first ever legal framework on AI proposed by the European Commission in 2021.

5.   Examining the AI trust intention–behavior gap

A central tenet to the importance of trust in the context of AI is that it promotes acceptance and adoption (AI HLEG, 2019). This is supported by a growing body of evidence that trust promotes the *intention* to adopt or use AI-enabled systems. For instance, trust has been demonstrated to promote intention to adopt autonomous vehicles (Panagiotopoulos & Dimitrakopoulos, 2018) and AI-enabled mobile banking (Payne, Peltier & Barger, 2018). However, few studies have investigated whether trust translates into behavioral outcomes such as adoption, cooperation, or compliance with AI systems. Indeed, some studies have been unable to find the expected relationship between trust and behavior in the context of cooperation with robots. For example, Robinette, Howard, and Wagner (2017) found a non-significant relationship between subjective trust and behavioral willingness to follow the advice of a robot in a simulated evacuation context (escaping a virtual maze under time pressure). Another study found that while faulty robot behavior negatively impacted participants' perceptions of robot trustworthiness and reliability, this did not always reduce their cooperation with the robot's request (Salem et al., 2015).

In short, empirical evidence for the assertion that trust is important for AI behavioral adoption and acceptance is sparse and mixed, highlighting the need for further research to test this assumed relationship. Developing a deeper understanding of the processes that translate perceptions of trustworthiness and trusting intentions into behavior is an important avenue for future research. Perceived risk may be one boundary condition that helps explain when trust does not influence relevant outcomes. The studies discussed previously which failed to find the expected relationship between trust and behavioral outcomes did so in scenarios where risk was manipulated. Robinette and colleagues (2017) found that trust did not correlate with behavioral cooperation in a low-risk context but did in a high-risk context. Similarly, Salem et al. (2015) note that while faulty robot behavior may negatively influence perceptions of trustworthiness and reliability, this may not influence cooperation when following the robot's instructions would not result in harm (i.e., is not risky).

Trust theory identifies risk as central to trust (e.g., Mayer et al., 1995), and highlights that trust matters most under conditions of risk (Rousseau et al., 1998). When perceived risk is low, factors other than trust (e.g., convenience) are likely to become more salient in predicting behavioral outcomes, such as use and adoption. Further investigation into how risk may moderate the influence of trust relevant to other factors that influence use and cooperation is warranted.

6.   Enhancing the rigor and context-sensitivity of AI trust
      research and measurement

Measurement issues may contribute to and exacerbate some of the issues raised in the five future research directions discussed so far. There is considerable variability in how trust in AI is operationalized (Glikson & Woolley, 2020; Lockey et al., 2021). Indeed, it is difficult to isolate the antecedents of trust in some of the papers included in Glikson and Woolley's (2020) review, as trust was not always measured in line with commonly accepted definitional features. In some instances, trust was equated with constructs such as affect or liking (e.g., Zhang et al., 2010), attraction to (e.g., Bickmore, Vardoulakis & Schulman, 2013), and general perceptions of AI (e.g., Haring et al., 2016).

Studies that do investigate trust, and use measurement scales, rarely provide sufficient psychometric details to give confidence that it is measured appropriately. Over-reliance on single-item measures has been noted as a particular limitation in the human–robot interaction literature (Schaefer, 2016). Single-item measurement may be appropriate when a construct is unidimensional, unambiguous to the respondent, and narrow in scope (e.g., Bergkvist & Rossiter, 2007). However, this is not the case with trust, which is "central, superficially obvious, but essentially complex" (Blois, 1999, p. 197). Therefore, trust should generally not be measured as a single item, unless authors can provide a convincing rationale for doing so.

Context is also likely to play an important role in the choice of measurement. Previous work on trust in technology demonstrates divergence in the constructs used to measure technology trust beliefs. Some scholars have used the human-like constructs of ability, benevolence, and integrity to measure technology trust beliefs, while others have used system-like constructs such as functionality, helpfulness, and reliability (Lankton, McKnight & Tripp, 2015). Lankton et al. (2015) found that when a technology is perceived as high in humanness (Facebook and Microsoft Access were chosen as high and low humanness technologies, respectively), human-like trust constructs had a stronger influence on outcomes. When the technology was perceived as low in humanness, system-like trust constructs had a stronger influence. A recent review of the empirical literature examining the antecedents of trust in AI demonstrated that representation, whether an AI is embodied, virtual, or embedded, differentially impacts trust in AI (Glikson & Woolley, 2020). Human-like trust constructs may be more applicable to embodied and virtual AI systems, which have a physical form or anthropomorphized features such as an avatar or voice. Conversely, embedded AI, where AI characteristics are invisible to users, could be better suited to system-like trust constructs. AI representation also influences trust dynamics, with trust in robotic AI tending to start low yet increasing over time, while trust in virtual and embedded AI was usually found to start high and decrease over time. Hence, care needs to be taken when extrapolating the findings on trust in one type of AI representation to another, or from trust in humans to trust in AI.

Another context-related measurement consideration that requires attention is the purpose of the AI application. Our recent work demonstrates that people are more trusting of AI used in the context of healthcare, where the purpose is to support disease diagnosis and treatment, than in the context of Human Resources, where the purpose is to support recruitment and performance management (Gillespie et al., 2021). We also asked people the extent to which they trust AI in general, and this was more trusted than AI in HR but less trusted than AI in healthcare. This raises the important related question of whether AI can be meaningfully studied as a general construct or requires a specific application or context. This is an issue for debate given continuing contention and divergence around the issue of what AI fundamentally is, across different groups of stakeholders and research communities (Krafft et al., 2020). Our view is that discussion of AI without proper contextualization may be actively unhelpful. Contemporary discourses about AI often rely on the *potential* of what AI *could* do, rather than existing capabilities, stoking unrealistic assumptions and irrational fears (Elish & Boyd, 2018). For example, Shank and DeSanti (2018) suggest that the general population considers AI to be aware and capable of morally unjust action. Such erroneous assumptions could ultimately undermine trust and acceptance of AI-enabled systems, and these could be exacerbated in contexts where AI is "black boxed," making explainability difficult. We recommend future research clearly ground and contextualize the examination of AI appropriately, as some applications of AI have significant trust challenges and are high risk (e.g., facial recognition use in policing), while others have fewer challenges and risks (e.g., customer service chatbots). Future research using methodologies that examine people's lived experiences and interactions with AI systems in naturally occurring contexts is essential to advancing understanding of trust in AI.

Conclusion

In proposing these directions for future research, our overall goal is to encourage scholars to advance understanding of trust in AI by taking a holistic, rigorous, and contextualized approach that embraces the real-world complexity and nuances of trusting AI systems in practice. Given the widespread benefits and risks of this powerful suite of technologies, coupled with the increasing investment in and ubiquitous nature of AI, and the limited general awareness and understanding of its use, advancing an evidenced-based understanding of trust in, and the trustworthiness of, AI use in organizations and society has never been more critical.

References

AI HLEG (2019). *Ethics Guidelines for Trustworthy AI*. European Commission. https://digital-strategy.ec.europa.eu/en/library/ethics-guidelines-trustworthy-ai.

Bachmann, R., & Inkpen, A. C. (2011). Understanding institutional-based trust building processes in inter-organizational relationships. *Organization Studies, 32*(2), 281–301. https://doi.org/10.1177/0170840610397477.
Bergkvist, L., & Rossiter, J. R. (2007). The predictive validity of multiple-item versus single-item measures of the same constructs. *Journal of Marketing Research, 44*(2), 175–184. https://doi.org/10.1509%2Fjmkr.44.2.175.
Bickmore, T. W., Vardoulakis, L. M. P., & Schulman, D. (2013). Tinker: a relational agent museum guide. *Autonomous Agents and Multi-agent Systems, 27*(2), 254–276. https://doi.org/10.1007/s10458-012-9216-7.
Blois, K. J. (1999). Trust in business-to-business relationships: an evaluation of its status. *Journal of Management Studies, 36*(2), 197–215. https://doi.org/10.1111/1467 -6486.00133.
Brundage, M., Avin, S., Wang, J., Belfield, H., Krueger, G., Hadfield, G., ... & Anderljung, M. (2020). Toward trustworthy AI development: mechanisms for supporting verifiable claims. *arXiv preprint.* https://arxiv.org/abs/2004.07213.
Culley, K. E., & Madhavan, P. (2013). A note of caution regarding anthropomorphism in HCI agents. *Computers in Human Behavior, 29*(3), 577–-79. https://doi.org/10 .1016/j.chb.2012.11.023.
Curtis, C., Gillespie, N., & Lockey, S. (2023). AI-deploying organizations are key to addressing 'perfect storm' of AI risks. *AI and Ethics, 3,* 145–153. https://doi.org/10 .1007/s43681-022-00163-7.
de Visser, E. J., Monfort, S. S., McKendrick, R., Smith, M. A., McKnight, P. E., Krueger, F., & Parasuraman, R. (2016). Almost human: anthropomorphism increases trust resilience in cognitive agents. *Journal of Experimental Psychology Applied, 22*(3), 331–349. https://doi.org/10.1037/xap0000092.
de Visser, E. J., Peeters, M. M. M., Jung, M. F., Kohn, S., Shaw, T. H., Pak, R., & Neerincx, M. A. (2020). Towards a theory of longitudinal trust calibration in human–robot teams. *International Journal of Social Robotics, 12,* 459–478. https:// doi.org/10.1007/s12369-019-00596-x.
Dietvorst, B., Simmons, J. P., & Massey, C. (2015). Algorithm aversion: people erroneously avoid algorithms after seeing them err. *Journal of Experimental Psychology: General, 144*(1), 114–126. http://dx.doi.org/10.1037/xge0000033.
Elish, M. C., & Boyd, D. (2018). Situating methods in the magic of Big Data and AI. *Communication Monographs, 85*(1), 57–80. https://doi.org/10.1080/03637751.2017 .1375130.
European Commission (2021). *Proposal for a Regulation of the European Parliament and of The Council: Laying Down Harmonised Rules on Artificial Intelligence (Artificial Intelligence Act) and Amending Certain Union Legislative Acts.* https://op.europa .eu/ en/ publication -detail/ -/ publication/ e4c43528 -ccfc -11ea -adf7 -01aa75ed71a1/ language-en.
Gillespie, N., Curtis, C., Bianchi, R., Akbari, A., & Fentener van Vlissingen, R. (2020). *Achieving Trustworthy AI: A Model for Trustworthy Artificial Intelligence.* Sydney: The University of Queensland and KPMG. https://doi.org/10.14264/ca0819d.
Gillespie, N., Lockey, S., & Curtis, C. (2021). *Trust in Artificial Intelligence: A Five Country Study.* Sydney: The University of Queensland and KPMG. https://doi.org/ 10.14264/e34bfa3.
Glikson, E., & Woolley, A. W. (2020). Human trust in artificial intelligence: review of empirical research. *Academy of Management Annals, 14*(2), 627–660. https://doi .org/10.5465/annals.2018.0057.

Haring, K. S., Silvera-Tawil, D., Watanabe, K., & Velonaki, M. (2016, November). The influence of robot appearance and interactive ability in HRI: a cross-cultural study. In *International Conference on Social Robotics* (pp. 392–401). Cham: Springer. https://doi.org/10.1007/978-3-319-47437-3_38.

IDC (2021, February 23). *IDC Forecasts Improved Growth for Global AI Market in 2021*. https://www.idc.com/getdoc.jsp?containerId=prUS47482321.

Jobin, A., Ienca, M., & Vayena, E. (2019). The global landscape of AI ethics guidelines. *Nature Machine Intelligence, 1*(9), 389–399. https://doi.org/10.1038/s42256-019-0088-2.

Jordan, M. I., & Mitchell, T. M. (2015). Machine learning: trends, perspectives, and prospects. *Science, 349*(6245), 255–260. https://doi.org/10.1126/science.aaa8415.

Kim, T., & Song, H. (2021). How should intelligent agents apologize to restore trust? Interaction effects between anthropomorphism and apology attribution on trust repair. *Telematics and Informatics, 61*, 101595. https://doi.org/10.1016/j.tele.2021.101595.

Knowles, B., & Richards, J. T. (2021, March). The sanction of authority: promoting public trust in AI. In *Proceedings of the 2021 ACM Conference on Fairness, Accountability, and Transparency* (pp. 262–271). https://doi.org/10.1145/3442188.3445890.

Kohn, S. C., Quinn, D., Pak, R., de Visser, E. J., & Shaw, T. H. (2018). Trust repair strategies with self-driving vehicles: an exploratory study. *Proceedings of the Human Factors and Ergonomics Society Annual Meeting, 62*(1), 1108–1112. https://doi.org/10.1177%2F1541931218621254.

Krafft, P. M., Young, M., Katell, M., Huang, K., & Bugingo, G. (2020, February). Defining AI in policy versus practice. In *Proceedings of the AAAI/ACM Conference on AI, Ethics, and Society* (pp. 72–78). https://doi.org/10.1145/3375627.3375835.

Lankton, N. K., McKnight, D. H., & Tripp, J. (2015). Technology, humanness, and trust: rethinking trust in technology. *Journal of the Association for Information Systems, 16*(10), article 1. https://doi.org/10.17705/1jais.00411.

Lewis, J. D., & Weigert, A. (1985). Trust as a social reality. *Social Forces, 63*(4), 967–985. https://doi.org/10.1093/sf/63.4.967.

Lockey, S., Gillespie, N., Holm, D., & Someh, I. A. (2021, January). A review of trust in artificial intelligence: challenges, vulnerabilities and future directions. In *Proceedings of the 54th Hawaii International Conference on System Sciences* (pp. 5463–5472). https://doi.org/10.24251/HICSS.2021.664.

Long, C. P., & Sitkin, S. B. (2018). Control-trust dynamics: identifying shared perspectives and charting conceptual faultlines. *Academy of Management Annals, 12*, 725–751.

Mayer, R. C., Davis, J. H., & Schoorman, F. D. (1995). An integrative model of organizational trust. *Academy of Management Review, 20*(3), 709–734. https://doi.org/10.2307/258792.

McKnight, D. H., Carter, M., Thatcher, J. B., & Clay, P. F. (2011). Trust in a specific technology: an investigation of its components and measures. *ACM Transactions on Management Information Systems (TMIS), 2*(2), 1–25. https://doi.org/10.1145/1985347.1985353.

Mittelstadt, B. (2019). Principles alone cannot guarantee ethical AI. *Nature Machine Intelligence, 1*(11), 501–507. https://doi.org/10.1038/s42256-019-0114-4.

OECD (2019). *Artificial Intelligence in Society*. Paris: OECD Publishing. https://doi.org/10.1787/eedfee77-en.

Panagiotopoulos, I., & Dimitrakopoulos, G. (2018). An empirical investigation on consumers' intentions towards autonomous driving. *Transportation Research Part C: Emerging Technologies, 95,* 773–784. https://doi.org/10.1016/j.trc.2018.08.013.

Park, S. (2020). Multifaceted trust in tourism service robots. *Annals of Tourism Research, 81,* 102888. https://doi.org/10.1016/j.annals.2020.102888.

Payne, E. M., Peltier, J. W., & Barger, V. A. (2018). Mobile banking and AI-enabled mobile banking: the differential effects of technological and non-technological factors on digital natives' perceptions and behavior. *Journal of Research in Interactive Marketing, 12*(3), 328–346. https://doi.org/10.1108/JRIM-07-2018-0087.

Raisch, S., & Krakowski, S. (2021). Artificial intelligence and management: the automation–augmentation paradox. *Academy of Management Review, 46*(1), 192–210. https://doi.org/10.5465/amr.2018.0072.

Rieder, G., Simon, J., & Wong, P. H. (2021). Mapping the stony road toward trustworthy AI: expectations, problems, conundrums. In M. Pelillo & T. Scantamburlo (Eds.), *Machines We Trust: Perspectives on Dependable AI* (pp.27–40). Cambridge, MA: MIT Press.

Rinta-Kahila, T., Someh, I., Gillespie, N., Gregor, S., & Indulska, M. (2021). Algorithmic decision making and system destructiveness: a case of automatic debt recovery. *The European Journal of Information Systems, 31*(3), 313–338. https://www.tandfonline.com/doi/full/10.1080/0960085X.2021.1960905.

Robinette, P., Howard, A. M., & Wagner, A. R. (2017). Effect of robot performance on human–robot trust in time-critical situations. *IEEE Transactions on Human-Machine Systems, 47*(4), 425–436. https://doi.org/10.1109/THMS.2017.2648849.

Rousseau, D. M., Sitkin, S. B., Burt, R. S., & Camerer, C. (1998). Not so different after all: a cross-discipline view of trust. *Academy of Management Review, 23*(3), 393–404. https://doi.org/10.5465/amr.1998.926617.

Salem, M., Lakatos, G., Amirabdollahian, F., & Dautenhahn, K. (2015, March). Would you trust a (faulty) robot? Effects of error, task type and personality on human-robot cooperation and trust. In *2015 10th ACM/IEEE International Conference on Human-Robot Interaction (HRI)* (pp. 1–8). IEEE. https://doi.org/10.1145/2696454.2696497.

Schaefer, K. E. (2016). Measuring trust in human–robot interactions: development of the "trust perception scale-HRI". In R. Mittu, D. Sofge, A. Wagner, & W. Lawless (Eds.), *Robust Intelligence and Trust in Autonomous Systems* (pp. 191–218). Boston, MA: Springer.

Shank, D. B., & DeSanti, A. (2018). Attributions of morality and mind to artificial intelligence after real-world moral violations. *Computers in Human Behavior, 86,* 401–411. https://doi.org/10.1016/j.chb.2018.05.014.

Shao, Z., Guo, Y., Li, X., & Barnes, S. (2020). Sources of influences on customers' trust in ridesharing: why use experience matters? *Industrial Management & Data Systems, 120*(8), 1459–1482. https://doi.org/10.1108/IMDS-12-2019-0651.

Söllner, M., Hoffmann, A., & Leimeister, J. M. (2016). Why different trust relationships matter for information systems users. *European Journal of Information Systems, 25*(3), 274–287. https://doi.org/10.1057/ejis.2015.17.

Spadaro, G., Gangl, K., Van Prooijen, J. W., Van Lange, P. A., & Mosso, C. O. (2020). Enhancing feelings of security: how institutional trust promotes interpersonal trust. *PloS One, 15*(9), e0237934. https://doi.org/10.1371/journal.pone.0237934.

Stewart, K. J. (2003). Trust transfer on the world wide web. *Organization Science, 14,* 5–17. https://doi.org/10.1287/orsc.14.1.5.12810.

van der Werff, L., Blomqvist, K., & Koskinen, S. (2021). Trust cues in artificial intelligence. In N. Gillespie, C. A. Fulmer, & R. J. Lewicki (Eds.), *Understanding Trust in Organizations: A Multilevel Perspective* (pp.307–333). New York: Routledge.

Weibel, A., Den Hartog, D., Gillespie, N., Searle, R., Six, F., & Skinner, D. (2016). How do controls impact employee trust in the employer? *Human Resource Management, 55*(3), 437–462.

Weller, A. (2017). Transparency: motivations and challenges. *arXiv preprint.* https://arxiv.org/abs/1708.01870.

Yamagishi, T., & Yamagishi, M. (1994). Trust and commitment in the United States and Japan. *Motivation and Emotion, 18*(2), 129–166. https://doi.org/10.1007/BF02249397.

Zhang, T., Kaber, D. B., Zhu, B., Swangnetr, M., Mosaly, P., & Hodge, L. (2010). Service robot feature design effects on user perceptions and emotional responses. *Intelligent Service Robotics, 3*(2), 73–88. https://doi.org/10.1007/s11370-010-0060-9.

Zuboff, S. (2015). Big other: surveillance capitalism and the prospects of an information civilization. *Journal of Information Technology, 30*(1), 75–89.

Zucker, L. G. (1986). Production of trust: institutional sources of economic structure, 1840–1920. *Research in Organizational Behavior, 8*, 53–111. http://psycnet.apa.org/psycinfo/1988-10420-001.

3 Linking trust constructs with computer science-based decision-making systems

Lucca Eloy, Philip Bobko, and Leanne Hirshfield

Introduction

Imagine a trio of Air Force pilots flying three F-18s on a complex mission. As part of a heterogeneous human–agent team (HAT), each pilot (i) interacts with other pilots, (ii) controls and receives information from external unmanned aerial vehicles, and (iii) receives support from autonomous decision aid technologies and other support systems (e.g., auto-pilot, heads-up display). Also assume that the human pilots' helmets and flight suits are embedded with non-invasive neurophysiological sensors, which provide real-time information about pilot social, cognitive, and affective states. Using these signals, the autonomous support systems can then assist the humans in real time (e.g., by suggesting handoff of some activities to other entities) by sensing when the pilots become stressed or overloaded, or when they do not have appropriate trust in other human or artificial teammates.

Given recent advances in artificial intelligence (AI) and biomedical engineering, the above vision is close to becoming a reality. Our chapter describes an interdisciplinary research agenda for achieving this vision for HATs, with emphasis on sensing/building appropriate trust and reliance. As Wickens points out in his classical textbook on engineering psychology and human performance, "there is probably no variable more important in the human–agent interaction than that of trust" (Wickens et al., 2013, p. 388). We start by describing how adaptive systems can be realized by theoretically and empirically linking computer science (CS)-based intelligent systems with trust constructs. We use as a primary example a decision-making framework called a partially observable Markov decision process (POMDP), which can model the decision-making of individuals as they act and attempt to maximize performance in uncertain environments.

In our opening example, a pilot support system built as a POMDP could monitor neurophysiological data from pilots ("observations") to estimate pilot levels of trust and workload ("states") and choose an action ("actions") to maximize performance and safety ("rewards"). Foundational research on trust can inform what actions the system should take to influence pilot trust, and whether increasing or decreasing trust would be more helpful given the current estimated state (De Visser et al., 2020).

Our chapter proceeds as follows: After providing an introduction to POMDPs, we describe (i) recent, initial work that embeds trust and related theory into POMDP-based systems, (ii) other examples of social science work focusing on human performance that would benefit from this approach, and (iii) cutting-edge neurophysiological metrics that help identify individual and team states relating to trust and reliance in real time. These states are crucial for selecting actions that optimize human and team performance. We conclude our chapter with some thoughts regarding a research agenda for building AI systems of the future—using the full potential of trust-sensitive POMDPs that are grounded in neurophysiological measurements.

Introduction to partially observable Markov decision processes

While there are many algorithms from the machine learning and pattern recognition domains that can be applied to intelligent systems, we focus here on POMDPs because they are particularly well suited for the design of adaptive systems, where there are often many uncertainties in the environment (e.g., human, team, and environmental states), and where the cost of making an inappropriate adaptation can be high (Chanel et al., 2020). Figure 3.1 depicts the main components of a POMDP, which we detail in this section.

First, an optimal policy is computed from prior data to maximize the potential reward probability. During the interaction, the agent receives an observation from the sensors and updates its belief state based on this observation and its prior belief. From the "learned" policy it then determines the best action based on this belief state. The agent acts, and the human's internal state transitions to a new state depending on this action and the prior state. The agent receives a reward of varying magnitude depending on this transition, which can be used to update the policy.

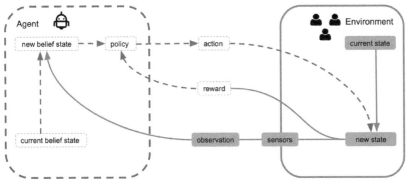

Source: The authors

Figure 3.1   Schematic of a POMDP

In complex "real-world" scenarios the true state is usually unobservable; the agent cannot directly measure a human's trust level. The POMDP, or partially observable Markov decision process, attempts to incorporate this uncertainty into its design. That is, POMDPs model environments where the agent receives indirect observations about the "true" state of nature—and must make decisions based on what state it *believes* the system is currently in. In our AI assistant example, a useful, indirect observation might be whether or not the human recently accepted the AI's recommendation (e.g., if the driver had taken a recommended turn, the AI might infer the driver's trust level is high).

A POMDP model (Figure 3.1) is formally defined by a set of underlying states S, a set of possible actions A, a set of observations Ω, transition probabilities between states T, a reward function R, observation probabilities O, and a discount factor γ that determines whether immediate or future rewards should be prioritized. The reward function R defines the reward for taking an action that results in a given state transition, and O defines the conditional probability of each possible observation being present given the current state. At each time period, the agent receives an observation o and estimates its *belief* of the current underlying state using the probability distribution O, the last action, and the previous belief state. Figure 3.1 illustrates the cyclical process of a POMDP in a human–agent interaction.

A POMDP is "solved" by identifying which action to take at each belief state to earn the greatest total reward, known as a *policy*. Based on the pre-defined reward values, certain state transitions (e.g., "low trust" → "high trust") are deemed more beneficial than others and thus prioritized in an optimal policy.

Due to the inherent uncertainty and reliance on probability distributions, computing a single optimal policy is often computationally intractable. Thus, POMDPs are solved in practice using mathematical approximations, for which several algorithms exist. The computationally rigorous field of approximation, though crucial in practice, is beyond the scope of this chapter.

Related work using POMDPs in the trust domain

Given its generalizability and ability to incorporate uncertainty, POMDPs are increasingly gaining traction in the HAT-trust domain. The shared goal of these efforts is to properly calibrate trust to maximize team performance by avoiding under- or over-reliance on the robot or agent. This implies rewarding higher team performance on the task, rather than unilaterally rewarding higher levels of trust. Chen et al. (2018) used an experimental task where a human and a robotic arm worked together to clear objects of ranging fragility from a table. They found that a robot using a trust-aware POMDP planner would first clear easier (less fragile but lower reward) objects in order to increase the participant's trust, before moving on to the more difficult targets. When compared to a trust-agnostic planner that targeted high-reward objects first, the trust-aware POMDP decreased human intervention (where the human partner chooses not to rely on the robot) by 71–100 percent for the various objects. This is a clear example of how the reward structure in a POMDP can influence both a human's actions as well as an agent's suggested actions.

Research on dynamic trust-modulation systems using a POMDP framework is rapidly shifting from theory to implementation. Among these studies, varying agent transparency is commonly used as an action to modulate trust levels, as research suggests that transparency encourages a human operator to appropriately calibrate their reliance on the agent depending on its level of certainty in the task (Kunze et al., 2019; see Bhaskara et al., 2020 for review). This calibration—decreasing trust in situations of low certainty and increasing trust in situations of high certainty—makes human–agent teams more efficient by allowing the automation to take over when able.

In one of the first completed efforts to build such a system, Akash et al. (2020) implemented a POMDP-based agent assistant for a simulated reconnaissance task with the goal of calibrating user trust and workload by varying transparency (low/medium/high) to optimize human performance. Recall that in addition to the chosen states, actions, and rewards, a POMDP requires pre-defined sets of (1) transition probabilities between states and (2) observation probabilities. Data from an initial experiment using the same reconnaissance task *sans* intelligent agent was used to compute the probability distribution of state transitions and observations. These distributions parameterized the human trust and workload models, from which an optimal policy was "learned" offline. The model's reward function was defined to reward human accuracy (regardless of the agent's recommendation) and response time. Participants assisted by the POMDP achieved higher accuracy than participants assisted by agents with static low and medium transparency levels. Participants in the static high-transparency condition, however, had the highest average accuracy score but slower response time than those in the POMDP conditions. The researchers' methodology suggests that the accuracy–response time tradeoff can be further tuned by reweighting the reward function to favor one or the other. Although these results do not outperform a traditional static-transparency system in every case, they validate a novel method of translating behavioral measures into a combined trust and workload probabilistic model that can be tuned according to task-specific performance goals.

Intelligent trust-modulation system technology is still in its infancy, and it is encouraging to see researchers beginning to implement and test these systems with human subjects. In existing work, trust and workload are estimated from behavioral data such as response time, compliance with agent recommendations, and agent reliability. Estimating POMDP parameters from these measures requires causal assumptions and several simplifications of human trust and teaming dynamics (e.g., a causal relationship of trust on compliance must be assumed). We propose that improvements can be made with a more robust measure of social, cognitive, and affective human states using neurophysiological sensors. Below, we outline a research agenda to estimate human trust and other relevant processes by using machine learning and methods grounded in neuroergonomics research (for more on neuroergonomics, see Ayaz & Dehais, 2018; Dehais et al., 2020; Parasuraman & Rizzo, 2006).

Trust research in this book that might benefit from links with POMDP models

Regarding the current book, Lockey and Gillespie (Chapter 2) provide a review of other factors that can influence trust in AI agents. Given the flexible POMDP trust-modulation framework, these additional factors could be added as available input for an agent to appropriately calibrate an operator's trust levels. Similarly, Lyons, Scheutz, and Jessup (Chapter 10) discuss the similarities and differences between human–human trust and human–agent trust across multiple disciplines. The experimental evidence and various models presented in this chapter can inform how a trust-aware agent might interact with humans individually and in teams. Evidence from these existing bodies of work on human–agent trust should therefore be applied to improve the efficacy of these intelligent adaptive systems. In addition, implementing and experimenting with these systems can simultaneously inform human–agent trust research by observing trust and performance outcomes. The POMDP model in particular is a formalization of a decision-making system into a computational/mathematical problem. Thus, observing the potential solutions, or optimal policies, that arise from these models may reveal how particular actions most effectively manipulate trust in certain contexts.

Wagner (Chapter 13) details a great example of an application that could take advantage of the POMDP approach. Trust in evacuation robots could be improved with context-aware systems that provide transparency explanations or modify the robot's behavior according to the human's levels of trust, stress, fear, and so on. The ability to dynamically calibrate trust might prove particularly effective in high-risk situations where individuals may have drastically different responses to an evacuation robot.

We also want to draw attention to Brewer, Torres, Celeya, and Pitaes' cognitive-physiological theory of trust (Chapter 7). They propose that the human brain makes trust decisions by computing a potential "expected value" of rewards that result from each decision and selecting the path of greatest reward. This mechanism can clearly be represented as a POMDP, which likewise is solved by maximizing expected future rewards. We believe this supports the case for using POMDPs to model decision-making under uncertainty, particularly with respect to trust, as it may closely mirror the human brain's processes. Furthermore, implementing and testing POMDPs can help to directly model and test their theory of decision-making.

Lastly, we note that the real-time, objective measurement of humans' trust states is imperative for building effective trust-sensitive POMDPs. Bio-technology sensors will be essential for collecting these observations, and ultimately for formulating the belief states that make up the POMDP formulation. But the interpretation of raw neurophysiological sensor data is only as good as one's ability to extract meaning from that raw data. There is a need for the interdisciplinary trust community to gain shared understanding of the neurophysiological correlates of trust. To that end, Wu and Krueger (Chapter 14) provide an excellent review of related literature to date, collated across many disciplines and empirical studies, about the neurophysiological correlates of trust.

Measuring trust-related POMDP states via neurophysiological sensors

We focus this section on neural correlates of trust in the brain, and the measurement modalities that show the most promise at measuring those neural correlates under normal working conditions. A detailed review of brain measurement, and the neural correlates of trust, distrust, and suspicion, may be found in Hirshfield et al. (2019). Although functional magnetic resonance imaging (fMRI) is the gold standard for precise measurements of the functioning human brain, the fMRI magnet is quite expensive to use per participant, and it requires participants to lie in a loud constrictive magnet, with extremely limited movement. By building on foundational fMRI research identifying the neural correlates of trust and other cognitive, social, and affective states in the brain, researchers have shown that the non-invasive electroencephalograph (EEG) and functional near-infrared spectroscopy (fNIRS) devices hold great potential for measurement of these states in ecologically valid contexts. These modalities can be particularly useful for human–human and human–agent teaming contexts where states like trust are particularly relevant.

fMRI has been used to measure the neural correlates of trust and distrust in a number of studies, providing an invaluable technique that recent fNIRS researchers have used as a roadmap in this domain (Krueger et al., 2007; Dimoka, 2010; Bhatt et al., 2012; Fett et al., 2014). Hirshfield et al. (2019) detail some of the primary brain regions implicated across a wide swath of trust fMRI studies. The findings in these efforts can be linked to a myriad of functional brain regions, which are involved in a range of human mental processes, including error monitoring, emotion regulation, cognitive load, reward processing, as well as a paradigm called "Theory of Mind" (ToM) focused on how people perceive the intentions of others in relation to their own thoughts and actions. More specifically, brain regions typically linked to ToM reasoning include the medial prefrontal cortex, anterior cingulate cortex (ACC), and the bilateral temporoparietal junction (TPJ) (Mahy et al., 2014).

Building on the fMRI findings noted above, the non-invasive EEG and fNIRS measurement modalities have substantial potential for measurement of trust (and related social, cognitive, affective states) during naturalistic interactions with human and agent teammates. EEG uses electrodes placed on the scalp to measure the electrical potentials caused by neurons firing in the brain. The devices have extremely high temporal resolution, but they often suffer from poor signal to noise ratio and a low spatial resolution. In contrast, but in a complementary manner, fNIRS measures the slower occurring hemodynamic responses that occur in the brain following neuronal activation. The modality works by pulsing near infrared light into the brain cortex, while powerful light detectors are used to infer hemodynamic responses based on the measurement of light reflected back out of the brain. Thus, the combination of both fNIRS and EEG has much potential for obtaining real-time measurement of social, cognitive, affective states in the human performance domain. Since fNIRS remains in the nascent stage, only a handful of studies have used the device to measure the complex social science constructs, such as trust and suspicion, in the brain. One notable exception was a recent study that used fNIRS to measure brain activation of two individuals during a face-to-face economic exchange (Tang et al., 2016). The researchers found the right TPJ brain region to be more active during increased intentionality and collaborative interactions among the individuals, which is in line with the prior fMRI research described above. A handful of studies have also used EEG to measure trust in the brain (Rudoy & Paller, 2009; Hahn et al., 2015; Ma et al., 2015; Wang et al., 2016), but the poor spatial resolution of EEG makes it difficult to precisely locate functional brain regions associated with trust (Hahn et al., 2015). However, it is notable that loss of interpersonal trust causes a violation in people's expectations, which is measurable via the error-related negativity (ERN), an event-related potential (ERP) in EEG data that occurs within milliseconds of the expectation violation (Ma et al., 2015). (For more information on the ERN in EEG data, see Ferrez & Millán, 2005; Hajcak et al., 2004; Vi & Subramanian, 2012.)

Since fNIRS and EEG measure activity in complementary ways, we suggest that hybrid approaches which combine EEG and fNIRS sensors will ultimately provide the clearest picture of changing trust states (Hirshfield et al., 2009; Fazli et al., 2012; Putze et al., 2014; Naseer & Hong, 2015; Kwon et al., 2020). For example, EEG can measure the quickly occurring ERN that occurs in the ACC when one person violates another's expectations (loss in trust), while high-density fNIRS can provide spatially accurate measures to access regions of interest regarding ToM, cognitive load, and emotion regulation (among others), where slower hemodynamic responses can be precisely measured. These measurements of trust dynamics can then be fed into a POMDP as observations, allowing the model to assess the human's current state and act accordingly. Furthermore, we have made recent progress characterizing the effects of agent transparency and reliability behaviors on human trust and neural activity via fNIRS (Eloy et al., 2022), and can build upon this work to inform how agents can best modulate trust under different contexts. This approach would build upon the POMDP studies discussed above, adding a more robust and directly informative set of observations than the purely behavioral measures used in previous attempts.

Some future research agendas for realization of trust-sensitive POMDPs

We end our chapter by describing a path forward for the research community to harness the full potential of trust-sensitive POMDPs that are grounded in neurophysiological measurements, in order to build AI systems of the future. We summarize this research agenda by posing several thoughts and directions for future work.

First and foremost, POMDPs can only learn and be integrated into HAT systems by learning from vast amounts of data. Thus, there is an immediate need for curation of large datasets, for training of the data-hungry POMDPs to learn the policy, and there is a need at the lower level to train supervised classification models to predict trust-related states from bio-technology sensors. One way to achieve larger training datasets can come from data sharing amongst labs. However, for datasets to be combined amongst labs and various projects there is a need as a community to place greater emphasis on adapting shared trust-related construct definitions, operationalizations, and measurement techniques.

We also call for more empirical research that models the inherent cyclical nature of team processes. The model in Figure 3.1 fits that nature—and POMDPs are thus examples of these iterative processes. More generally, note that classic theories of group development and team processes have been modified/updated to incorporate feedback loops. For example, Tuckman's (1965) five-stage model of group formation (forming, storming, norming, performing, adjourning), has been updated by focusing solely on storming, norming, and performing and, to the point, adding a cyclical feedback loop (see Karriker, 2005 for review). As another example, the classic input–process–output (IPO) model (see Mathieu et al., 2018 for review and discussion) has been modified by Ilgen et al. (2005) to be "IMOI"—where IMOI stands for input–mediator–output–input. The second "I" emphasizes the cyclical feedback nature.

In addition, in our POMDP model, we purposively incorporated a lens of trust as a mediating, explanatory variable. The iterative nature of POMDPs (and the trust lens) is also consistent with a recent review and analysis of the trust in automation literature (Chiou & Lee, 2021). Those authors suggest that trust changes as people interact with agents and, as the authors note in their abstract, "Much research … neglects relational aspects of increasingly capable automation." Again, consistent with our focus on POMDP models, we call for

research that continues to view team processes and trust as emergent characteristics that evolve (potentially quickly and iteratively) across time.

Lastly, we note that our chapter focused on the blending of advanced
decision-making algorithms from computer science with theoretical and
empirical work focused on the construct of trust. To achieve ambitious
interdisciplinary research like that posed in this chapter, there is a need to
raise our next generation of social and computer scientists with the interdisciplinary skillsets and breadth of knowledge that will allow them to build
decision-making algorithms that are empirically supported and theoretically
sound. We look forward to the results from the cross-fertilizations of these
disciplines.

References

Akash, K., McMahon, G., Reid, T., & Jain, N. (2020). Human trust-based feedback
control: dynamically varying automation transparency to optimize human–machine
interactions. *IEEE Control Systems Magazine, 40*(6), 98–116.

Ayaz, H., & Dehais, F. (Eds.) (2018). *Neuroergonomics: The Brain at Work and in
Everyday Life.* Cambridge, MA: Academic Press.

Bhaskara, A., Skinner, M., & Loft, S. (2020). Agent transparency: a review of current
theory and evidence. *IEEE Transactions on Human–Machine Systems, 50*(3),
215–224.

Bhatt, M. A., Lohrenz, T., Camerer, C. F., & Montague, P. R. (2012). Distinct contributions of the amygdala and parahippocampal gyrus to suspicion in a repeated bar-
gaining game. *Proceedings of the National Academy of Sciences, 109*(22), 8728–8733.

Chanel, C. P., Roy, R. N., Dehais, F., & Drougard, N. (2020). Towards mixed-initiative
human–robot interaction: assessment of discriminative physiological and behavioral
features for performance prediction. *Sensors, 20*(1), article 296.

Chen, M., Nikolaidis, S., Soh, H., Hsu, D., & Srinivasa, S. (2018). Planning with trust
for human–robot collaboration. In *Proceedings of the 2018 ACM/IEEE International
Conference on Human–Robot Interaction* (pp. 307–315). https:// doi .org/ 10 .1145/
3171221.3171264.

Chiou, E. K., & Lee, J. D. (2021). Trusting automation: designing for responsivity and
resilience. *Human Factors, 65*(1). https://doi.org/10.1177/00187208211009995.

De Visser, E. J., Peeters, M. M., Jung, M. F., Kohn, S., Shaw, T. H., Pak, R., & Neerincx,
M. A. (2020). Towards a theory of longitudinal trust calibration in human–robot
teams. *International Journal of Social Robotics, 12*(2), 459–478.

Dehais, F., Lafont, A., Roy, R., & Fairclough, S. (2020). A neuroergonomics approach to
mental workload, engagement and human performance. *Frontiers in Neuroscience,
14*, article 268.

Dimoka, A. (2010). What does the brain tell us about trust and distrust? Evidence from
a functional neuroimaging study. *MIS Quarterly, 34*(2), 373–396.

Eloy, L., Doherty, E. J., Spencer, C. A., Bobko, P., & Hirshfield, L. (2022). Using
fNIRS to identify transparency- and reliability-sensitive markers of trust across

multiple timescales in collaborative human–human–agent triads. *Frontiers in Neuroergonomics, 3,* article 10. https://doi.org/10.3389/fnrgo.2022.838625.

Fazli, S., Mehnert, J., Steinbrink, J., Curio, G., Villringer, A., Müller, K. R., & Blankertz, B. (2012). Enhanced performance by a hybrid NIRS–EEG brain computer interface. *Neuroimage, 59*(1), 519–529.

Ferrez, P. W., & Millán, J. D. R. (2005). You are wrong!—automatic detection of interaction errors from brain waves. In *Proceedings of the 19th International Joint Conference on Artificial Intelligence.* https://infoscience.epfl.ch/record/83269?ln=en.

Fett, A. K. J., Gromann, P. M., Giampietro, V., Shergill, S. S., & Krabbendam, L. (2014). Default distrust? An fMRI investigation of the neural development of trust and cooperation. *Social Cognitive and Affective Neuroscience, 9*(4), 395–402.

Hahn, T., Notebaert, K., Anderl, C., Teckentrup, V., Kaßecker, A., & Windmann, S. (2015). How to trust a perfect stranger: predicting initial trust behavior from resting-state brain-electrical connectivity. *Social Cognitive and Affective Neuroscience, 10*(6), 809–813.

Hajcak, G., McDonald, N., & Simons, R. F. (2004). Error-related psychophysiology and negative affect. *Brain and Cognition, 56*(2), 189–197.

Hirshfield, L., Bobko, P., Barelka, A., Sommer, N., & Velipasalar, S. (2019). Toward interfaces that help users identify misinformation online: using fNIRS to measure suspicion. *Augmented Human Research, 4*(1), 1–13.

Hirshfield, L. M., Chauncey, K., Gulotta, R., Girouard, A., Solovey, E. T., Jacob, R. J., … & Fantini, S. (2009, July). Combining electroencephalograph and functional near infrared spectroscopy to explore users' mental workload. In *International Conference on Foundations of Augmented Cognition* (pp. 239–247). Berlin, Heidelberg: Springer.

Ilgen, D. R., Hollenbeck, J. R., Johnson, M., & Jundt, D. (2005). Teams in organizations. *Annual Review of Psychology, 56,* 517–543.

Karriker, J. H. (2005). Cyclical group development and interaction-based leadership emergence in autonomous teams: an integrated model. *Journal of Leadership & Organizational Studies, 11*(4), 54–64.

Krueger, F., McCabe, K., Moll, J., Kriegeskorte, N., Zahn, R., Strenziok, M., … & Grafman, J. (2007). Neural correlates of trust. *Proceedings of the National Academy of Sciences, 104*(50), 20084–20089.

Kunze, A., Summerskill, S. J., Marshall, R., & Filtness, A. J. (2019). Automation transparency: implications of uncertainty communication for human–automation interaction and interfaces. *Ergonomics, 62*(3), 345–360.

Kwon, J., Shin, J., & Im, C. H. (2020). Toward a compact hybrid brain–computer interface (BCI): performance evaluation of multi-class hybrid EEG-fNIRS BCIs with limited number of channels. *PLoS One, 15*(3), e0230491.

Ma, Q., Meng, L., & Shen, Q. (2015). You have my word: reciprocity expectation modulates feedback-related negativity in the trust game. *PloS One, 10*(2), e0119129.

Mahy, C. E., Moses, L. J., & Pfeifer, J. H. (2014). How and where: theory-of-mind in the brain. *Developmental Cognitive Neuroscience, 9,* 68–81.

Mathieu, J. E., Wolfson, M. A., & Park, S. (2018). The evolution of work team research since Hawthorne. *American Psychologist, 73*(4), 308–321.

Naseer, N., & Hong, K. S. (2015). fNIRS-based brain–computer interfaces: a review. *Frontiers in Human Neuroscience, 9,* article 3.

Parasuraman, R., & Rizzo, M. (Eds.) (2006). *Neuroergonomics: The Brain at Work* (Human Technology Interaction Series, vol. 3). New York: Oxford University Press.

Putze, F., Hesslinger, S., Tse, C. Y., Huang, Y., Herff, C., Guan, C., & Schultz, T. (2014). Hybrid fNIRS-EEG based classification of auditory and visual perception processes. *Frontiers in Neuroscience, 8,* article 373.

Rudoy, J. D., & Paller, K. A. (2009). Who can you trust? Behavioral and neural differences between perceptual and memory-based influences. *Frontiers in Human Neuroscience, 16.* https://www.frontiersin.org/articles/10.3389/neuro.09.016.2009/full.

Tang, H., Mai, X., Wang, S., Zhu, C., Krueger, F., & Liu, C. (2016). Interpersonal brain synchronization in the right temporo-parietal junction during face-to-face economic exchange. *Social Cognitive and Affective Neuroscience, 11*(1), 23–32.

Tuckman, B. W. (1965). Developmental sequence in small groups. *Psychological Bulletin, 63*(6), 384–399.

Vi, C., & Subramanian, S. (2012, May). Detecting error-related negativity for inter-action design. In *Proceedings of the SIGCHI Conference on Human Factors in Computing Systems* (pp. 493–502). https://doi.org/10.1145/2207676.2207744.

Wang, Y., Zhang, Z., Jing, Y., Valadez, E. A., & Simons, R. F. (2016). How do we trust strangers? The neural correlates of decision making and outcome evaluation of generalized trust. *Social Cognitive and Affective Neuroscience, 11*(10), 1666–1676.

Wickens, C. D., Helton, W. S., Hollands, J. G., & Banbury, S. (2013). *Engineering Psychology and Human Performance.* Abingdon: Routledge.

4   Trust in science: considering whom to trust for knowing what is true

Rainer Bromme and Friederike Hendriks

Introduction

In the beginning of 2020 when the first reports of the Coronavirus disease (COVID-19) frightened the world, it became rapidly clear that taking effective action against the evolving pandemic would depend upon the general public as well as decision-makers on all levels being willing to rely on science (Bromme et al., 2022). The COVID-19 pandemic is an illustrative example of an issue revealing that public trust in science is integral for confronting global challenges; thus, we use it for elaborating why and for whom trust in science[1] matters, but also for reflecting on the conditions and pitfalls of citizens' *informed* trust judgments.

The Mayer, Davis, and Schoorman (MDS) model of trust (MDS, 1995) provides a fruitful starting point (for a more elaborate discussion, see Mayer & Mayer, Chapter 1) for summarizing the main components of trust[2] (see Blöbaum, 2021; PytlikZillig & Kimbrough, 2016). In theory, *trust* is the voluntary dependence of a *trustor* on the actions of a *trustee*. The *choice* to trust (in principle, the trustor could choose not to rely on the trustee's critical action) rests on expectations, namely, ascriptions of *trustworthiness*. The trustee's action is beneficial for achieving the trustor's *goals*, who is not able to achieve these using his/her own capabilities. This reliance implies *risk*: the trustor

---

[1]   In this chapter, the notion *science* is used in the broad sense of the German concept of *Wissenschaft*, including the sciences of the natural world, the social world (social science), and the cultural world (humanities). The case of the COVID-19 pandemic exemplifies that all these disciplinary perspectives are required for a research-based understanding of the pandemic and its effects on the world.

[2]   Our perspective on trust in science is based on *psychological* research and informed by *epistemological* and *sociological* perspectives on trust in science.

doesn't have *full control over the provision of the expected action* or over its *quality*. Insofar the trustor accepts a *vulnerability* when choosing to trust. Here, *trust* is characterized as a *social relationship*, when in other work, trust is considered a *process*, with a focus on the *development* and the *use* of the above-mentioned expectations (about the trustor) for making goal-directed decisions (Blöbaum, 2021).

Trust in science

In the following section, we will use the "Hydroxychloroquine controversy" (see also, Berlivet & Löwy, 2020) to specify these components for *trust in science*. In March 2020, the French microbiologist Professor Didier Raoult published a study claiming that Hydroxychloroquine (a Malaria drug) was highly effective for treating COVID-19. Rapidly, Raoult's results became well known and were picked up by politicians in France and the U.S.A. (especially President Trump and media leaning to him). Simultaneously, the study was scrutinized by other researchers, who pointed to methodological shortcomings. Just a few weeks later, the journal which had accepted the paper, in a fast-track procedure, retracted it. Further studies then corroborated the lack of effectiveness of Hydroxychloroquine treatment against COVID-19 (Lee et al., 2021).

Risk

This case shows how "trust in science" can be simultaneously crucial and fragile. When the pandemic emerged, the nature and epidemiology of the disease and its possible treatments were not well understood, but it became clear that the pathogen was a new version of the well-known coronavirus family. Therefore, researchers worldwide were able to come up with provisional (albeit, not univocal) answers regarding the virus' containment and its treatment. However, there was little evidence yet to back up these claims (epistemic uncertainty) and implementing measures of prevention based on these predictions were costly (and were deeply affecting personal freedom). Therefore, by trusting Raoult's claims, the *risk* for the trustor is the probability of being (by intention or not) misinformed about the *veracity of a claim* about *a critical issue*, which seemed to have been the case when citizens as well as political leaders trusted the claims of the (later retracted) Hydroxychloroquine study.

Epistemic trust

When Raoult published his findings, all stakeholders were *epistemically* dependent on this expert (as from other experts' claims). There might be variance among researchers about the criteria for accepting a claim as "true," as it was in the just mentioned case (Berlivet & Löwy, 2020), especially when the critical issue is directly implemented into practical application. For example, scientists and general practitioners might use different thresholds for accepting a treatment as effective. Furthermore, uncertainty is a central feature of science, allowing only for tentative determination of "truth." However, especially in cases in which the epistemic risk (believing a false claim) is connected to a personal or societal risk (patients' health), trust in science relies on the tightening of conventions for deciding whether to accept a claim as true (Wilholt, 2013). Raoult refused tightening of the methodological conventions and even argued against randomized controlled trials (Berlivet & Löwy, 2020).

When it comes to a medical practitioner (as trustor) and the researcher (for example, Raoult) as trustee, the *epistemic* nature of the risk is obvious. Patients, however, have limited *choice* about the medical treatment on first glance because their knowledge and understanding of alternatives might not allow a truly informed decision. What is their *epistemic* risk and which vulnerability do they accept? Patients legally must agree to being treated in a certain way. Furthermore, the cognitive and the emotional acceptance of a treatment matters for its clinical effectiveness. Such acceptance is not only based on *epistemic* trust, because patients must rely on the medical system in non-epistemic ways (e.g., instruments' quality used for treatment). Nevertheless, the final justification of any treatment is based on the assumed veracity of the claim that this treatment is more effective than an alternative or no treatment.

Citizens who are not directly affected by COVID-19, but interested in news about the pandemic also have a *choice* in whether to believe in Raoult's (vs. his critics') claims, facing the *risk* to accept a claim as true which is (on empirical grounds) false. This risk is even greater when the issue at stake matters for the general understanding of the natural or social world. In the case of the Hydroxychloroquine controversy, claims of effectiveness came along with further, far-reaching claims about the future course of the pandemic and measures to take against it. In fact, when it comes to the public understanding of science, vulnerability does not only come along with the risk of believing false claims, but also with integrating these beliefs into a larger worldview. If claims are justified by evidence, believing them results in a rational and science-based view of the world. Otherwise, the epistemic risk of believing false claims intertwines with more fundamental societal and individual risks (in the case of a pandemic, health risks for the individual and the community). Recent debates about post-truthism as a societal challenge (Lewandowsky et al., 2017) allow for the conclusion that this is a serious problem.

Instrumental trust

Beside its *epistemic* nature, trust in science can have an *instrumental* function. *Instrumental trust* refers to the expectation that the trustee's actions work toward the goals of the trustor. This conceptual distinction mirrors different roles of scientists in society, namely, as researchers (producers of valid knowledge) and as public advisers (brokers of valid knowledge; Pielke, 2007). Scientific advice often is embedded in public discourses, for example about the acceptability of negative side effects of Hydroxychloroquine. Thus, trust in science may be instrumental for the individual by informing personal decisions.

It is an empirical question if people's trust in science has an *epistemic* or an *instrumental* focus. This question could be answered only if the conceptual distinction suggested here is also reflected within research designs and survey items, which is not always the case. Most surveys on trust in science put an emphasis on instrumental trust, when for example asking about citizens' approval of spending tax money for science, or when asking whether science makes life easier (Castell et al., 2014; National Science Board, 2018). In contrast, asking respondents whether they believe that science has sufficiently understood the causes of climate change, or whether there is scientific consensus about this issue (Pasek, 2018), are examples of a focus on *epistemic* trust.

In some instances, instrumental trust might superimpose epistemic trust, as is argued in the cultural cognition literature (Kahan et al., 2011). Epistemic trust judgments rely on an assertion that an expert has the ability, integrity, and benevolence to make "true" claims (see below). However, a persons' general worldview may not only affect her social and technological risk perception, but also her trustworthiness ascriptions to experts, when basing them on value similarity rather than the experts' epistemic trustworthiness.

The trustee

In trust research it is well established that trustors differentiate conceptually between individuals, groups, and institutions as trust object (Blöbaum, 2021), which could be, respectively, single scientists, research labs, or universities. In fact, the COVID-19 pandemic has brought a few scientists to the center of public attention. In Germany, for example, a virologist (Prof. Christian

Drosten, working at an established hospital in Berlin) was expert advisor not only to the Federal government but also in a podcast with millions of listeners (Kupferschmidt, 2020; see also Fahy, 2015 for examples of scientist celebrities from other domains).

People furthermore trust science as an *abstract* entity because science contributes to the everyday understanding of the social world, just as politics or religion (Cervantes et al., Chapter 16). What "science" or "research" as an abstract entity means is an empirical question: German respondents most often mentioned (in this order) medicine, general ideas about science and its importance, technology, environmental issues, and physics/space research (Ziegler et al., 2018).

Often, experiences with science are *mediated*, that is, journalists, public relations officers, teachers, or science museum designers (Schäfer, 2016) could also serve as trustees. The Internet helps attract more diverse audiences but also offers opportunities for science communication to diverse actors. For example, citizens could act as mediators of approved scientific knowledge (as in Wikipedia) but also as partisans of science denialism, for example regarding vaccination in the context of the COVID-19 pandemic (Nguyen & Catalan-Matamoros, 2020). If these sources of science-related information are seen as the ultimate trustees, or as stand-ins for someone else (usually a scientist) who guarantees for the veracity of a claim is an empirical question.

Trustworthiness

The MDS model (1995) assumes that people ascribe trustworthiness to the trustee on the dimensions expertise, integrity, and benevolence, impacting their willingness to trust (Hamm et al., 2019). These may be based on pre-existing beliefs and on inferences following indicative cues (Landrum et al., 2015). For trustworthiness ascriptions to experts, people make differentiated judgments depending on cues relating to these three dimensions, indicating that the dimensions are, albeit interrelated, clearly distinct from each other (Hendriks et al., 2015). *Expertise* refers to the trustees' knowledge and skill. *Integrity* refers to adherence to the professions' rules. *Benevolence* means considering the interests of the trustor or, more generally, the positive impact of scientists' work on society. Besley and colleagues (2020) reassessed how "perceptions of scientists" are measured, integrating items from 40 studies (published in well-established science communication journals) and find a fourth dimension beyond expertise, integrity, and benevolence they call *openness* (represented by items like respectful–disrespectful, willing–unwilling to explain decisions).

While the dimensions expertise, benevolence, and integrity replicate well in the context of science, their meaning is specific to this context. For example, the dimension of integrity typically is understood as the trustees' adherence to values and principles which are shared by the trustor (Hamm et al., 2019). Applied to science, these values and principles are those shared by the scientific community. Laypersons must not necessarily have a deep understanding of them, but a general sense that adherence to scientific conventions is vital to produce true and unbiased knowledge.

Why trust is inevitable in people's encounters with science

In modern societies, scientific knowledge is inevitable for citizens' personal problem solving and for an understanding of the natural and the social world. Many different disciplines and scientific fields contribute to the scientific understanding of today's problems, such as climate change or the global pandemic response. But this understanding is fundamentally constrained by an elaborated division of cognitive labor. It takes years to acquire the skills and the understanding necessary for judging about the "truth" of scientific knowledge, resulting in a set of highly specialized fields and disciplines. Insofar as this is true, people must rely on the testimony of experts about what is true (*dependence*). Regarding many issues of interest (e.g., whether a treatment against COVID-19 is effective) decisions cannot be based alone on one's own (as laypersons) capabilities for understanding of what is true and what is false. Most people do not have the expertise, the resources, and the time for valid first-hand judgments. Instead, one's reliance on experts must be based on second-hand judgment about whom to trust (*expectations*, Bromme & Goldman, 2014), even though believing experts for knowledge comes with the *risk* to acquire false beliefs. In that sense, the relationship between citizens and science is *inevitably* a relationship of trust (or distrust) in science, whenever people refer to scientific knowledge (in discourse, for personal decision making, or for their personal understanding of the social and the natural world).

Challenges for *informed* epistemic trust

Inspired by the concept of patients' informed decision making (Bekker et al., 1999), we have suggested the notion of informed trust as a concept for a knowledge-based and rational process of trust (Bromme, 2020; see also

Bromme & Gierth, 2021 on the relationship between rationality and trust). A main challenge for informed trust is that science can be conceived as an epistemic as well as a social endeavor (Hendriks et al., 2016). When we refer to science as an epistemic endeavor, we refer to data, knowledge, methods, rules, and regulated ways of discourse aimed at both the production and the critique of "truth." In empirical disciplines, "truth" starts with theoretical notions about the research object which are constrained by data. Simultaneously, science refers to the social endeavor in which individuals and organizations collaboratively produce and negotiate "truth." To do this effectively, scientists rely on each other,[3] based on conventions, which are closely upheld, and controlled by others (and penalized if not). In this sense, what is accepted as "true" is based on a consensus among scientists, which is not arbitrary but regulated by methods and conventions and has to align with the available data. Establishing a consensus "against evidence" is not possible, at least not in the long run.

Even this humble description[4] of science immediately reveals one of the main challenges of informed trust: For judgments of informed trust in science, it is necessary to consider and weigh up information on both the epistemic and the social nature of science. In the easiest case, this means judgments about scientists' expertise, integrity, and benevolence, to identify the most trustworthy expert. However, trust in science also relies on more general expectations about science and its processes. Accepting that climate change is real because there is a consensus among the vast majority of climate scientists is not in accordance with the everyday understanding of reality and truth: One would not accept that it is raining when the majority of their neighbors agree about the weather. Only if one understands the role of consensus in science, it would be rational to believe a claim based on consensus. Thus, understanding scientific consensus has been considered a "gateway belief" for accepting the present state of scientific knowledge about climate change (van der Linden, 2021). However, the duality of the epistemic and the social side of science can also be a gateway for science denialism (Kienhues et al., 2020). Strategies to undermine trust in scientists and in science include that there are alternative scientists having their own consensus, and even the outright rejection of the duality by insisting on an idea of immediate truth, appealing to people's intuitions and personal experience (Boudry et al., 2015). Furthermore, scandals

---

[3]   This is why trust is also essential among scientists (Hardwig, 1991; Wilholt, 2013). Here, we do not cover the role of trust *among* scientists and *within* science.

[4]   This is a condensed view of science and scientific knowledge production is based on recent philosophy of science (see, for example, Oreskes, 2020).

like climategate (hacked emails by U.K. scientists seemed to imply scientific misconduct, but the scientists were later exonerated) imply scientists' own violation of epistemic and social values and thus may lead to a loss of trust in science; moreover, such cases are strategically used by science denialists to attack science (Collins & Nerlich, 2016).

Fostering citizens' informed trust judgments

The dimensions of trustworthiness are informative for reflecting on challenges in making judgments of *informed* trust. Beyond this, they inform implications for science communication to foster such judgments. In the following, we outline a few examples.

Expertise

People use superficial indicators for determining scientists' expertise about a topic, as for example a professorship or doctorate in a relevant discipline (Hendriks et al., 2015), an affiliation to a well-known university, and even the use of technical terms (Thon & Jucks, 2016). These cues can inform judgments about "whom to trust," especially for distinguishing between pseudo-science and science. However, from the notion of the cognitive division of labor, it follows that expertise is graded, relative to the breadth of a topic (Bromme & Thomm, 2016). Thus, judging experts' *pertinence* (as a specific feature of expertise) is vital for identifying the expert most knowledgeable about the topic of interest. Science communication could use information on the disciplinary structure of science (highlighting also boundaries of expertise) to inform citizens' reasoning about experts' pertinence. Furthermore, the *reputation* of an expert (indicated by prestige within the scientific community and the number of relevant publications and their citations) is a reasonable indicator for expertise from the social side of science.

Integrity

Transparency in research processes have been considered (at least within science) a signifier of trustworthiness through fostering replicability and reproducibility (Peels & Bouter, 2021), a central argument of the Open Science movement. Science communication could thus inform judgments about the integrity of scientists by transparency about research processes (Jamieson et al., 2019). Empirical results show that when a university or company commits to transparent research practices in a public statement, they were trusted more than in the absence of such a statement (Landrum et al., 2018). Similarly, a scientist's integrity might be positively affected, if he/she performs self-criticism of research methodology (Altenmüller et al., 2021b).

However, science communication addressing low replicability within a discipline may lead to lower trust compared to a condition of comparably high replicability (Wingen et al., 2019), or a control condition (Anvari & Lakens, 2019). Importantly, the two cited studies were not successful in repairing such loss of trust by providing information about reforms (here, the open science movement in psychology). Ophir and Jamieson (2021) found that trust in science may benefit the belief that science is self-correcting, even if news stories about science are problem-focused. These results show why it is so important to explore and support *people's beliefs about science as a social system* (Ophir & Jamieson, 2021).

Benevolence

This dimension is related to Merton's norm of disinterestedness: Scientists should not be influenced by extrinsic (e.g., profit, prestige) motivations. In fact, citizens prefer intrinsic motivations (e.g., being curious, wanting to help) over extrinsic motivations for scientists (Johnson & Dieckmann, 2020). Cues pointing to the possibility of vested interests typically reduce trust in science or scientists' claims (Besley et al., 2017, Gierth & Bromme, 2020). However, when a researcher has a personal connection to a research topic (a vegan scientist studying perceptions of veganism), he/she is perceived as being more trustworthy, but only when participants held a favorable view of the topic (Altenmüller et al., 2021a).

These results raise the question whether there can be a disinterested researcher. In fact, many historical examples show the influence of moral and political values on science (Allchin, 1999), sometimes in a deeply troubling way, as in the case of the Tuskegee syphilis study. In consequence of such cases, there might be deeply rooted mistrust in science (Pierre, 2020). When establishing the veracity of knowledge claims—the epistemic function of science—a disinterestedness in aims and values (beyond epistemic values, as for example objectivity) should be expected to justify the ascription of trust. However, in the choice of research questions or the assignment of monetary resources, moral and/or political values are sometimes unavoidable (Douglas, 2000), and may even justify trust, for example when science aims at identifying health risks (Wilholt, 2013). Again, informed trust could resolve this tension by understanding science as both an epistemic and a social endeavor (including organized skepticism).

Conclusion

The MDS trust model and related models conceptualize trust as a social process between trustor and trustee, benefitting the trustors' understanding of and agency in the world, based on his/her belief systems (knowledge). Insofar, trust in science can be conceptualized similar to trust in other contexts. However, the division of cognitive labor leads to a specific form of vulnerability: The trustor can only achieve a partial understanding of the world, based on only fragments of scientific knowledge (Keil, 2019). While there is no need to understand the world in depth, the trustor could rely on experts to gain knowledge (the epistemic function of science), and gain agency (the instrumental function of science), if these experts are trustworthy (this, the trustor can only infer). In this chapter, we have focused on these functions of trust by elaborating the concept of *epistemic* trust. It might be worthwhile to study the triangle of trustor, trustee, and belief systems (which are not fully represented within an individual's cognitive systems) in other contexts; for example, cognitive development (Harris, 2012), religion (Cervantes et al., Chapter 16), and dynamical systems (Long & Sitkin, Chapter 6).

References

Allchin, D. (1999). Values in science: an educational perspective. *Science & Education 8*, 1–12. https://doi.org/10.1023/A:1008600230536.

Altenmüller, M. S., Lange, L. L., & Gollwitzer, M. (2021a). When research is me-search: how researchers' motivation to pursue a topic affects laypeople's trust in science. *PLoS ONE, 16*(7). https://doi.org/10.1371/journal.pone.0253911.

Altenmüller, M. S., Nuding, S., & Gollwitzer, M. (2021b). No harm in being self-corrective: self-criticism and reform intentions increase researchers' epistemic trustworthiness and credibility in the eyes of the public. *Public Understanding of Science.* https://doi.org/10.1177/09636625211022181.

Anvari, F., & Lakens, D. (2019). The replicability crisis and public trust in psychological science. *Comprehensive Results in Social Psychology, 3*(3), 266–286. https://doi.org/10.1080/23743603.2019.1684822.

Bekker, H., Thornton, J., Airey, C., Connelly, J., Hewison, J., Robinson, M., et al. (1999). Informed decision making: an annotated bibliography and systematic review. *Health Technology Assessment, 3*(1). https://discovery.ucl.ac.uk/id/eprint/15902/1/15902.pdf.

Berlivet, L., & Löwy, I. (2020). Hydroxychloroquine controversies: clinical trials, epistemology, and the democratization of science. *Medical Anthropology Quarterly, 34*(4), 525–541. https://doi.org/10.1111/maq.12622.

Besley, J. C., Lee, N. M., & Pressgrove, G. (2020). Reassessing the variables used to measure public perceptions of scientists. *Science Communication.* https://doi.org/10.1177/1075547020949547.

Besley, J. C., McCright, A. M., Zahry, N. R., Elliott, K. C., Kaminski, N. E., & Martin, J. D. (2017). Perceived conflict of interest in health science partnerships. *PLoS ONE, 12*(4). https://doi.org/10.1371/journal.pone.0175643.

Blöbaum, B. (2021). Some thoughts on the nature of trust: concept, models and theory. In B. Blöbaum (Ed.), *Trust and Communication in a Digitized World* (pp. 3–28). Wiesbaden: Springer.

Boudry, M., Blancke, S., & Pigliucci, M. (2015). What makes weird beliefs thrive? The epidemiology of pseudoscience. *Philosophical Psychology, 28*(8), 1177–1198. https://doi.org/10.1080/09515089.2014.971946.

Bromme, R. (2020). Informiertes vertrauen: eine psychologische perspektive auf vertrauen in wissenschaft. In M. Jungert, A. Frewer, & E. Mayr (Eds.), *Wissenschaftsreflexion. Interdisziplinäre Perspektiven zwischen Philosophie und Praxis* (pp. 105–134). Paderborn: Mentis.

Bromme, R., & Gierth, L. (2021). Rationality and the public understanding of science. In M. Knauff & W. Spohn (Eds.), *The Handbook of Rationality* (pp. 767–776). Cambridge, MA: MIT Press.

Bromme, R., & Goldman, S. R. (2014). The public's bounded understanding of science. *Educational Psychologist, 49*(2), 59–69. https://doi.org/10.1080/00461520.2014.921572.

Bromme, R., Mede, N., Thomm, E., Kremer, B., & Ziegler, R. (2022). An anchor in troubled times: trust in science before and within the COVID-19 pandemic. *PLoS ONE*. https://doi.org/10.1371/journal.pone.0262823.

Bromme, R., & Thomm, E. (2016). Knowing who knows: laypersons' capabilities to judge experts' pertinence for science topics. *Cognitive Science, 40*, 241–252. https://doi.org/10.1111/cogs.12252.

Castell, S., Charlton, A., Clemence, M., Pettigrew, N., Pope, S., Quigley, A., Navin Shah, J., & Silman, T. (2014). Public attitudes to science 2014. *Ipsos MORI*, 202. http://www.ipsos-mori.com/Assets/Docs/Polls/pas-2014-main-report.pdf.

Collins, L. C., & Nerlich, B. (2016). Uncertainty discourses in the context of climate change: a corpus-assisted analysis of UK national newspaper articles. *Communications, 41*(3), 291–313. https://doi.org/10.1515/commun-2016-0009.

Douglas, H. (2000). Inductive risk and values in science. *Philosophy of Science, 67*(4), 559–579. https://doi.org/10.1086/392855.

Fahy, D. (2015). *The New Celebrity Scientist*. Lanham, MD: Rowman & Littlefield.

Gierth, L., & Bromme, R. (2020). Beware of vested interests: epistemic vigilance improves reasoning about scientific evidence (for some people). *PLoS ONE, 15*(4). https://doi.org/10.1371/journal.pone.0231387.

Hamm, J., Smidt, C., & Mayer, R. (2019). Understanding the psychological nature and mechanisms of political trust. *PLoS ONE*. https://doi.org/10.1371/journal.pone.0215835.

Hardwig, J. (1991). The role of trust in knowledge. *The Journal of Philosophy, 88*(12), 693–708.

Harris, P. (2012). *Trusting What You're Told: How Children Learn From Others*. Cambridge, MA: The Belknap Press of Harvard University Press.

Hendriks, F., Kienhues, D., & Bromme, R. (2015). Measuring laypeople's trust in experts in a digital age: the Muenster epistemic trustworthiness inventory (METI). *PLoS ONE, 10*(10). https://doi.org/10.1371/journal.pone.0139309.

Hendriks, F., Kienhues, D., & Bromme, R. (2016). Trust in science and the science of trust. In B. Blöbaum (Ed.), *Trust and Communication in a Digitized World: Models and Concepts of Trust Research* (pp. 239–251). Cham: Springer. https://doi.org/10 .1007/978-3-319-28059-2.

Jamieson, K. H., McNutt, M., Kiermer, V., & Sever, R. (2019). Signaling the trust-worthiness of science. *Proceedings of the National Academy of Sciences, 116*(39), 19231–19236. https://doi.org/10.1073/pnas.1913039116.

Johnson, B. B., & Dieckmann, N. F. (2020). Americans' views of scientists' motivations for scientific work. *Public Understanding of Science, 29*(1), 2–20. https://doi.org/10 .1177/0963662519880319.

Kahan, D. M., Jenkins-Smith, H., & Braman, D. (2011). Cultural cognition of scientific consensus. *Journal of Risk Research, 14*(2), 147–174. https://doi.org/10.1080/ 13669877.2010.511246.

Keil, F. C. (2019). How do partial understandings work? In S. Grimm (Ed.), *Varieties of Understanding* (pp. 191–208). New York, Oxford: Oxford University Press.

Kienhues, D., Jucks, R., & Bromme, R. (2020). Sealing the gateways for post-truthism: reestablishing the epistemic authority of science. *Educational Psychologist, 55*(3), 144–154. https://doi.org/10.1080/00461520.2020.1784012.

Kupferschmidt, K. (2020). How the pandemic made this virologist an unlikely cult figure. *Science, 19*. https://doi.org/10.1126/science.abc5095 M4.

Landrum, A. R., Eaves, B. S., & Shafto, P. (2015). Learning to trust and trusting to learn: a theoretical framework. *Trends in Cognitive Sciences, 19*(3), 109–111. https://doi .org/10.1016/j.tics.2014.12.007.

Landrum, A. R., Hilgard, J., Lull, R. B., Akin, H., & Hall Jamieson, K. (2018). Open and transparent research practices and public perceptions of the trustworthiness of agricultural biotechnology organizations. *Journal of Science Communication, 17*(2), 1–33. https://doi.org/10.22323/2.17020204.

Lee, Z., Rayner, C. R., Forrest, J. I., Nachega, J. B., Senchaudhuri, E., & Mills, E. J. (2021). The rise and fall of hydroxychloroquine for the treatment and prevention of COVID-19. *The American Journal of Tropical Medicine and Hygiene, 104*(1), 35–38. https://doi.org/10.4269/ajtmh.20-1320.

Lewandowsky, S., Ecker, U., & Cook, J. (2017). Beyond misinformation: understanding and coping with the post-truth era. *Journal of Applied Research in Memory and Cognition, 6*, 353–369. https://doi.org/10.1016/j.jarmac.2017.07.008.

Mayer, R. C., Davis, J. H., & Schoorman, F. D. (1995). An integrative model of organizational trust. *Academy of Managment Review, 20*(3), 709–734. https://doi.org/10 .2307/258792.

National Science Board (2018). Science and engineering indicators 2018. https://www .nsf.gov/statistics/indicators/.

Nguyen, A., & Catalan-Matamoros, D. (2020). Digital mis/disinformation and public engagment with health and science controversies: fresh perspectives from Covid-19. *Media and Communication, 8*(2), 323–328. https://doi.org/10.17645/mac.v8i2.3352.

Ophir, Y., & Jamieson, K. H. (2021). The effects of media narratives about failures and discoveries in science on beliefs about and support for science. *Public Understanding of Science*. https://doi.org/10.1177/09636625211012630.

Oreskes, N. (2020). *Why Trust Science?* Princeton, NJ: Princeton University Press.

Pasek, J. (2018). It's not my consensus: motivated reasoning and the sources of scientific illiteracy. *Public Understanding of Science, 27*(7), 787–806. https://doi.org/10.1177/ 0963662517733681.

Peels, R., & Bouter, L. (2021). Replication and trustworthiness. *Accountability in Research*, 1–11. https://doi.org/10.1080/08989621.2021.1963708.

Pielke, R. J. (2007). *The Honest Broker: Making Sense of Science in Policy and Politics*. Cambridge: Cambridge University Press.

Pierre, J. M. (2020). Mistrust and misinformation: a two-component, socio-epistemic model of belief in conspiracy theories. *Journal of Social and Political Psychology*, *8*(2), 617–641. https://doi.org/10.5964/jspp.v8i2.1362.

PytlikZillig, L. M., & Kimbrough D. K. C. (2016). Consensus on conceptualizations and definitions of trust: are we there yet? In E. Schockley, T. M. S. Neal, L. M. PytlikZillig, & B. H. Bornstein (Eds.), *Interdiciplinary Perspectives on Trust: Towards Theoretical and Methodological Integration* (pp. 17–47). Cham: Springer.

Schäfer, M. S. (2016). Mediated trust in science: concept, measurement and perspectives for the "science of science communication". *Jcom – Journal of Science Communication*, *15*(5). https://doi.org/10.22323/2.15050302.

Thon, F. M., & Jucks, R. (2016). Believing in expertise: how authors' credentials and language use influence the credibility of online health information. *Health Communication*. https://doi.org/10.1080/10410236.2016.1172296.

van der Linden, S. (2021). The Gateway Belief Model (GBM): a review and research agenda for communicating the scientific consensus on climate change. *Current Opinion in Psychology*. https://doi.org/10.1016/j.copsyc.2021.01.005.

Wilholt, T. (2013). Epistemic trust in science. *The British Journal for the Philosophy of Science*, *64*(2), 233–253. https://doi.org/10.1093/bjps/axs007.

Wingen, T., Berkessel, J. B., & Englich, B. (2019). No replication, no trust? How low replicability influences trust in psychology. *Social Psychological and Personality Science*, *11*(4), 454–463. https://doi.org/10.1177/1948550619877412.

Ziegler, R., Kremer, B., & Weißkopf, M. (2018). *Medizin und neue Technologien, Analysen und Erkenntnisse, Intelligenz und Ausdauer – Welche Vorstellung hat die Bevölkerung von Wissenschaft und Forschenden? Ergebnisse der offenen Fragestellungen im Wissenschaftsbarometer 2017*. https:// www .wissenschaft -im -dialog .de/ fileadmin/ user_upload/ Projekte/ Wissenschafts barometer/ Dokumente _17/ WiD-Wissenschaftsbarometer_Hintergrundpapier_Vorstellung_Wissenschaft _Forschende.pdf.

5   Trust in autonomous technology: the machine or its maker?

Kimberly M. Wingert and Roger C. Mayer

Recent advances in technology have led to increasing innovation in the use of autonomous systems, allowing people to focus on and prioritize other actions and decisions (Boeing, 2021). In addition to Boeing's autonomous sea, aerial, and space systems, the market for autonomous vehicles is expected to grow substantially over the next decade (e.g., Precedence Research, 2020; Research and Markets, 2020). The U.S. Department of Transportation (2019) has recognized the importance of this growth and recently invested $60 million in grant funding to test the safety of autonomous vehicles on the road. While some see this as a logical and valuable development of current technology that will cut costs and increase efficiency for consumers, others are skeptical about having their safety and security under the control of automated technology.

Although researchers have been studying the factors that affect how much one trusts automation for some time (e.g., Lee & See, 2004), in this chapter we question what the trust referent actually is: is the relevant trust referent the *technology itself*, or the *maker* of the technology (e.g., Tesla and the people working at Tesla)? Additionally, we summarize some early empirical research we have conducted to investigate whether trusting other people in general, trusting autonomous machines (e.g., self-driving cars), and trusting the makers of autonomous machines are different from one another. We posit that trust formation is different across different possible autonomous technology-related referents, and is likely dependent on different processes across referents. Further, it is possible that some of the findings in the literature that connect trust to automation may be due to the trustee grouping the technology and the maker of the technology together when considering their willingness to trust automation.

Autonomous systems

Lee and See (2004, 50) define automation as "technology that actively selects data, transforms information, makes decisions, or controls processes." An autonomous system[1] can thus be defined as an instance of automation where the goal of the system is defined. For example, an automobile that is able to drive itself is an example of an autonomous system. Despite the potential of such technology to improve human performance (Boeing, 2021; Lee & See, 2004), not everyone is willing to rely on such technology. Recent failures of autonomous systems, such as the Boeing 737 MAX crash that took 157 lives (Synced, 2019), do little to increase people's willingness to rely on automation. Given the recent and expected increase in the use of such technology, researchers have increasingly focused on understanding what determines whether an individual will trust an autonomous system (e.g., Lee & See, 2004).

Trust

In this chapter we define trust as "the willingness of a party to be vulnerable to the actions of another party based on the expectation that the other will perform a particular action important to the trustor, irrespective of the ability to monitor or control that other party" (Mayer et al., 1995; see also Mayer & Mayer, Chapter 1). As shown in the model presented in the overview chapter, Mayer et al. (1995) proposed that trust is determined by perceptions of trustworthiness (ability, benevolence, and integrity) of the trustee, as well as a trustor's inherent willingness to trust others (propensity to trust). Further, the authors proposed that the likelihood or propensity of an individual to trust other people in general can enhance or moderate the effect of ability, benevolence, and integrity on trust in that party. Inherent in this model is the assumption that trust involves an identifiable "other party," or referent, to which the individual makes themselves vulnerable (e.g., Mayer et al., 1995).

---

[1]   Others refer to Artificial Intelligence (AI) agents (e.g., see Singh & Mayer, Chapter 8), which are what we define to be an autonomous system. This system is embedded within a broader sociotechnical system that encompasses people (e.g., the organization if the autonomous system is implemented in that organization: see Chopra & Singh, 2018; Singh, 2014; Singh & Mayer, Chapter 8). Considerations of the broader sociotechnical system may introduce additional trust referents (e.g., the maker may not be the same as the organization implementing the autonomous system) but would be specific to a given context.

An example provided by Mayer et al. (1995) addressing the necessity of a relationship with an identifiable "other party" was a situation in which a farmer plants crops with the expectation that there will be sufficient rain for the crops to grow. Although there are systems in place for predicting the weather, those systems and the people reporting data from those systems do not actually control the weather. As noted by the authors, the farmer does not actually trust the weather, but rather takes a risk on what the weather will do based on the potential gains from the crops (Deutsch, 1958). This example highlights a potential issue with research on trust in autonomous systems. Does an autonomous system qualify as an identifiable other party, or do people simply take a risk on how the system will perform in a given context? In the sections that follow, we evaluate the claim that an individual can trust an autonomous system.

Autonomous systems as an identifiable "other party"

Humans anthropomorphize objects or systems for a number of reasons. A study by Waytz et al. (2010) indicated that one reason that people anthropomorphize is to make something appear more predictable and understandable. This same study further indicated that neural activation in response to evaluating the mental capacity of unpredictable gadgets is similar to neural activation when mentalizing about humans (e.g., see Jenkins et al., 2008; Mitchell et al., 2006). Further, this neural activation was related to explicit anthropomorphism ratings. However, as noted in Mayer et al. (1995), while prediction and trust provide a means of reducing complexity and uncertainty (Lewis & Weigert, 1985), trust goes beyond predictability (Deutsch, 1958). One example provided in Mayer et al. (1995) clearly illustrates why this must be true. If a superior in a work environment were to always blame an employee for bad news the employee had to deliver, the superior's behavior would be predictable but the employee would be less likely to choose to deliver the bad news. Thus, if the reason for attributing human characteristics to an autonomous system is to make it seem more predictable, it does not necessarily follow that these attributions will qualify the system as something the person can choose to trust.

Lee and See (2004) similarly cite work demonstrating that people respond to technology as if it were human (e.g., Reeves & Nass, 1996). The authors draw on work such as this to support the notion that emotion and attitude may influence not only relationships between humans, but also relationships between humans and automation. Further, the authors define trust as an attitude and argue that automation can be categorized as an agent to which trust can be attributed. Lee and See (2004) also cite work by Sheridan (1975) and Sheridan and Hennessy (1984) who argue that trust is an important determinant of the relationship between people and automation. Further, Sheridan and Hennessy (1984) argue that perceived trustworthiness determines the behavior of the human in interacting with the system. However, it is unclear if an object or system itself can have benevolence, and the ability and integrity of a system may be inherently tied to the maker of the system and not to the system itself.

Trust and autonomous systems

Mayer et al. (1995) proposed that trust is determined by characteristics of the trustee and of the trustor. The characteristics of the trustee relevant to a trustor making a trust decision include three factors of perceived trustworthiness: ability, benevolence, and integrity. In order to evaluate the claims made by Sheridan and Hennessy (1984; see also Lee & See, 2004) that a system can be trustworthy, it is important to consider how each of these factors of trustworthiness may relate to an autonomous system. If any one of these factors does not apply to autonomous systems, then this would imply that the basis for decisions to trust is different across *objects or systems* on the one hand, and *people in general* or even the *makers* of the object or system on the other hand. Next, we consider the definition of each of these factors as outlined in Mayer et al. (1995), and then discuss the appropriateness of evaluating an autonomous system along this dimension of trustworthiness.

Ability is defined as "that group of skills, competencies, and characteristics that enable a party to have influence within some specific domain" (Mayer et al., 1995, 717). As noted by these authors, ability is specific to a given domain or area in which that the referent is expected to perform. As an example, a pharmacist may be up to date on all the latest medications, what they are used for, their interactions with other medications, and their potential side effects. However, this pharmacist would not be qualified to perform surgery because that is outside of their domain. Similarly, an autonomous system is created to serve a function. An automobile with the ability to drive itself would certainly not make a good airplane. On the surface these considerations between ability in people and ability in autonomous systems seem reasonably comparable; however, these considerations may not tell the entire story.

On the one hand, Lyons, Scheutz, and Jessup (Chapter 10) summarize work that demonstrates that perceived ability of an autonomous agent is higher when it is more accurate. However, they also found that when the script indicated that the autonomous agent had higher benevolence toward certain people, it was only perceived as higher in ability when a person was behind the scenes controlling the decisions. Additionally, when faced with the decision of determining the ability of an autonomous system that is unfamiliar to an individual, it seems likely that this person will seek information from sources other than interacting with the system itself. Deciding that a self-driving car has the ability to get to a destination safely can be costly if the underlying computer program directing the car to respond in certain ways to external stimuli is meaningfully flawed. To determine this ability prior to experiencing it, it is likely that people will instead first consider the ability of the *maker* of the autonomous system.[2] If a given maker of an autonomous system is judged to have low ability, then it would stand to reason that a person would be unwilling to assume that the vehicle itself should have the ability to drive safely to the destination.

On the other hand, given the relative novelty of such autonomous technology, there may be no meaningful information about the maker of the autonomous system in this context. In this case, it is possible that an individual may determine the ability of the autonomous system via other means such as conversations with those who have used the system and can attest to how well the system performs. From these two points we can infer that there are two potential referents in judging the ability of the system: the system itself, and the maker of the system. To disentangle the contributions of each of these to perceptions of trustworthiness and examine how these perceptions influence decisions to trust, it is important to measure perceptions of both referents in empirical studies.

Benevolence is defined as "the extent to which a trustee is believed to want to do good to the trustor, aside from an egocentric profit motive" (Mayer et al., 1995, 718). Mayer et al. (1995, 719) further clarify that "benevolence is the perception of a positive orientation of the trustee toward the trustor." If an individual decided to give out a scholarship to pay for someone's education so that the student can excel despite difficult life circumstances, the recipient may judge the benefactor to be high in benevolence. It is noteworthy that the person awarding the scholarship does not profit from doing this for the student; they are simply acting in the student's best interests. Based on the above definition, it is unclear if an object or system can have benevolence.

---

[2]   More established and familiar systems such as planes on autopilot may generate slightly less focus on the maker of the system compared to novel autonomous systems (such as self-driving cars) because sufficient familiarity with the system and common use of the system may be more informative in determining reliance.

An autonomous system does not have an orientation toward an individual outside of what it was programmed to do. Thus, in the case of an autonomous system it seems more relevant to question whether the *maker* of the autonomous system has benevolence toward the trustor. A maker of an autonomous system can want to do good for the trustor independent from their potential to earn profit. Although Lee and See (2004) summarize research to conclude that emotional and attitudinal considerations are similarly relevant in considering relationships with autonomous systems, it is unclear that this would extend to the domain of benevolence. Lyons et al. (Chapter 10) summarize research whereby an autonomous agent is deemed to have benevolence, particularly when participants are told that the autonomous agent has a self-sacrificing social intent and has higher levels of autonomy to implement this intent. However, an autonomous agent is still driven by how it was programmed. Thus, by failing to account for the two separate referents (the maker of the system and the system itself), any actual judgments of benevolence of a system would be confounded with judgments of the benevolence of the maker of the system. Once again, to disentangle the contributions of judgments of the benevolence of each of the referents to perceptions of trustworthiness and examine how these perceptions influence decisions to trust, it is important to measure perceptions of both referents in empirical studies.

The third factor contributing to perceptions of trustworthiness is integrity. Perceptions of integrity are determined by how well a trustee "adheres to a set of principles that the trustor finds acceptable" (Mayer et al., 1995, 719). As noted in Mayer et al. (1995), it is both the adherence to principles as well as the fact that the trustor finds the principles acceptable that jointly determine perceptions of integrity. If an individual is committed to the principle of seeking profit no matter what, this party would not be judged to have high integrity unless the trustor also values this (finds this principle acceptable: Mayer et al., 1995: 719). In the case of an autonomous system, it can be argued that the system adheres to a set of principles if it was programmed to adhere to those principles. Additionally, it is entirely possible that the trustor could value these principles. Taken literally then, it is possible that an autonomous system could operate with integrity as defined in this section and in Mayer et al. (1995). However, the system itself doesn't actually have intent, and the integrity of the system is defined by how the *maker* of the system has created the autonomous system to be and how well it can execute its programming. That is, although Lyons et al. (Chapter 10) indicates that social intent manipulations affect perceived integrity, we posit that it is likely that people still understand that the autonomous system was programmed to have that intent and they may be considering both the system itself and the maker of the system in these judgments. Thus, once again it is important to measure perceptions of integrity of both the autonomous system itself and of the maker of the system to determine if it is appropriate to claim that a system can be trustworthy (e.g., Sheridan & Hennessy, 1984).[3]

The three factors of trustworthiness define characteristics of the trustee that are relevant for making decisions about whom (or what) to trust. Based on the preceding section, a trustor's consideration of trustworthiness of a person, autonomous system, or maker of an autonomous system may develop weighting the three factors (Ability, Benevolence, Integrity) differently. It is thus unclear if the basis for trust decisions is the same for a person, an autonomous system, or the maker of an autonomous system. The fact that these perceptions regarding the system itself have been confounded with the maker of the system in the literature may partially help explain why authors such as Lee and See (2004) concluded that it is appropriate to consider trust in a system as a defining feature of the relationship between a person and that system, just as trust is a defining feature of relationships between people. Such authors may believe studies they cited have measured reactions to an autonomous system, but the individual may be shifting between considering the system itself and the maker of the system (when they cannot draw inferences based on the system itself). To keep the individual from doing this, the distinction between the system itself and the maker must be brought to participants' awareness, and perceptions of the trustworthiness of the system and perceptions of trustworthiness of the maker of the system should be measured separately, allowing these variables both to separately predict reliance on the system. Studies that have combined these two sources of variability—which may be based on qualitatively different kinds of evaluations—may dismiss as error a relationship that could explain variation in trust.

Propensity to trust

The characteristics of the trustee discussed above are not the only factors that ultimately determine a trustor's decision to trust in a given situation. Characteristics of the trustor are also important. Mayer et al. (1995) define propensity to trust as "a general willingness to trust others." As noted by the

---

[3]   We note an important distinction in this analysis that differs from that of Singh and Mayer (Chapter 8). Their analysis is focused on trusting a *sociotechnical* system that includes AI; by definition such a system has people involved so a trustor's perception of the system's benevolence and integrity are more straightforward and appropriate.

authors, this general willingness to trust other people helps determine decisions to trust, especially in the absence of information about the trustworthiness of the trustee. Additionally, Mayer et al. propose that propensity to trust can enhance the effect of factors of trustworthiness on decisions to trust.

The same question raised in the section covering the factors of trustworthiness is again raised here: What is the most appropriate referent for this general willingness to trust? In the experience of these authors, some people seem—from their words and behavior—not to trust an autonomous system in a situation involving much risk. Other people show the same sort of hesitation regarding trusting large for-profit corporations. While Mayer et al. (1995) describe the willingness to trust people in general, we submit that a focus on how much a trustor is willing to trust autonomous systems in general is likely to be distinct from propensity to trust people. To best predict trust in a *given* autonomous system, we question whether the most appropriate propensity referent is the autonomous system itself, the *maker* of the autonomous system, or both? In other words, when examining how much a trustor is willing to be vulnerable to a *particular autonomous system*, is there an appropriate analog to propensity to trust other people? We believe research is needed to evaluate whether the general willingness to trust other people translates into a general willingness to trust autonomous systems and their makers. Is the trustor's *general willingness to trust autonomous systems* and/or *general willingness to trust the makers* of such complex autonomous systems a distinct, and perhaps even a better predictor of trust in a specific autonomous system (e.g., a self-driving taxicab that is in front of them)?

We focused our initial empirical research on investigating whether propensity to trust other people, autonomous systems, and makers of autonomous systems were distinct from one another. Before we could evaluate whether propensity to trust autonomous systems and/or propensity to trust makers of such systems can help make better predictions about how much risk a trustor is willing to take with, for example, an autonomous vehicle in front of them, some more basic research was needed. First, we needed measures of propensity to trust for all three referents, and to statistically test whether they were (as we suggest above) distinct from one another.

We started with existing survey items that measured *propensity to trust people in general*. An example of a question from this survey is "Most people can be counted on to do what they say they will do" (Mayer and Davis, 1999: 136; Rotter, 1967). Participants answered each question by indicating how much they agreed with each statement on a scale from 1 (Disagree) to 7 (Agree). Next, we adapted this scale so that a second version of the scale included questions referring to autonomous systems as the referent (instead of people in general), and another version included questions referring to the makers of autonomous systems as the referent. An example question from the *propensity to trust autonomous systems* scale is "Most autonomous systems can be counted on to do what they are supposed to do." An example question from the *propensity to trust makers of autonomous systems* scale is "Most makers of autonomous systems can be counted on to create a product that does what they claim it will do."

The original measure for propensity to trust people in general was developed focused on a referent of people in general. People can make conscious decisions and take internally determined action. Some of the items that have traditionally been used to measure propensity reflect this. For our analysis we used only questions that could reasonably be adapted to autonomous systems and makers of autonomous systems. One statistical method for evaluating survey measures is to examine how the items "load," or how the items' intercorrelations group them together. These patterns of loadings, or factor structures, were compared for the three scales. Examining propensity to trust across each of these referents revealed that the factor structure was similar for people in general and makers of autonomous systems and different than either of those for the autonomous systems themselves. This finding is consistent with our expectation that different referents would be considered differently even in this early general willingness to trust. Given the work outlined thus far in the chapter, we expect that more differences will arise in considerations of trustworthiness across the different referents.

Despite the tendency of humans to anthropomorphize and respond to technology as if it were human (e.g., Reeves & Nass, 1996; see also Lee & See, 2004), it does not necessarily follow that trust is derived similarly across people and machines. Further, it is possible that there are additional referents beyond those mentioned here. For example, asking about the maker of an autonomous system may involve an evaluation of the person or company, on the one hand, and the country in which the product was made, on the other hand, or who implemented the autonomous system (e.g., corporation or government), or who is operating or maintaining the autonomous system. There may also be differences across autonomous systems created by the same maker (e.g., different models of self-driving cars by the same company).

These issues deserve further exploration and may improve the ability of trust to predict trust behaviors such as reliance on technology (e.g., Lee & See, 2004). Other issues that may influence trust include human flaws in assessments of cause and effect, and their determinations of the agency of an automated system. For example, a downdraft could cause a rocket to land in the wrong place in error and people could interpret this as a missile attack when actually the error was due to an act of nature.

Additionally, there may be differences in reliance depending on how much control an autonomous system has and the consequences of failure. In the case of a self-driving car, the car would have total control, and a failure could result in death. By contrast, management of fewer components (e.g., lane assist to steer but the driver is still in control) likely has less serious consequences, but involves the trustor monitoring the system and thus likely isn't truly reflective of only trust in the system. Thus, even if control is associated with differences in reliance it may not necessarily be driven by trust, but by the level of perceived risk (see Mayer et al., 1995; see also Mayer & Mayer, Chapter 1).

Interdisciplinary considerations and conclusion

In the present chapter we have provided one perspective on important future directions for trust research. Other perspectives presented in this book similarly provide valuable insight into this topic and suggest avenues for interdisciplinary work. Close to the present topic, Lockey and Gillespie (Chapter 2) highlight unique risks and vulnerabilities involved when considering trust in artificial intelligence. These authors address some of the same concerns that we have posed here (e.g., is benevolence and integrity relevant in the absence of agency?), but extend the concepts presented here in notable ways (e.g., who are the stakeholders and what motivates them to trust optimally?). Another chapter by Singh and Mayer (Chapter 8) presents a scorecard for applying ability, benevolence, and integrity constructs to dimensions of AI which the U.S. National Science Foundation is interested in pursuing. This is an important step toward evaluating some of the questions asked in this chapter. Wagner (Chapter 13) extends beyond the considerations of the present chapter and addresses the question of whether humans will decide to rely on evacuation robots in an emergency situation.

Our chapter addresses the importance of carefully considering the referent when conducting research on trust. Although Bromme and Hendriks (Chapter 4) do not reference autonomous systems, these authors draw a similar parallel within the realm of science. That is, these authors critically note that when considering trust in science it is important to distinguish between trust in science itself, and trust in the scientists presenting the research. Similarly, Boettcher (Chapter 11) notes the difficulties faced in developing trust between state parties during the formation of nuclear nonproliferation agreements. This author discussed means by which trust could be developed and how to bridge gaps in trust so that negotiations will be successful. In this context, it is also critically relevant to consider the trust referent. Specifically, the trustor may be considering the state, political leaders, or the type of government when making trust decisions.

The present chapter considers why close attention to the referent of trust is important within the domain of trusting autonomous systems. We concluded by noting several other works in this book wherein the same challenges exist. Future research should consider the relevant referent(s) carefully, and create sufficiently sensitive measures that measure trustworthiness of and trust in each of these referents.

References

Boeing (2021). From seabed-to-space. https://www.boeing.com/defense/autonomous -systems/index.

Chopra, A. K., & Singh, M. P. (2018, December). Sociotechnical systems and ethics in the large. In *Proceedings of the 2018 AAAI/ACM Conference on AI, Ethics, and Society* (pp. 48–53). https://dl.acm.org/doi/proceedings/10.1145/3278721.

Deutsch, M. (1958). Trust and suspicion. *Journal of Conflict Resolution, 2*(4), 265–279. https://doi.org/10.1177/002200275800200401.

Jenkins, A. C., Macrae, C. N., & Mitchell, J. P. (2008). Repetition suppression of ventromedial prefrontal activity during judgments of self and others. *Proceedings of the National Academy of Sciences, 105*(11), 4507–4512. https://doi.org/10.1073/pnas .0708785105.

Lee, J. D., & See, K. A. (2004). Trust in automation: designing for appropriate reliance. *Human Factors, 46*(1), 50–80. https://doi.org/10.1518/hfes.46.1.50_30392.

Lewis, J. D., & Weigert, A. (1985). Trust as a social reality. *Social Forces, 63*(4), 967–985. https://doi.org/10.2307/2578601.

Mayer, R. C., & Davis, J. H. (1999). The effect of the performance appraisal system on trust for management: a field quasi-experiment. *Journal of Applied Psychology, 84*(1), 123–136. https://doi.org/10.1037/0021-9010.84.1.123.

Mayer, R. C., Davis, J. H., & Schoorman, F. D. (1995). An integrative model of organizational trust. *Academy of Management Review, 20*(3), 709–734. https://doi.org/10 .5465/amr.1995.9508080335.

Mitchell, J. P., Macrae, C. N., & Banaji, M. R. (2006). Dissociable medial prefrontal contributions to judgments of similar and dissimilar others. *Neuron, 50*, 655–663. https://doi.org/1016/j.neuron.2006.03.040.

Precedence Research (2020, October 1). Autonomous vehicle market will garner growth 63.5% by 2027. https://www.globenewswire.com/news-release/2020/10/01/2102335/ 0/en/Autonomous-Vehicle-Market-will-Garner-Growth-63-5-by-2027.html.

Reeves, B., & Nass, C. (1996). *The Media Equation: How People Treat Computers, Television, and New Media Like Real People and Places*. New York: Cambridge University Press.

Research and Markets (2020, December 28). Global autonomous cars market (2020 to 2030) – opportunities and strategies with COVID-19 growth and change. https://www.globenewswire.com/news-release/2020/12/28/2150806/0/en/Global-Autonomous-Cars-Market-2020-to-2030-Opportunities-and-Strategies-with-COVID-19-Growth-and-Change.html.

Rotter, J. B. (1967). A new scale for the measurement of interpersonal trust. *Journal of Personality*, 35(4), 651–665. https://doi.org/10.1111/j.1467-6494.1967.tb01454.x.

Sheridan, T. B. (1975). Considerations in modeling the human supervisory controller. *IFAC Proceedings*, 8(1), 223–228. https://doi.org/1016/s147406670(17)67555-4.

Sheridan, T. B., & Hennessy, R. T. (1984). *Research and Modeling of Supervisory Control Behavior*. Washington, DC: National Academy.

Singh, M. P. (2014). Norms as a basis for governing sociotechnical systems. *ACM Transactions on Intelligent Systems and Technology (TIST)*, 5(1), 1–23.

Synced (2019, March 14). Boeing 737 MAX crashes raise public distrust of autonomous systems. https://syncedreview.com/2019/03/14/boeing-737-max-crashes-raise-public-distrust-of-autonomous-systems/.

U.S. Department of Transportation (2019, September 18). U.S. Secretary of Transportation announces automated driving system demonstration grant winners. https://www.transportation.gov/briefing-room/us-secretary-transportation-announces-automated-driving-system-demonstration-grant#:~:text=Chao%20today%20announced%20nearly%20%2460,ADS)%20on%20our%20nation's%20roadways.&text=Automation%20offers%20the%20potential%20to,other%20travelers%20sharing%20the%20road.

Waytz, A., Morewedge, C. K., Epley, N., Monteleone, G., Gao, J., & Cacioppo, J. T. (2010). Making sense by making sentient: effectance motivation increases anthropomorphism. *Journal of Personality and Social Psychology*, 99(3), 410–435. https://doi.org/10.1037/a0020240.

6 Trust attractors: a dynamical systems approach to trust research

Chris P. Long and Sim B. Sitkin

Introduction

Building and maintaining trust within and across organizations leads individuals to confront a challenging, complicated set of dynamics. Individuals who trust exhibit "a psychological state comprising the intention to accept vulnerability based upon positive expectations of the intentions or behavior of another" (Rousseau et al., 1998: 395). Trust produces significant and positive effects on many job-related attitudes such as satisfaction, commitment, and support in ways that positively influence other attitudes, cognitions, emotions, behaviors, and performance outcomes (Davis et al., 2000). Trust facilitates economic and social exchanges (Arrow, 1974; Granovetter, 1985) where competition exists and where conflicts hold the potential to significantly compromise cooperative dynamics (Deutsch, 1973).

Although scholars have made significant progress outlining the general nature and predictors of trust (Colquitt, Scott, & LePine, 2007; Mayer, Davis, & Schoorman, 1995), our understanding of how trust develops over time has lagged in three key areas. First, the cross-sectional methodologies adopted by most trust researchers have provided episodically oriented "snapshots" of why particular forms of trust exist at points in time. Second, current trust research provides only very general ideas about the dynamic nature of trust evolution (and devolution) processes (Fulmer & Gelfand, 2012; Gillespie, Fulmer, & Lewicki, 2021). Third, while recent scholarship in multi-level trust dynamics has increased (e.g., Gillespie et al., 2021), the models that scholars use to explain trust development continue to focus primarily on single analytical levels. As a result, these models fail to capture the complex milieu of individual, relational, institutional, and environmental factors that concurrently influence trust development processes and outcomes across contexts and situations as they evolve.

The relatively narrow scope of our trust theories creates a dilemma in that scholars have a limited understanding of how to promote the forms and levels of trust that are most effective for different situations. For example, interpersonal trust research often fails to reflect the situational and environmental factors that influence micro- and meso-level trust dynamics (Mishra & Mishra, 2013). These limitations have hampered scholars' understandings of how trust of others persists over time and within environments where trustors typically receive significant amounts of conflicting information about trustee trustworthiness.

In this chapter, we address these issues by conceptualizing how trust attractors influence trust relations at multiple analytical levels. Consistent with research on dynamical systems and conflict (Coleman, 2021; Coleman et al., 2007), we identify trust attractors as change-resistant attitude patterns that are initially developed and reinforced through the interactions of related psycho-social, institutional, contextual, and environmental factors. Because they provide ways to satisfy attributional processes, trust attractors can initially draw trustors into integrated cognitive, relational, and behavioral repertoires. Over time, the levels of comfort and certainty that trust attractors create produce resilient attitude patterns and propensities that influence subsequent trust development processes.

Our overall objective is to introduce trust attractors and related concepts of dynamical systems theory to trust scholars. It is our hope that these ideas might motivate scholars to use this research in ways that will help them answer persistent questions regarding the enduring nature of certain types of trusting (and distrusting) relationships. Understanding trust attractors can provide important insights and more complete pictures of complex, multi-level trust dynamics. By unmasking persistent and recognizable patterns of factors that influence how trust develops, this perspective holds the potential to recalibrate our understanding of how trustors' attitudes persist across a range of trust dimensions.

Embracing the complexity of trust development

Current perspectives on trust development suggest that trust builds iteratively over time as actors (trustors and trustees) evaluate their own vulnerabilities against the willingness and ability of their exchange partners to address their needs, interests, and desires (Lewicki, Tomlinson, & Gillespie, 2006). In interpersonal relationships, researchers argue that trust results from a series of judgments about another's trustworthiness across three dimensions: ability, benevolence, and integrity (Mayer et al., 1995; Rousseau et al., 1998). Ability reflects trustee competence on dimensions that are critical to the trustor. Benevolence captures the concern of trustees about trustor welfare and interests. Integrity describes trustor evaluations of how consistently trustees fulfill promises and meet trustor value-based expectations.

Trust is typically portrayed as initially forming from cognitive assessments, followed by more relational assessments as trustors conduct knowledge-based evaluations, and finally more identification-based evaluations (Lewicki & Bunker, 1996; McAllister, 1995; Rousseau et al., 1998; Shapiro, Sheppard, & Cheraskin, 1992). Research has found that individual dispositional characteristics and accumulated experiences generate emotional reactions that influence these cognitions (Colquitt et al., 2007; Mayer et al., 1995; Rousseau et al., 1998; Shapiro et al., 1992). Research also suggests that trust development is affected by numerous organizational or institutional factors that surround interpersonal exchanges (Bijlsma-Frankema, Sitkin, & Weibel, 2015; Fulmer & Gelfand, 2012; Gillespie & Dietz, 2009; Mishra & Mishra, 2013; Sitkin, 1995).

Introducing a dynamical systems perspective

Despite its long history, key questions about trust development continue to perplex and intrigue scholars. Most behavior-based research on trust developmental processes assumes that trust begins at a zero-point and then either increases or decreases over time based on evaluations that partners make (e.g., Lewicki & Bunker, 1996). Over the past ten years, scholars have begun to examine how contextual factors influence these processes (Mishra & Mishra, 2013) and present multi-level perspectives that examine trust development processes across analytical levels (e.g., Gillespie et al., 2021). However, these perspectives are not yet widespread and are only beginning to integrate cognitive, emotional, group, and organizational-level perspectives on how trust initially forms and changes over time (Fulmer & Gelfand, 2012).

As work on these topics continues, we propose that *dynamical systems theory* may assist scholars in developing models of trust development. Dynamical systems theory outlines how distinct factors can evolve into organized patterns that are remarkably stable and resistant to change (Holland, 2000; Nowak & Vallacher, 1998; Vallacher, Read, & Nowak, 2002). Over the last several decades, researchers have increasingly used dynamical system models to explain a wide range of psychological and sociological processes from identity maintenance, to decision-making, to social movements, and polling patterns (Vallacher & Nowak, 2007; Thelen & Smith, 1994). Recently, dynamical systems perspectives have been used to examine intractable conflicts that are strongly resistant to well-meaning and well-planned remediation efforts (e.g., Coleman, 2021).

At the heart of dynamical systems theory are "attractors" which are patterns of states or behaviors to which systems converge over time. Attractors "attract" system elements into cognitive, emotional, and behavioral repertoires that eventually evolve and coalesce to form stable sets of patterned states. When not in an attractor-type state, the cognitive, emotional, and behavioral elements of the system may be more easily influenced to change and develop because they exist in more random (i.e., less patterned) ways. However, when a system achieves an attractor-like state, these elements array into a patterns that foster a coherent sense of meaning and become self-sustaining, mutually reinforcing, and resistant to change (Vallacher et al., 2010).

When in the psychological hold of an attractor, individuals expend less cognitive and emotional energy because cognitive dissonance ebbs, emotional labor required to align feelings and thoughts is reduced, and experiences with others feel familiar, effective, and coherent (Vallacher et al., 2010). Individuals often find it difficult to move away from attractor states because doing so requires them to marshal energies to alter strongly believed, deeply felt, and logical (for them) ways of thinking. As a result, attractor-based systems will tend to be resilient and return to their primary states even after external influences temporarily alter them (Vallacher, Nowak, Froehlich, & Rockloff, 2002).

To illustrate how attractor dynamics work, we utilize the case of someone who is in the throes of a chemical addiction. The attractor state produced by a chemical addiction is often so strong that someone feels that they would rather die than put in the work necessary to unshackle themselves from their addiction (Vallacher, Read, & Nowack, 2002). This often occurs because the state of chemical addiction itself is an attractor that is comprised of cognitive schemas and emotional responses that feel familiar and, at times, functional or even comfortable. In addition to enabling their chemical dependency, the addict creates social structures that align with and support their addictive behaviors—and serve as hard-to-scale barriers to pursuing alternatives. After living in this state for even a short while, addicts often come to see this state as normal. As a result, individuals are attracted to being in this state, are unmotivated to abandon it because there are so many things that they need to change to get them out of it, and—even if motivated to leave—may find it too challenging to overcome the barriers to exit.

Two key characteristics of attractors

Coleman (2021) and others (e.g., Coleman et al., 2007) have graphically illustrated the attractor concept, as we do in Figure 6.1. They ask readers to imagine a ball on a hilly landscape that represents the current state of a system. The two basins in the figure represent two system attractors (i.e., Attractor 1 and Attractor 2). Each basin has breadth and depth characteristics that influence its capacity to capture and hold the ball (Vallacher et al., 2010).

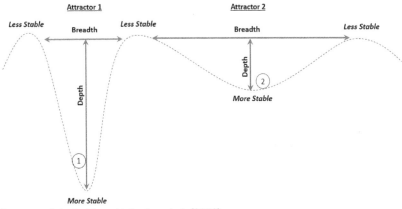

Source: Adapted from Vallacher et al. (2010)

Figure 6.1   A simple landscape with two attractors

Attractor depth

The depth of each basin represents its strength or resistance to change. The deeper a basin's depth represents the more resistant the attractor is to any single countervailing factor (event or experience) (Vallacher et al., 2010). The depth of a basin is determined by how tightly the factors supporting the attractor are integrated. Taut patterns of thoughts, emotions, behaviors, and environmental variables create consistent patterns that can more effectively "block out" individual pieces of countervailing information. In Figure 6.1, notice that a ball is sitting in the basin of Attractor 1 which is deeper and therefore more resistant to change than Attractor 2.

Using our addiction example, Attractor 1 would be able to more strongly hold an addict in an attractor state. This is because this addiction is consistently reinforced by a tightly integrated collection of factors (e.g., one's addict friends, a similarly addicted spouse, easy access to drugs). To move the ball in Figure 6.1 to an alternative state (e.g., a lack of chemical dependency) will often require multiple, persistent forces (e.g., interventions, holistic treatments, new friends, new job) over extended periods of time. This dynamic explains how individuals will often remain in the grip of the attractor because doing so allows them to expend less perceived energy than they would have to expend working to achieve an alternative state (Coleman, 2021). Singular challenges that exhibit little interdependence with other factors are often experienced as shallow or superficial countervailing forces that cannot effectively dislodge an individual from the grip of an attractor state.

Attractor breadth

The breadth of each basin represents the range of countervailing influences that can readily be rationalized to support and reinforce the attractor state. In Figure 6.1, the basin of Attractor 2 is wider than the basin of Attractor 1. Wider basins can readily accomodate a broader range of information that challenge the predominant attractor-based perspective because individuals in that state can rationalize that information into thoughts, emotions, and behaviors that align with the prevalent attractor view (Coleman, 2021).

Using our addiction example, a wider attractor can accommodate and render superficial a more diverse range of information, people, and situations that challenge the addiction. For example, individuals' addictions often seem impervious to anti-addiction public service announcements, negative health reports, admonishments from friends, and even repeated incarcerations. This is because current addicts often encounter this information as singular, countervailing forces that fail to address the complexity of their current context. Moreover, the sheer volume and perceived ubiquitousness of these influences are often diffused to a point where their potential powers to motivate changes in addicts' thoughts, feelings, and behaviors are undermined.

In addition to depth and breadth dynamics, research suggests that several "laws" govern the operations of dynamical systems. For example, these systems are strongly determined by founding conditions and tend to move toward consistency, coherence, and integration over time. In addition, while dynamical systems and the relationships they foster are generally resistant to routine environmenal influences, they can be destabilized by large shocks that alter their basic interaction rules (Coleman, 2021).

Using dynamical systems theory to examine trust development

By employing a dynamical systems perspective, researchers can increase their understanding of basic trust dynamics while they chart new lines of investigation into how trust is developed and maintained over time. Several factors inherent in trust development processes manifest patterns of coherence, consistency, and stability that often result from discrete but related and mutually reinforcing sets of individual, group, and organizational-level factors (Gillespie et al., 2021). Due to how essential trust is for many social systems, a dynamical systems perspective can help scholars understand how individual features of these systems cohere and modulate to promote, evolve, and attain the relatively stable, attractor-like states that can affect trust development and maintenance.

While dynamical systems perspectives have been used to examine intractable conflicts for some time, this work highlights elements that can also be used to explain features endemic to trusting relationships. First, the literature on protracted intractable conflicts (Lewicki, Gray, & Elliott, 2003) provides scholars with ways of disaggregating the multi-dimensional and multi-level environments within which trust is often developed and maintained (Cook, 2001; Long, 2021). Second, research on resolving intractable conflicts offers insights concerning factors that are inherent to trust development: morality, identity, fairness, self-determination, and authority (Coleman, 2003). Third, similar to trust dynamics, intractable conflicts initially develop around significant social and economic exchanges that eventually expand to permeate how individuals experience many other aspects of their lives (Coleman, 2021; Deutsch, 1973).

Attractors can be used to explain how members of one organization come to trust members of another organization. For example, as members of a group maintain an effective and very positive close partnership with another group, its members may come to believe and find it difficult (if not impossible) to conceptualize a similarly effective partnership with a different group. Over time, members of this group may come to depend on, feel good about, and develop strong norms, routines, and shared resources that reinforce this partnership. If we ask members of both groups the level of confidence that they have in this partnership, many members would state that they "trust" members of this other organization, suggesting that patterned trust behaviors, beliefs, and feelings are holding members of this group in a trust attractor.

If we dig a little deeper, we believe we would find members of this organization actively working to maintain this partnership in order to sustain the trust perceptions, attitudes, feelings, and routines that this partnership produces. As group members collectively acknowledge and publicly espouse the importance of trust, the trust that members have in one another may increase the intensity of these attitudes. By virtue of group members' shared experiences and overall interpretations of mission, even individuals who were initially reluctant are likely to develop trusting attitudes as they grow in their affinity for and confidence in the counsel of their team members.

In situations like these, dynamical systems perspectives can illuminate how trust develops and deepens as the individual, group, and organizational factors that directly and indirectly support certain forms of trust cohere and become institutionalized in the minds of trustors and trustees. When this happens, key enablers (e.g., anticipated reciprocity, benevolent dealings) no longer impact trust independently but create an ecosystem that sustains trusting attitudes (Carver & Scheier, 1999) through self-reinforcing interpersonal relationships and social structures that surround those relationships.

A current example of this phenomenon can be found in the insular polar groups that have formed in societies around the world. Those who take moderate positions are much more open to new and divergent information sources that shift individual and collective attitudes, beliefs, norms, and actions. In contrast, radicalization at the extremes can be more characterized by positive feelings toward in-group members and negative feelings toward out-group members. This hard-to-break insular trust is precisely the sort of situation that a dynamical systems view can help to explain.

In relationships like these, trust emerges from interacting forces consistent with those described as attractor dynamics. Even when conflicts emerge between group members that threaten intra-group harmony, individual and collective forces that exist within these groups often move to quell the negative impacts of these conflicts and pull the group back toward trust. At the individual level, these collections of forces direct group members to rationalize their differences with each other and motivate them to re-establish and re-commit to group agreements. The efforts individuals make are often reinforced at the group level by effective conflict-management routines and norms that require group members to resolve or ignore their disagreements in order to cooperate on achieving collective goals.

As intra-group trust strengthens, any one factor (e.g., disagreement) is not likely to terminate or even significantly lessen the trust that group members have in each other because this trust is bolstered by psychological and social mechanisms that perpetuate and support group members trusting and supporting one another. Once the members of a trusting group have stabilized the ways they think about, feel, and behave toward one another, the cognitive, affective, and behavioral patterns that have come to constitute and define their relationships also help to sustain trust over time and across varied circumstances.

Dynamical systems insights into trust development

Research on dynamical systems holds the potential to significantly and fundamentally alter our understanding of how trust is developed and maintained over time in the minds, exchanges, and relationships of trustors and trustees. Measurement development studies by Cummings and Bromiley (1996) and Clark and Payne (1997) find that individuals conjoin their cognitive and affect-based trust evaluations. This suggests that once individuals begin to trust others, the dimensions of their trust evaluations and responses tend to converge in ways that mirror dynamics of attractors. Thus, while scholars have theorized that cognitions, emotions, and behaviors influence trust through different mechanisms, a dynamical perspective could shed light on how individuals' conjoined cognitions and emotions are influenced by trustors' desires to maintain their trusting state.

Research on dynamical systems can also generate insights about the levels and forms of trust that exist at the beginning of relationships. While most behavior-based research on trust developmental processes assumes that trust begins at a zero-point and then either increases or decreases over time based on the level of cooperation that develops between exchange partners (e.g., Lewicki & Bunker, 1996), other scholars argue that common values, similar attitudes, positive affect, and strong cultural norms often lead trustors to exhibit high levels of trust from the beginning of exchange relationships (Kramer, 1999). By incorporating ideas about the convergence of multiple factors, dynamical system perspectives may help researchers disaggregate and recalibrate their ideas about where trust begins, how quickly it develops, and how it adapts over time.

Additional advances in trust perspectives

Arguably, the most compelling reasons trust researchers should consider a dynamical systems approach are that the levels of faith and confidence that many trustors exhibit across time and situations often seem to defy simple attributional processes and rational calculations (Weber, Malhotra, & Murnighan, 2004). As trust becomes embedded in the trustors' cognitions, emotions, behaviors, expectations, and values, data that should lessen trust or lead to distrust is often interpreted (or reinterpreted—or even misinterpreted) in ways that increase trust. This suggests that trustors' desires to maintain coherent and consistent experiences of trust tend to generate processes that reinforce, sustain, deepen, and insulate trustors' trusting attitudes over time (Newman, 1996).

When a trustor is in the hold of a trust attractor, they may reframe negative information about their team members in ways that they can interpret as positive (Vallacher, Read, and Nowack, 2002). By altering how they interpret past as well as the future interactions they anticipate, dynamics such as these can directly influence individuals' decisions to trust (Brewer et al., Chapter 7). At a collective level, multiple social and structural dynamics develop and sustain routines, norms, or ways of thinking that reinforce the reframed calibration of negative information. For example, individuals within strong organizational cultures often resist outside pressures for change while they encourage each other to adopt shared norms and values (Kenrick, Li, & Butner, 2003). Notably, groupthink dynamics lead team members to engage numerous processes that foster trust with each other, discount disconfirming information, and disparage opposing groups (Janis, 1983).

The effects of contextual factors on trust development represent another topical area that may benefit significantly from dynamical systems research. While current research examining the influence of various contextual factors on trust remains relatively limited (e.g., Mishra & Mishra, 2013), existing perspectives do suggest that trust may vary significantly in level (i.e., high–low) and form (calculative, relational, and institutional) based on the influences of various contextual factors. Research that employs a dynamical perspective can illuminate how socio-technical systems that surround trustors provide the supports for various trust attractors. These investigations may bolster those who have argued that interpersonal trust can be reinforced by institutional mechanisms (e.g., Bijlsma-Frankema et al., 2015; Sitkin, 1995) such as team-based cultures (Miles & Creed, 1995), or legal systems at the socio-cultural level (Fukuyama, 1995). These research efforts may assist in answering questions about what specific contextual mechanisms actually influence trust development across situations.

Research using dynamical systems' perspectives should seek to identify the relevant factors in these processes and then work to map their interconnections. Due to the potential complexity of elements, their mechanisms, and their interconnections, scholars will need to take time to disaggregate the structures of trust attractors to clearly identify their component parts. Ultimately, trust research that does this can illuminate how various cognitive, affective, and contextual factors combine to generate integrative effects on trustors experiences, emotions, behaviors, and outcomes.

References

Arrow, K. J. (1974). *The Limits of Organization.* New York: W.W. Norton & Company.

Bijlsma-Frankema, K., Sitkin, S., & Weibel, A. (2015). Distrust in the balance: emergence and development of inter-group distrust in a court of law. *Organization Science, 26*(4), 1018–1039.

Carver, C. S., & Scheier, M. F. (1999). Control theory: a useful conceptual framework for personality-social, clinical, and health psychology. In R. F. Baumeister (Ed.), *The Self in Social Psychology* (pp. 299–316). London: Psychology Press.

Clark, M. C., & Payne, R. L. (1997). The nature and structure of workers' trust in management. *Journal of Organisational Behaviour, 18,* 205–224.

Coleman, P. T. (2003). Characteristics of protracted, intractable conflict: towards the development of a meta-framework–I. *Peace and Conflict, 9,* 1–37.

Coleman, P. T. (2021). *The Way Out.* New York: Columbia University Press.

Coleman, P. T., Vallacher, R. R., Nowak, A., & Bui-Wrzosinska, L. (2007). Intractable conflict as an attractor: presenting a model of conflict, escalation, and intractability. *American Behavioral Scientist, 50,* 1454–1475. https:// doi .org/ 10 .1177/ 0002764207302463.

Colquitt, J. A., Scott, B. A., & LePine, J. A. (2007). Trust, trustworthiness, and trust propensity: a meta-analytic test of their unique relationships with risk taking and job performance. *Journal of Applied Psychology, 92*(4), 909–927.

Cook, K. S. (Ed.) (2001). *Trust in Society.* New York: Russell Sage.

Cummings, L. L., & Bromiley, P. (1996). The Organizational Trust Inventory (OTI): development and validation. In R. M. Kramer & T. R. Tyler (Eds.), *Trust in Organizations: Frontiers of Theory and Research* (pp. 302–330). Thousand Oaks, CA: Sage.

Davis, J. H., Schoorman, F. D., Mayer, R. C., & Tan, H. H. (2000). The trusted general manager and business unit performance: empirical evidence of a competitive advantage. *Strategic Management Journal, 21,* 563–576.

Deutsch, M. (1973). *The Resolution of Conflict.* New Haven, CT: Yale University Press.

Fukuyama, F. (1995). *Trust: The Social Virtues and the Creation of Prosperity.* New York: Free Press.

Fulmer, C. A., & Gelfand, M. J. (2012). At what level (and in whom) we trust. *Journal of Management, 38*(4). https://doi.org/10.1177/0149206312439327.

Gillespie, N. & Dietz, G. (2009). Trust repair after an organization-level failure. *Academy of Management Review, 34*(1), 127–145.

Gillespie, N., Fulmer, A., & Lewicki, R. (2021). *Understanding Trust in Organizations: A Multilevel Perspective.* New York: Routledge.

Granovetter, M. (1985). Economic action and social structure: the problem of embeddedness. *American Journal of Sociology*, 91(3), 481–510.

Holland, J. H. (2000). *Emergence: From Chaos to Order*. Oxford: Oxford University Press.

Janis, I. L. (1983). *Groupthink*. Boston, MA: Houghton Mifflin.

Kenrick, D. T., Li, N. P., & Butner, J. (2003). Dynamical evolutionary psychology: individual decision rules and emergent social norms. *Psychological Review*, 110(1), 3–28.

Kramer, R. M. (1999). Trust and distrust in organizations: emerging perspectives, enduring questions. *Annual Review of Psychology*, 50, 569–598.

Lewicki, R. J., & Bunker, B. B. (1996). Developing and maintaining trust in work relationships. In R. Kramer & T. R. Tyler (Eds.), *Trust in Organizations: Frontiers of Theory and Research* (pp. 114–139). Thousand Oaks, CA: Sage.

Lewicki, R. J., Gray, B., & Elliott, M. (Eds.) (2003). *Making Sense of Intractable Environmental Conflicts: Concepts and Cases*. Washington, DC: Island Press.

Lewicki, R. J., Tomlinson, E. C., & Gillespie, N. (2006). Models of interpersonal trust development: theoretical approaches, empirical evidence, and future directions. *Journal of Management*, 32(6), 991–1022.

Long, C. P. (2021). "Cascading Influences and Contextualized Effects: A Model of Multilevel Control-Trust Dynamics." Understanding Trust in Organizations: A Multilevel Perspective (SIOP Organizational Frontiers Series) 1st Edition (First ed., pp. 87-120). New York, NY: Routledge.

Mayer, R. C., Davis, J. H., & Schoorman, F. D. (1995). An integrative model of organizational trust. *Academy of Management Review*, 20, 709–734.

McAllister, D. J. (1995). Affect- and cognition-based trust as foundations for interpersonal cooperation in organizations. *Academy of Management Journal*, 38, 24–59.

Miles, R. E., & Creed, W. D. (1995). Organizational forms and managerial philosophies: a descriptive and analytical review. *Research in Organizational Behavior*, 17, 333–372.

Mishra, A. K., & Mishra, K. E. (2013). The research on trust in leadership: the need for context. *Journal of Trust Research*, 3(1), 59–69.

Newman, D. V. (1996). Emergence and strange attractors. *Philosophy of Science*, 63(2), 245–261.

Nowak, A., & Vallacher, R. R. (1998). *Dynamical Social Psychology*. New York: Guilford Press.

Rousseau, D., Sitkin, S., Burt, R., & Camerer, C. (1998). Not so different after all: a cross-discipline view of trust. *Academy of Management Review*, 23(3), 393–404.

Shapiro, D., Sheppard, B. H., & Cheraskin, L. (1992). Business on a handshake. *Negotiation Journal*, 8, 365–377.

Sitkin, S. B. (1995). On the positive effect of legalization on trust. In R. J. Bies, R. J. Lewicki, & B. H. Sheppard (Eds.), *Research on Negotiations in Organizations* (pp. 185–217). Greenwich, CT: JAI Press.

Thelen, E., & Smith, L. B. (1994). *A Dynamic Systems Approach to the Development of Cognition and Action*. Cambridge, MA: MIT Press.

Vallacher, R. R., & Nowak, A. (2007). Dynamical social psychology: finding order in the flow of human experience. In A. W. Kruglanski & E. T. Higgins (Eds.), *Social Psychology: Handbook of Basic Principles* (2nd edn, pp. 734–758). New York: Guilford Press.

Vallacher, R. R., Coleman, P. T., Nowak, A., & Bui-Wrzosinska, L. (2010). Rethinking intractable conflict: the perspective of dynamical systems. *American Psychologist*, 65, 262–278.

Vallacher, R. R., Nowak, A., Froehlich, M., & Rockloff, M. (2002). The dynamics of self-evaluation. *Personality and Social Psychology Review, 6,* 370–379. https:// doi .org/10.1207/S15327957PSPR0604_11.

Vallacher, R. R., Read, S. J., & Nowak, A. (2002). The dynamical perspective in personality and social psychology. *Personality and Social Psychology Review, 6*(4), 264–273.

Weber, J. M., Malhotra, D., & Murnighan, J. K. (2004). Normal acts of irrational trust: motivated attributions and the trust development process. *Research in Organizational Behavior, 26,* 75–101.

7 Perceptions of trustworthiness and decisions to trust are determined by anticipation of future states

Gene A. Brewer, Alexis Torres, Xavier Celaya, and Margarida Pitaes

A cognitive-physiological theory of perceptions of trustworthiness and decisions to trust

A central theme of this book is that trust is necessary for forming secure social bonds, maximizing utility when interacting with humans and autonomous systems, and developing functional norms for guiding interactions in the future.[1] Despite the clear value of understanding trust, our current understanding of the cognitive psychology of trust is limited. The primary aim of this chapter is to highlight the fact that perceptions of trustworthiness and decisions to trust reflect dynamics between three complementary cognitive-physiological systems that are necessary for behavioral manifestations of trust (i.e., perceptual, mentalizing, and decision-making systems). A secondary aim of this review is to develop a cognitive theory linking perceptions of trustworthiness to decisions to trust in terms of their core reliance on anticipatory thinking. Our theory assumes that these systems interact and that perceptions of trustworthiness and decisions to trust are mediated by information processing in the central nervous system. A third aim of this review is to connect our theory of trust behavior to a larger literature on trust. Understanding trust behavior not only requires understanding the cognitive-physiological system underpinning this process, but also requires understanding information exchange between trustors and trustees.

---

[1] The preparation of this chapter was supported by the Air Force Office of Scientific Research (Grant ID No. 4RT0319) to GAB, the Fundação para a Ciência e Tecnologia research fellowship awarded to MP, and by a generous donation to our laboratory for the study of mentalizing behaviors from Steve Neumann.

Operationally defined, we follow from the tradition of viewing trust as a willingness to be vulnerable to a person or party under conditions where a trustor cannot monitor the behavior of a trustee (Mayer, Davis, & Schoorman, 1995). In this definition, there are several important constituents that warrant further definition. The trustor is defined as the person who is making the decision whether or not to trust. The trustee is the person or party that is expected to behave a certain way in the future. Importantly, our view considers the trustor to always be a human but that the trustee can belong to an ever-increasing set of objects that we place our trust in including other humans, animals, intelligent systems, and even abstract systems with fuzzy boundaries (e.g., government). Beyond these distinctions, we also highlight the difference between a perception of trustworthiness and a decision to trust. This distinction is characterized by the cognitive processes that constitute these two processes. A decision to trust, and confidence in this decision, is a natural outcome of the perception of trustworthiness plus predictions about the trustees' behaviors when they cannot be monitored along with the trustor's trait level of propensity to trust.

How do humans render these types of decisions to trust? What factors influence these trust decisions? How can we identify good versus bad trust decisions? Answers to these questions, and many more, can be found in the cognitive and cognitive neuroscience literature where there is a growing body of work examining future-oriented processes in behavior and the brain (Bar, 2011; Szpunar, Spreng, & Schacter, 2014). Our central claim is that the human cognitive system is designed to make predictions about the future—a form of anticipatory thinking—and this design allows people to consider a variety of possible trustee behaviors that may happen in the future. These possible future behaviors are more versus less likely, and then decision processes compute a type of expected value that takes the reward/punishment into account with the likelihood of future behavior for us to maximize our chances of reward and minimize our chances of punishment when deciding whether or not to trust.

Perceptions of trustworthiness unfold in two different, but complimentary, ways. Immediate perceptions of trustworthiness happen implicitly and are governed by evolutionary, cultural, and personal experiences. For example, facial characteristics are known to influence trustor estimates of a trustee's trustworthiness and these influences emerge very early in cognitive processing (Olivola, Funk, & Todorov, 2014). Alternatively, focused effort can be used to develop a perception of trustworthiness which we refer to as a more explicit process governed by concentration and attention to features of the trustee, the context, and the reward/punishment contingencies of the decision to trust. These two forms of trust dovetail with a well-established tradition of automatic versus controlled cognitive processes (Schneider & Shiffrin, 1977; Shiffrin & Schneider, 1977). We will discuss these two systems in turn.

Automatic appraisals of trustworthiness

Studies that investigated the underlying factors of the trustworthiness dimension showed that it is highly correlated with emotional facial expressions (i.e., a happy–angry dimension). Based on a series of studies, Todorov and colleagues concluded that evaluation of emotionally neutral faces is an extension of functionally adaptive mechanisms for interpreting others' emotional expressions (Engell, Todorov, & Haxby, 2010). Specifically, in the absence of emotional cues broadcasting others' behavioral intentions, judgments of trustworthiness are an attempt to predict approach/avoidance behaviors (Todorov & Engell, 2008). In the social psychology and cognitive literature, trust appraisals have been conceptualized as an individual's attempt to infer others' intentions, and, thus, decide whether to approach or avoid that individual (Anderson et al., 2013). Using a data-driven computer model to manipulate facial trustworthiness, Todorov and colleagues concluded that trustworthiness judgments are derived from subtle facial features signaling approach/avoidance intentions. As the facial features become more exaggerated in the negative direction (−8 SD), the faces were mostly classified as angry, whereas, as the trustworthy facial features become more exaggerated in the positive direction (+8 SD), the faces were mostly classified as happy (Todorov, 2008; Todorov & Duchaine, 2008). The trustworthiness dimension is based on emotion overgeneralization, that is, faces that structurally resemble angry faces are to be avoided and thus perceived as untrustworthy, whereas faces that structurally resemble happy faces are to be approached and thus perceived as trustworthy (Said et al., 2009; Slepian, Young, & Harmon-Jones, 2017; Zebrowitz, Kikuchi, & Fellous, 2010). Secord (1958) has suggested that personality inferences from emotions occur through temporal extension whereby people, upon detecting a temporary emotional facial expression on others, misattribute the transient cue to a fixed trait. That is, inferences from subtle cues related to emotional states (e.g., anger) may be inappropriately generalized to inferences of personality dispositions (e.g., untrustworthiness). Zebrowitz and colleagues (2010) extended this assumption into emotional overgeneralization, suggesting that this dispositional misattribution seems to also happen when target faces are actually expressionless, but merely structurally resemble emotional expressions. Based on trait judgments of emotionally neutral faces, recent studies found that specific facial characteristics are associated with trustworthiness inferences (e.g., nose and cheekbone salience), suggesting that faces with certain features (e.g., pronounced cheekbones) appeared to be more (un)trust-worthy (Todorov, Baron, & Oosterhof, 2008).

Evidence supporting the hypothesis that trustworthiness judgments are asso-ciated with overgeneralized perceptions of expressions of anger and happiness also comes from different literatures (Engell et al., 2010). By manipulating both facial features and the emotionality of a face, Oosterhof and Todorov (2008) showed that dynamic changes from neutral to angry or happy expressions are perceived as more intense when accompanied by congruent changes in structural features (i.e., from a trustworthy to untrustworthy face, or vice versa, respectively). In the same vein, Engell and colleagues (2010) suggested that the brain's adaptation to expressions of anger results in higher evaluations of trust-worthiness, whereas adaptation to expressions of happiness results in lower evaluations of trustworthiness. Neuroimaging findings also support the idea that a common neural system is engaged during inferences of facial trustwor-thiness and expressions signaling approach. These studies found a nonlinear pattern of amygdala responses to both highly trustworthy and highly untrust-worthy faces (Said, Baron, & Todorov, 2009; Todorov et al., 2008), closely mirroring previous research reporting increased amygdala activation to happy and angry faces compared to neutral faces (Pessoa et al., 2002).

The emotion overgeneralization hypothesis predicted by this body of research seems to account for rapid, yet not necessarily accurate, judgments of trustwor-thiness (Engell et al., 2010; Oosterhof & Todorov, 2008; Said, Sebe, & Todorov, 2009; Todorov et al., 2015). From this point of view, to the extent that such impressions are formed by automatic extrapolation and (mis)interpretation of physiognomic features cuing emotional messages about others' intentions, and that there is variability in the information that individuals extract from faces, it is not surprising that they are not accurate. Impressions from facial appearance involve a subjective evaluative component (Kuzmanovic et al., 2012), making it not expected to see a relationship between raters' judgments and targets' behaviors or self-reports of personality.

Specific to judgments of trustworthiness, studies suggest that the detection of trustworthiness involves an unreflective (e.g., Todorov et al., 2005), uninten-tional (e.g., Todorov & Uleman, 2004), and intuitive character (Porter et al., 2008; Willis & Todorov, 2006). The intuitive way in which we evaluate others is not fully understood, yet has a powerful impact on our daily lives (both as raters/trustors and as targets/trustees). Identifying the factors affecting such automatic judgments can provide much insight that can be used in the countless social interactions that may be influenced by our first impressions. Considering the crucial role that trustworthiness judgments play in social interactions, the intuitive character involved in such inferences assumes relevant importance. In the same way, although evaluations from faces are fairly consistent across perceivers, the consistency is far from perfect and a large proportion of variance in these judgments remains unaccounted for (Todorov et al., 2015). Recent empirical work suggests that some of this variance may be attributed to individual differences (Engell, Haxby, & Todorov, 2007; Todorov, Said, & Verosky, 2011). For instance, trustworthiness impression seems to be affected by the rater's mood (Forgas & East, 2008), personality (Adolphs, 2002), degree of trait anxiety (Willis, Dodd, & Palermo, 2013) or by the priming approach or avoidance motivation states (Forster et al., 2006). To completely understand trust-based interactions, research must consider not only the characteristics of the partner that make him or her trustworthy but also the observer effects that contribute to individual variation in such judgments. However, we know very little about the sources of idiosyncratic variance in trustworthiness evaluation (but see Todorov et al., 2013; Todorov et al., 2015). Traditionally, the focus of trustworthiness perception research has been on the cues in the face that signal trustworthiness evaluations across perceivers. Previous studies shed light on the cognitive and neural mechanisms underlying the ability to discriminate facial properties conveying social signals, but the underlying processes supporting individual differences remain poorly understood.

Controlled assessments of trustworthiness

The human memory system possesses the unique ability to reconstruct and re-experience past events (Johnson, 2006; Tulving, 1983). This declarative system is highly flexible insofar that we are also able to exercise the ability to project oneself "forward in time to pre-experience an event" before the event occurs (Atance & O'Neill, 2001, 537). Tulving (2004) has described this ability to mentally place oneself forward in time as a hallmark of human existence. The use of declarative memories to simulate the outcome of events that have yet to occur is known as episodic future thinking (Atance & O'Neill, 2001). Episodic future thinking provides a trajectory of action that allows for individuals to simulate multiple outcomes and adjust motivation accordingly to remain goal-oriented but this can only be attainable with knowledge of the past. Recently, researchers have conducted experiments to investigate and decode the neural networks responsible for mental time travel, as well as the extent to which these areas contribute (Addis, Wong, & Schacter, 2007; Buckner & Carroll, 2007; Schacter, Addis, & Buckner, 2008; Szpunar, Watson, & McDermott, 2007). The findings from these studies indicate that the neural regions such as the prefrontal cortex and the medial temporal lobe that are responsible for envisioning the future are the areas that are employed to remember past events and many of these brain regions are implicated in controlled and effortful forms of cognitive processing.

Okuda and colleagues suggest a theoretical explanation, that the episodic memory network facilitates the recapitulation of perceptual context, in which these cortical and subcortical structures are critical for both remembering past events and envisioning the future (Okuda et al., 2003). Thus, episodic information is useful (perhaps necessary) for creating representations of event-based prospective memories which are to be carried out in the future. Researchers in the field refer to the neural machinery responsible for both simulating future events and remembering past events as a core network. Evidence of the shared utility of these regions is sourced from amnesic and lesion patients, in which when these individuals suffered from episodic memory deficits, their ability to personally plan for the future also showed deficits (Talland, 1964; Tulving, 1983; Klein, Loftus, & Kihlstrom, 2002). In addition, Okuda and colleagues (2003) instructed participants to freely talk about their near or distant future or past during a PET scan where they found evidence of shared activity for previous and future experiences in parts of the prefrontal cortex, medial temporal lobe, right hippocampus, and bilateral parahippocampal gyrus.

Although several findings pointed to the same direction, a criticism of the field was a concern that the comparison between past and future events was confounded by differences in the levels of detail. To resolve this, Addis and colleagues (2007) utilized the temporal dynamics of functional magnetic resonance imaging (fMRI) to their advantage by splitting the past and future task into two components: the first being a construction phase where participants generate a past or event in response to an event cue (e.g., "car") and the second where participants elaborate as much detail as possible. Addis and colleagues found that during the construction phase, past and future events shared activity in posterior visual areas and left hippocampus; however, the elaboration phase additionally illustrated past–future activity overlap in the medial temporal area (hippocampus and parahippocampal gyrus), prefrontal cortex, posterior cingulate, and retrosplenial cortex (Addis et al., 2007). Lastly, some studies not only found shared activation for past and future thinking, but interestingly found higher activation for future events compared to past events (Okuda et al., 2003; Addis et al., 2007; Szpunar et al., 2007). What does this all mean? Addis and colleagues hypothesized that unlike remembering past events, envisioning future events undergoes a more intensive constructive process that requires active imagery which results in more activity for future events compared to past ones.

In times where an individual must contemplate whether or not to trust another, they likely try to remember similar situations and pull details from each to reconstruct anticipatory future events and this process relies on episodic future thinking. Interestingly, there is very little empirical research on the connection between episodic future thinking and trust behavior. However, several features of future thinking bear mention here that are clearly related to controlled aspects of contemplation that provide a basis for decisions regarding whether or not to trust. First, future thinking has been associated with theory of mind which refers to the ability to attribute mental states, feelings, and emotions to other people (Adornetti et al., 2021; Shanton & Goldman, 2010; Schurz et al., 2015). There are functional and neurological similarities between episodic future thinking and theory of mind which, in the context of considering whether or not to trust, indicates that a trustor may be simulating *both* the trustees' intentions along with the most plausible futures that are likely given the trust decision. These simulations could be incredibly useful for helping to make a decision about whether or not to trust because they incorporate features of the trustee, inferences about the intentions of the trustee, and plausible futures under conditions of a trust or no trust decision. It is known that individuals can consider multiple possible futures for themselves—a concept known as possible selves (Markus & Nurius, 1986). Thus, it is quite likely that trustors similarly contemplate possible futures conditionalized on whether or not they make a decision to put their faith in a trustee.

Making the decision to trust

The decision to trust may be an isolated event, but it is oftentimes more dynamic as the decision is sustained over extended periods or as the decision becomes recurrent. As individuals receive feedback, decision processes and the decision itself may change. We know that feedback is an influential factor in human decision-making—humans adapt to various types of implicit and explicit policies. Therefore, the outcome of a decision to trust is important to future decisions to trust. What other information drives the decision to trust and honor trust over prolonged periods? Snijders and Keren (2001) describe the importance of dispositional factors, anticipation factors, and situational factors in one's decision to trust the intentions of another.

Dispositional factors such as gender, age, socioeconomic status, prosocial vs pro-self behavior, and so on may determine whether a person is more or less likely to trust and honor trust in the long term. Findings on gender and trust have been mixed, with several reporting no effect of gender (e.g., Croson

& Buchan, 1999). However, others that investigate additional mitigating factors may be informative. One study found that decisions to trust differed across gender with women—showing a greater fear of exploitation and a less utilitarian perception of society—placing less trust in others regardless of their group affiliation (ingroup/outgroup) or expectation of reciprocity (Neary, 2009). Another study reported that in response to violations of trust, women—scoring higher in relational investment and higher in attitudinal trust following a transgression—are less likely to lose trust and are more likely to restore trust compared to their male counterparts (Haselhuhn et al., 2015). When playing a classic Prisoner's Dilemma style trust game against an opponent, participants who demonstrated prosocial behaviors tended to be more trustful in their opponent as compared to their pro-self counterparts (Snijders & Keren, 2001). In a meta-analysis of trust behaviors by age across 38 countries, researchers found that age positively correlated with trust toward family, friends, neighbors, and strangers (Li & Fung, 2013).

Anticipation factors are based on the entity to be trusted and the impact of one's decision to trust said entity. For example, this may include familiarity, kinship relation, how much the entity resembles oneself, appearance, behavior, and assumptions about possessing certain characteristics. Individuals who show a reputation for prosocial behavior tend to be perceived as more trustworthy by opponents during trust games (Snijders & Keren, 2001). Researchers have found that appearance, reputation, and the inferred personality of the alter play a major role in decisions to trust. That is, individuals will place greater trust in alters with certain facial features but they will also take into account behavioral patterns and update their decisions to trust (Li et al., 2017; Chang et al., 2010; Yu, Saleem, & Gonzalez, 2014). Neuroimaging research underscores the importance of anticipation factors in trust decisions: alpha oscillatory brain activity is associated with predictions about a trustee to be continuously trusted and decisions to trust based on actions of the trustee and beliefs about the trustee. Alpha activity is influenced by features of the trustee—specifically, group membership and behaviors that signal trustworthiness—and predict one's continuous decisions to trust (Blais et al., 2019).

Situational factors describe contexts where trust may be more or less likely to develop. One consideration is culture. Alongside the advent of the internet, we have witnessed a growth in a subculture of distrust, conspiracy, and paranoia (Aupers, 2012). Aupers (2012) argues that this subculture is a response to existential insecurity and ontological insecurity, which may overlap with religious and political affiliations, perceived or real unfairness of social and economic systems, and modernization. Within these subcultures, one may develop confirmation bias, which will generally inform decisions to trust or distrust certain entities. Li and Fung (2013) report that trust across age groups is moderated by contextual factors such as culture, values, income inequality, formal justice systems, and country-level development status. Situational factors may also be more circumstantial. For example, an individual may base their decision to trust on a moment-to-moment risk assessment. That is, risk of a future transgression versus honoring trust, and what is at stake. The risk assessment may be informed by one's conception of the alter, patterns of behavior, who is watching, perceived intentionality and potential for reciprocity, and the factors discussed above (Snijders & Keren, 2001). However, more recent research has questioned whether or not trust can extend across cultural boundaries (Hall et al., 2015). In this work it was shown that cultural outgroups who signal commitment to their group (e.g., a religious outgroup member expressing high levels of commitment to their group—known as costly signaling) is perceived as being *more* trustworthy by outgroup members. In unpublished research on this topic, we have shown that this increase in outgroup trust based on costly signaling is driven predominantly by increases in perceived integrity.

Theoretical advancement

Trust can be cognitively framed in terms of a trustor's prediction of future behavior of a trustee, features of the trustor and trustee that govern this prediction, and decision-making dynamics that weigh these predictions. Our theory dovetails with prior work examining the neural correlates of trust, trustworthiness, and trust behaviors that have emphasized the role of mentalizing (inferring the thoughts, emotions, or intentions of others) in decisions to trust (Borum, 2010; Krueger et al., 2007; Stanley et al., 2011; Stanley et al., 2012). The theory is based on a fundamental assumption that much of cognitive and neural processes are devoted to anticipatory thinking. From this perspective, the cognitive system can be used to render effective trust decisions based on a combination of relatively automatic evaluations of trustworthiness based on perceptual features of a trustee (e.g., facial characteristics) and relatively controlled assessments of possible futures conditionalized on whether or not a decision to trust has been made. The decision-making dynamic is likely governed primarily by the anticipated reward–punishment value associated with those future states along with any other possible consequences. While the entirety of this review has focused on human-to-human trust interactions, we believe that the theory also has merit for better understanding human-to-machine trust interactions. For example, what features of an autonomous system would lead to immediate impressions of trustworthiness, what experiences a person had with autonomous systems in the past that could bias their simulations of the future, and what types of decision-making dynamics must emerge to make a decision to trust a machine. Presently, there is little reason to believe that this process would fundamentally differ based on whether the trustee was a human or a machine.

In conclusion, deciding to trust seems to be based on multiple streams of information that are highly dependent on anticipatory states that have yet to occur. Future research on this topic could benefit from better integrating what is known regarding the psychology and neuroscience of episodic future thinking, mentalizing, anticipatory thinking, and trust.

References

Addis, D. R., Wong, A. T., & Schacter, D. L. (2007). Remembering the past and imagining the future: common and distinct neural substrates during event construction and elaboration. *Neuropsychologia*, *45*(7), 1363–1377.

Adolphs, R. (2002). Trust in the brain. *Nature Neuroscience*, *5*, 192–3.

Adornetti, I., Chiera, A., Altavilla, D., Deriu, V., Marini, A., Valeri, G., … & Ferretti, F. (2021). Self-projection in middle childhood: a study on the relationship between theory of mind and episodic future thinking. *Cognitive Processing*, *22*(2), 321–332.

Anderson, S. W., Bechara, A., Dam´sio, H., Tranel, D., & Dam´sio, A. R. (2013). Impairment of social and moral behavior related to early damage in human prefrontal cortex. *Social Neuroscience*, *2*, 1032–1037.

Atance, C. M., & O'Neill, D. K. (2001). Episodic future thinking. *Trends in Cognitive Sciences*, *5*(12), 533–539.

Aupers, S. (2012). "Trust no one": modernization, paranoia and conspiracy culture. *European Journal of Communication*, *27*(1), 22–34.

Bar, M. (Ed.) (2011). *Predictions in the Brain: Using Our Past to Generate a Future*. Oxford: Oxford University Press.

Blais, C., Ellis, D. M., Wingert, K. M., Cohen, A. B., & Brewer, G. A. (2019). Alpha suppression over parietal electrode sites predicts decisions to trust. *Social Neuroscience*, *14*(2), 226–235.

Borum, R. (2010). The science of interpersonal trust. Mental Health Law & Policy Faculty Publications, University of South Florida. https://digitalcommons.usf.edu/cgi/viewcontent.cgi?article=1573&context=mhlp_facpub.

Buckner, R. L., & Carroll, D. C. (2007). Self-projection and the brain. *Trends in Cognitive Sciences*, *11*(2), 49–57.

Chang, L. J., Doll, B. B., van't Wout, M., Frank, M. J., & Sanfey, A. G. (2010). Seeing is believing: trustworthiness as a dynamic belief. *Cognitive Psychology*, *61*(2), 87–105.

Croson, R., & Buchan, N. (1999). Gender and culture: international experimental evidence from trust games. *American Economic Review*, *89*(2), 386–391.

Engell, A. D., Haxby, J. V., & Todorov, A. (2007). Implicit trustworthiness decisions: automatic coding of face properties in the human amygdala. *Journal of Cognitive Neuroscience*, *19*(9), 1508–1519.

Engell, A. D., Todorov, A., & Haxby, J. V. (2010). Common neural mechanisms for the evaluation of facial trustworthiness and emotional expressions as revealed by behavioral adaptation. *Perception, 39*(7), 931–941.

Forgas, J. P., & East, R. (2008). On being happy and gullible: mood effects on skepticism and the detection of deception. *Journal of Experimental Social Psychology, 44,* 1362–1367.

Forster, J., Friedman, R. S., Ozelsel, A., & Denzler, M. (2006). Enactment of approach and avoidance behavior influences the scope of perceptual and conceptual attention. *Journal of Experimental Social Psychology, 42,* 133–146.

Hall, D. L., Cohen, A. B., Meyer, K. K., Varley, A. H., & Brewer, G. A. (2015). Costly signaling increases trust, even across religious affiliations. *Psychological Science, 26*(9), 1368–1376.

Haselhuhn, M. P., Kennedy, J. A., Kray, L. J., Van Zant, A. B., & Schweitzer, M. E. (2015). Gender differences in trust dynamics: women trust more than men following a trust violation. *Journal of Experimental Social Psychology, 56,* 104–109.

Johnson, M. K. (2006). Memory and reality. *American Psychologist, 61*(8), 760–771.

Klein, S. B., Loftus, J., & Kihlstrom, J. F. (2002). Memory and temporal experience: the effects of episodic memory loss on an amnesic patient's ability to remember the past and imagine the future. *Social Cognition, 20*(5), 353–379.

Krueger, F., McCabe, K., Moll, J., Kriegeskorte, N., Zahn, R., Strenziok, M., … & Grafman, J. (2007). Neural correlates of trust. *Proceedings of the National Academy of Sciences, 104*(50), 20084–20089.

Kuzmanovic, B., Bente, G., von Cramon, D. Y., Schilbach, L., Tittgemeyer, M., & Vogeley, K. (2012). Imaging first impressions: distinct neural processing of verbal and nonverbal social information. *NeuroImage, 60,* 179–188.

Li, T., & Fung, H. H. (2013). Age differences in trust: an investigation across 38 countries. *Journals of Gerontology Series B: Psychological Sciences and Social Sciences, 68*(3), 347–355.

Li, T., Liu, X., Pan, J., & Zhou, G. (2017). The interactive effect of facial appearance and behavior statement on trust belief and trust behavior. *Personality and Individual Differences, 117,* 60–65.

Markus, H., & Nurius, P. (1986). Possible selves. *American Psychologist, 41*(9), 954–969.

Mayer, R. C., Davis, J. H., & Schoorman, F. D. (1995). An integrative model of organizational trust. *Academy of Management Review, 20*(3), 709–734.

Neary, J. P. (2009). Putting the "new" into new trade theory: Paul Krugman's Nobel Memorial Prize in economics. *Scandinavian Journal of Economics, 111*(2), 217–250.

Okuda, J., Fujii, T., Ohtake, H., Tsukiura, T., Tanji, K., Suzuki, K., … & Yamadori, A. (2003). Thinking of the future and past: the roles of the frontal pole and the medial temporal lobes. *Neuroimage, 19*(4), 1369–1380.

Olivola, C. Y., Funk, F., & Todorov, A. (2014). Social attributions from faces bias human choices. *Trends in Cognitive Sciences, 18*(11), 566–570.

Oosterhof, N. N., & Todorov, A. (2008). The functional basis of face evaluation. *Proceedings of the National Academy of Sciences, 105*(32), 11087–11092.

Pessoa, L., McKenna, M., Gutierrez, E., & Ungerleider, L. G. (2002). Neural processing of emotional faces requires attention. *Proceedings of the National Academy of Sciences, 99*(17), 11458–11463.

Porter, S., England, L., Juodis, M., Ten Brinke, L., & Wilson, K. (2008). Is the face a window to the soul? Investigation of the accuracy of intuitive judgments of the trustworthiness of human faces. *Canadian Journal of Behavioural Science/Revue canadienne des sciences du comportement, 40*(3), 171–177.

Said, C. P., Baron, S. G., & Todorov, A. (2009). Nonlinear amygdala response to face trustworthiness: contributions of high and low spatial frequency information. *Journal of Cognitive Neuroscience, 21*(3), 519–528.

Said, C. P., Sebe, N., & Todorov, A. (2009). Structural resemblance to emotional expressions predicts evaluation of emotionally neutral faces. *Emotion, 9*(2), 260–264.

Schacter, D. L., Addis, D. R., & Buckner, R. L. (2008). Episodic simulation of future events: concepts, data, and applications. *Annals of the New York Academy of Sciences, 1124*(1), 39–60.

Schneider, W., & Shiffrin, R. M. (1977). Controlled and automatic human information processing: I. Detection, search, and attention. *Psychological Review, 84*(1), 1–66.

Schurz, M., Kogler, C., Scherndl, T., Kronbichler, M., & Kühberger, A. (2015). Differentiating self-projection from simulation during mentalizing: evidence from fMRI. *PLoS ONE, 10*(3), e0121405.

Secord, P. F. (1958). Facial features and inference processes in interpersonal perception. In R. Tagiuri & L. Petrullo (Eds.), *Person Perception and Interpersonal Behavior* (pp. 300–315). Stanford, CA: Stanford University Press.

Shanton, K., & Goldman, A. (2010). Simulation theory. *Wiley Interdisciplinary Reviews: Cognitive Science, 1*(4), 527–538.

Shiffrin, R. M., & Schneider, W. (1977). Controlled and automatic human information processing: II. Perceptual learning, automatic attending and a general theory. *Psychological Review, 84*(2), 127–190.

Slepian, M. L., Young, S. G., & Harmon-Jones, E. (2017). An approach-avoidance motivational model of trustworthiness judgments. *Motivation Science, 3*(1), 91–97.

Snijders, C., & Keren, G. (2001). Do you trust? Whom do you trust? When do you trust? In S. Thye & E. Lawler (Eds.), *Advances in Group Processes* (Advances in Group Processes, vol. 18, pp. 129–160). Bingley: Emerald Group Publishing.

Stanley, D. A., Sokol-Hessner, P., Banaji, M. R., & Phelps, E. A. (2011). Implicit race attitudes predict trustworthiness judgments and economic trust decisions. *Proceedings of the National Academy of Sciences, 108*(19), 7710–7715.

Stanley, D. A., Sokol-Hessner, P., Fareri, D. S., Perino, M. T., Delgado, M. R., Banaji, M. R., & Phelps, E. A. (2012). Race and reputation: perceived racial group trustworthiness influences the neural correlates of trust decisions. *Philosophical Transactions of the Royal Society B: Biological Sciences, 367*(1589), 744–753.

Szpunar, K. K., Spreng, R. N., & Schacter, D. L. (2014). A taxonomy of prospection: introducing an organizational framework for future-oriented cognition. *Proceedings of the National Academy of Sciences, 111*(52), 18414–18421.

Szpunar, K. K., Watson, J. M., & McDermott, K. B. (2007). Neural substrates of envisioning the future. *Proceedings of the National Academy of Sciences, 104*(2), 642–647.

Talland, G. A. (1964). Self-reference: a neglected component in remembering: comment. *American Psychologist, 19*(5), 351–353. https://doi.org/10.1037/h0039768.

Todorov, A. (2008). Evaluating faces on trustworthiness: an extension of systems for recognition of emotions signaling approach/avoidance behaviors. *Annals of the New York Academy of Sciences, 1124,* 208–224.

Todorov, A., Baron, S. G., & Oosterhof, N. N. (2008). Evaluating face trustworthiness: a model-based approach. *Social Cognitive and Affective Neuroscience, 3*(2), 119–127.

Todorov, A., Dotsch, R., Porter, J. M., Oosterhof, N. N., & Falvello, V. B. (2013). Validation of data-driven computational models of social perception of faces. *Emotion, 13*(4), 724–738.

Todorov, A., & Duchaine, B. (2008). Reading trustworthiness in faces without recognizing faces. *Cognitive Neuropsychology, 25*(3), 395–410.

Todorov, A., & Engell, A. D. (2008). The role of the amygdala in implicit evaluation of emotionally neutral faces. *Social Cognitive and Affective Neuroscience*, *3*(4), 303–312.

Todorov, A., Mandisodza, A. N., Goren, A., & Hall, C. C. (2005). Inferences of competence from faces predict election outcomes. *Science*, *308*, 1623–1626.

Todorov, A., Olivola, C. Y., Dotsch, R., & Mende-Siedlecki, P. (2015). Social attributions from faces: determinants, consequences, accuracy, and functional significance. *Annual Review of Psychology*, *66*, 519–545.

Todorov, A. T., Said, C. C., & Verosky, S. C. (2011). Personality impressions from facial appearance. https:// bpb -us -w2 .wpmucdn .com/ voices .uchicago .edu/ dist/ f/ 3051/ files/2021/02/Todorov_HFP2011.pdf.

Todorov, A., & Uleman, J. S. (2004). The person reference process in spontaneous trait inferences. *Journal of Personality and Social Psychology*, *87*(4), 482.

Tulving, E. (1983). *Elements of Episodic Memory*. New York: Oxford University Press.

Tulving, E. (2004). How many memory systems are there? In D. A. Balota & E. J. Marsh (Eds.), *Cognitive Psychology: Key Readings* (pp. 362–378). London: Psychology Press.

Willis, J., & Todorov, A. (2006). First impressions: making up your mind after a 100-ms exposure to a face. *Psychological Science*, *17*(7), 592–598.

Willis, M. L., Dodd, H. F., & Palermo, R. (2013). The relationship between anxiety and the social judgements of approachability and trustworthiness. *PLoS ONE*, *8*(10), 1–6.

Yu, M., Saleem, M., & Gonzalez, C. (2014). Developing trust: first impressions and experience. *Journal of Economic Psychology*, *43*, 16–29.

Zebrowitz, L. A., Kikuchi, M., & Fellous, J. M. (2010). Facial resemblance to emotions: group differences, impression effects, and race stereotypes. *Journal of Personality and Social Psychology*, *98*(2), 175–189.

8 Toward a scorecard (and roadmap) for trustworthy AI implementation in organizations

Munindar P. Singh and Roger C. Mayer

Introduction

Due in part to the cost savings and efficiencies it can bring, the use of artificial intelligence (AI) is expanding and expected to expand greatly in the coming years. In this chapter, we consider the application of AI technologies in organizations. We are particularly interested in understanding the use of AI for purposes that benefit society so that this technology can provide ordinary people and businesses with the greatest assistance. To this end, we develop here a method to characterize the trustworthiness of AI technology deployed in organizations.

Specifically, in this chapter we apply the framework for trustworthiness proposed by Mayer, Davis, and Schoorman (1995; see also Mayer & Mayer, Chapter 1, for an overview of the model). In brief, trust is the willingness of a trustor (trusting party) to make itself vulnerable to a trustee (party to be trusted) for a particular task or purpose when the trustee cannot be monitored or controlled (Mayer et al., 1995). Whereas trust is an intention (i.e., a willingness) held by the trustor, trustworthiness is the trustor's evaluation of the trustee. The important outcome of trust is the trustor actually engaging in behavior that puts the trustor at risk (referred to as risk taking in the relationship, or RTR by Mayer et al. 1995).

Trustworthiness consists of three dimensions: the trustor's perceptions of the trustee's ability, benevolence, and integrity (ABI), which we explain briefly here and return to later in the chapter. Ability concerns how proficient the trustor deems the trustee to be at the task at hand. Benevolence concerns how strongly the trustor expects the trustee to seek the benefit of the trustor (i.e., to support the trustor's interests). Integrity concerns how consistently the trustor believes the trustee will follow values acceptable to the trustor. Thus, this approach separates perceived characteristics of the trustee (trustworthiness) from trust (a behavioral intention) and risk-taking behavior that makes the trustor vulnerable to the trustee (i.e., RTR).

As noted by Sheridan (2019) and others, trust in automation has been defined in a number of ways. AI is a particular type of automation. A recent meta-analysis including 65 articles on trust in AI defined trust as "the *reliance* by an agent that actions *prejudicial* to their well-being will not be undertaken by influential others" (Kaplan et al., 2021; emphasis added). This definition limits consideration of trust in at least two ways.

First, Kaplan and colleagues' definition focuses on trust being reliance. The *behavior of relying* on a technology—i.e., RTR—is influenced by factors other than trust, such as a lack of viable alternatives, and the perceived riskiness of the behavior. Moreover, reliance does not inherently provide any diagnostic information about *why* the trustor takes the risk of relying on the technology. Consideration of trust as a willingness to be vulnerable and trustworthiness as comprised of three perceptions of ability, benevolence, and integrity provides more insight into the reasons the trustor engages or does not engage in the RTR.

Second, Kaplan et al.'s (2021) definition is limited to consideration of the extent to which the trustor perceives prejudice toward the trustor. Using trustworthiness from Mayer et al. (1995), if a trustee has a prejudice toward the trustor, it would be reflected in the trustworthiness dimension of benevolence. If, for example, prejudice from the trustee were perceived by the trustor, measurement on a Likert-type scale would record strong disagreement with statements reflecting that the trustee cares about the trustor and would seek to protect the trustor's interests. Moreover, that would capture at best a portion of the continuum of benevolence. A lack of prejudice implies nothing more than a neutral orientation, which falls short of a perceived desire to do things to benefit the trustor, which is captured by the higher end of the benevolence scale. In addition to the trustee's orientation toward the trustor, ability and integrity as described above are focused on distinct issues. Thus, use of the three dimensions of trustworthiness enables us to consider a broader spectrum of reasons that might influence a trustor to either be willing or to avoid being vulnerable to the AI. We therefore adopt the Mayer et al. (1995) trust model for its diagnostic utility to delineate why a trustor might trust an AI technology (as deployed in an organization) to a greater or lesser extent.

Scope

In current and emerging applications in organizations, AI is often packaged with Big Data (technologies for acquiring, storing, querying, and manipulating vast amounts of data) to provide decision support. Examples of such AI applications in business include customer modeling and personalization, supply chain optimization, mortgage risk assessment, and trading futures. In other organizational settings, judicial settings are seeing widespread use of AI in predicting recidivism (i.e., return to the legal system of offenders) and sentencing guidelines, and in such areas as healthcare and finance it is being used for fraud detection. (Manyika, Silberg, and Presten, 2019) review some opportunities and risks associated with AI.

There are other instances of AI where it is embodied in physical artifacts such as robots and autonomous vehicles. Those applications are increasingly becoming prevalent with factory robots gaining improved capabilities and vehicles demonstrating self-driving capabilities (albeit not always safely). A wide-ranging review of human trust in AI notes that an important issue that affects trust in AI is tangibility, or the actual physical presence of the machine such as a robot. AI that is embedded in a physically tangible artifact such as a robot appears to be more trustworthy than when a physical object is not associated with it (Glikson & Woolley, 2020). Our framework could potentially, with or without extensions, cover such forms of AI, although we defer a consideration of them to future work.

Contributions in a nutshell

The U.S. National Science Foundation (NSF) is interested in research considering the impact of AI on people. For this purpose, the NSF recently introduced four dimensions of AI to be considered: fairness, ethics, accountability, and transparency (FEAT) [https://www.nsf.gov/pubs/2019/nsf19016/nsf19016.jsp]. They intentionally did not define these terms, encouraging instead researchers to define them as they deem warranted. Given the lack of widely agreed-upon definitions for these terms, we note some of the challenges to defining them and offer our own interpretations of them.

In this chapter, we use both ABI and FEAT as bases to evaluate AI technology deployments in organizations. Doing so leads us to identify exemplar questions in the resulting 3 × 4 grid. We posit that answering these questions will provide a fruitful basis for evaluating AI-based systems in terms of its trustworthiness in the eyes of those affected by it. We close with a discussion of some potentially valuable directions for investigation.

A sociotechnical stance on AI

> Any sufficiently advanced technology is indistinguishable from magic.
> —Arthur C. Clarke (1968)

In common usage, AI is framed as a set of mysterious artifacts that can magically solve problems. To end-users, the often-uncanny ability of AI to identify patterns and make predictions is nothing short of magical, echoing Arthur C. Clarke's famous dictum. Therefore, it is perhaps not surprising that users or end-users focus on the technical aspects of AI. Indeed, from the perspective of trust, that view is not entirely without merit because the ability associated with or ascribed to AI relies on its construction and function as a technical artifact. Viewing AI as a purely technical artifact makes it more difficult to ascribe integrity and particularly benevolence to it, however.

A second view of AI is through the so-called *intentional stance*, as described by Daniel Dennett (1987) and McCarthy (1990). The idea of the intentional stance is that we (as humans) may ascribe a mind to any technical artifact (e.g., see Wingert & Mayer, Chapter 5). Instead of seeking to understand the artifact in terms of its design or function, one would ascribe a mental state to it. In the usual approaches, one would use the so-called folk psychological concepts such as beliefs, knowledge, goals, and intentions to describe, understand, and explain observed behaviors of the artifact. In a famous example, we might view an old-fashioned (that is, not infused with AI in the modern sense) thermostat in intentional terms. We might state that the thermostat intends to raise the temperature to at least the set point. When it believes the temperature is below its set point, in accordance with its intention, it would turn the central furnace on to bring the temperature up. We might be able to explain when the thermostat malfunctions, for example, by determining that either its belief is wrong (the temperature is high enough so its sensor may be broken) or that its intention (reflecting raising the temperature) may be out of sync with the user's.

While the intentional stance remains the dominant view of AI within computer science, another influential formulation of it is as the *knowledge level* (Newell, 1982, 1992). This stance continues to be seen in recent work on the ethics of AI, for example, in building AI agents that demonstrate ethical reasoning (e.g.,

Bremner et al., 2019). An important benefit of this stance is that it can help combat complexity. Instead of having to contend with the incredible complexity of the construction of today's computing artifacts, we can form a rough and ready model of them in folk psychological terms—terms that are familiar to us as humans and help to mediate our normal interactions with other humans.

Because of its ascription of mental states to artifacts, the intentional stance makes it quite natural to talk of the benevolence and integrity of the artifacts. However, for our present purposes, such ascriptions can be misleading in that they hide the contributions of social actors, such as humans and organizations, in how AI interacts with ordinary people.[1] Specifically, although the intentional stance is couched in psychological language, it is very much a view of AI as a technical artifact—that is, divorced from its societal or organizational contexts. Moreover, the mysterious nature of AI as perceived by lay people is arguably made more prominent through the use of such psychological language.

In light of the foregoing, in this chapter, we consider AI implementations as part of a sociotechnical framework. The idea of a sociotechnical system was developed by Trist and Bamforth's (1951) famous studies of coal miners, referring to the combined relationship between the human and technical aspects of a workplace. For our purposes in this chapter, we think of the concrete computational notion of a sociotechnical system as formalized by Singh (2013). The AI is not a standalone artifact, whether or not we ascribe a mental state to it. AI as implemented in an organization therefore reflects, or ought to reflect, the purpose and goals of the organization. Its ability depends upon how effectively it meets its organizational purpose, for example, to serve the organization's stakeholders and help to solve their problems within a given domain. Its benevolence arises (or not) from not just the AI technology, but how well the AI in combination with the organizational backdrop takes its stakeholders' interests into account. Likewise, the system's integrity arises (or not) from how the AI technology and organization together respect societal and legal norms.

---

[1]   We recognize that Wingert and Mayer (Chapter 5) consider the technology artifact and the social actors associated with that artifact as described here may be considered separately. We acknowledge that future research to investigate whether such treatment would better explain reactions to AI is warranted.

Ability, benevolence, and integrity

A considerable amount of research on trust in and between organizations has been conducted since the mid-1990s. In this chapter we employ the framework of trust from Mayer, Davis, and Schoorman (1995), which has been widely adopted as a research framework. In the introductory chapter of this book the model is described in text and shown by a figure (Mayer & Mayer, Chapter 1), so our treatment of it here will focus more specifically on how trustworthiness applies to the evaluation of an AI-based system.

Mayer et al.'s (1995) theory states that the three main issues about a trustee that lead to a higher assessment of that party's trustworthiness are ability, benevolence, and integrity, often abbreviated as ABI. Ability addresses the issue of whether the trustee has the capacity to deliver what is needed in the context of the relationship at hand: is it capable of achieving the desired objectives? *Ceteris paribus*, if the trustee has strong ability, then the chances of a good outcome are better; if the trustee lacks ability to do what is needed, then it is likely unwise to make oneself vulnerable to that trustee.

Benevolence addresses the question to what extent the trustee will seek to protect the interests of the trustor. Typically, this focuses on the idiosyncratic relationship between the trustee and the trustor, but can be viewed more broadly. In a study of trust in the federal government, Hamm, Smidt, and Mayer (2019) operationalized benevolence as the perception of the extent to which the trustee (i.e., federal government) *cares about oneself and others similar to oneself*. It is noteworthy that when the trustee is as large and intangible as the federal government, it cannot be expected to develop a personal relationship with the trustor in the same way that another human would. For this purpose, Hamm and colleagues adapted benevolence to be directed toward not only the trustor, but also *others like the trustor*. They found that the perception of government benevolence viewed this way contributed to an individual's willingness to be vulnerable to the government in such ways as following recommendations to evacuate prior to a natural disaster, or to receive a vaccine in the face of a public health crisis. Furthermore, they found that operationalizing trust as the willingness to be vulnerable to the government was significantly more correlated with variables expected than is the well-established American National Election Studies measure that has been used in political science for decades. It therefore appears to be fruitful to consider AI from a perspective of its holding the interests of *the trustor and others like the trustor* as important.

The third factor about a trustee that the model describes is integrity. This addresses the question of how closely the trustee follows a set of values the trustor finds acceptable. An assessment of integrity necessitates two underlying assumptions. The first is that the trustor holds an acceptable set of values. If, for example, an AI algorithm were structured around the goal of short-term gain for the organization, to the extent that this was inconsistent with the trustor's expectations of how the system ought to behave, this would diminish the system's integrity. In addition, if the system did not reliably and consistently follow the set of values it purports to adhere to, that would also reduce the system's perceived integrity. Thus, the system's reliability affects the perception of its integrity.

It is important at this point to make two notes about this use of the Mayer et al. (1995) model. First, the theory was originally described using the language of "parties" to denote individuals. Soon afterwards, its authors explained that the model was intentionally designed to be isomorphic (Schoorman, Mayer, & Davis, 1996), meaning that the definition and conceptualization is the same across different levels of analysis (e.g., Rousseau, 1985). The constructs of trust and the three trustworthiness factors are not only applicable to interpersonal trust, but also to intergroup and interorganizational trust, and trust between these different levels of analysis. We therefore posit that it is appropriate to apply the model to a sociotechnical AI-based system, as it is simply a technologically enhanced system of people.

Second, we note here a distinction between integrity and benevolence. While integrity is the perception that the trustee adheres to an acceptable set of values, benevolence reflects a perception of the relationship between the trustee and the trustor. In some cases, benevolence and integrity are consistent, possibly to the point of being indistinguishable from one another. In other cases, however, the distinction between them is important. Consider, for example, that an AI controls the scheduling of trains in a city's transportation system. An affluent business executive may recognize that the scheduling priorities favor the executive at the expense of less affluent citizens. The executive would be likely to perceive the system as being benevolent. Whether that individual would see the system as having high integrity, however, would depend on how acceptable they found it that the transportation system was favoring the affluent rather than, for example, scheduling trains in a way that was most efficient for the most riders, or even scheduling that prioritized the transportation needs of the most disadvantaged. If so, the system would likely be perceived to have benevolence but not integrity. We suggest that there are enough situations in which judgments of the benevolence and integrity of an AI-based sociotechnical system can be expected to diverge that it is fruitful to consider these as separate factors in trust, as proposed in the Mayer et al. (1995) model.

As another way in which the ABI model can be applied to understand the trustworthiness of AI, Singh and Singh (2023) develop a model for trustworthiness of AI based on the ABI model but grounded in case law. The case law precedes AI but illustrates how similar considerations arise in human to human and human to organizational interactions.

Understanding fairness, ethics, accountability, and transparency

There is a rather extensive literature on how to define fairness, ethics, accountability, and transparency, and it is rife with criticisms about flaws in various definitional approaches. We first provide some brief notes about the difficulties in trying to define them, and then we approach them as they seem to make sense in our context.

As one example, Bennett and Keyes (2020) raise the question of what is the point of fairness? They draw on Hoffmann (2019), who points out that fairness is often modeled after U.S. anti-discrimination law. They point out that in seeking to redress disparities, no consideration is given to the effect on those who were previously advantaged. For a second example, consider defining ethics. Benke et al. (2020) raise the question of how to decide what should be deemed good or bad. The field of philosophy, which should form a basis to address this, seems to lack a clear, straightforward answer to this question.

It is beyond the scope of this chapter to thoroughly review the options for defining the four variables denoted by FEAT and the challenges to each of them. Rather, we note that this may in part be why the NSF intentionally did not define them but left that open to researchers. Below we seek to be clear about what we mean by each, recognizing that if future researchers take issue with any of our definitions and alter them, it will likely mean revisiting the questions within the matrix presented below.

We interpret Fairness in terms of how distributions of desirable outcomes are made, such as the parity in decision-making across demographic groups. Our use of Ethics is in terms of deserts, or the extent to which the AI makes decisions that favor those who deserve the favor. We understand Accountability in terms of how account-giving is provided, along with course correction of decision-making. Finally, we consider Transparency as being about the clarity and explanations provided about the decisions made by the AI.

ABI on FEAT: toward a scorecard

The combinations of each of the four factors of FEAT described above with each of the three factors of trustworthiness are described in Table 8.1. Consider a bank that deploys an AI approach for mortgage loan approvals. We can further refine the scorecard by considering the different stakeholders of an organization. A simple dichotomy is between internal (those who constitute the organization and are primarily responsible for carrying out its processes) and external stakeholders (those whom the organization serves or otherwise affects). For purposes of clarity in each cell, at this point in the chapter we develop these questions attempting to focus on only the cell's particular line and column. We revisit this issue at the chapter's end to open further possibilities for intriguing and illuminating research on trust in AI.

To motivate our scorecard, we turn to the notion of a critical question, as proposed by Walton, Reed, and Macagno (2008). A critical question raises a concern at the heart of the robustness of an argument, and answering a critical question helps complete an argument. Critical questions, in essence, reflect knowledge of important concerns that an expert can raise in critically evaluating a claim made by another person or in formulating a defensible claim of their own. For example, for practical reasoning (as to select an action), the relevant critical questions would concern the feasibility of the action or the relationship between that action and one's goals.

Accordingly, we identify critical questions pertaining to the trustworthiness of AI as deployed in an organization. We place these questions in a matrix whose rows are the ABI factors in trustworthiness and whose columns are the FEAT criteria for ethical AI. We further use these critical questions as a basis for a reasoned scorecard, wherein answers to the critical questions can be summed across rows or columns to arrive at a measure of trustworthiness of an AI deployment in an organization.

Table 8.1   Critical questions for understanding the trustworthiness of AI

	Fairness	Ethics	Accountability	Transparency
Ability	Does the AI have the data and hardware (e.g., sensors) to make equitable decisions? Is its programming sophisticated enough to enable it to do so?	Can the AI incorporate data in its decision-making that enables it to make just decisions; e.g., considering the personal situation of an application (children, credit history)? Does the AI have the capacity to incorporate feedback from external sources to improve the fairness of its decisions?	Does the AI assemble the data to justify its decision-making to the regulatory bodies and to prospectively take regulatory guidance about its decisions (e.g., loan approvals)? Does it make its decisions and their relationship to demographics known?	Does the AI have the ability to reveal its decision-making, e.g., through explicit criteria under which a decision (e.g., loan approval or denial) is made? Can it do it in an understandable fashion?
Benevolence	Is the AI programmed to learn to better help me or people like me?	Is the AI structured to help individual applicants, e.g., by finding mitigating circumstances for their credit lapses or acknowledging that as minority or immigrant applicants they may not have the family backing to co-sign a loan?	Does the AI seek to make any necessary corrections in light of any problems discovered?	Does the AI reveal elements of its decision-making and data to help the loan applicant and not, e.g., to mislead them? Does it provide info to help them be more successful in the future?

	Fairness	Ethics	Accountability	Transparency
Integrity	Does the AI compute the fairness criteria honestly, e.g., not altering the criteria or ranges over which the demographic distributions are computed?	Does the AI avoid misusing information obtained from applicants to hurt their prospects, especially optional information? What do people believe the system should morally have to do? What moral compass should the AI technology be built around?	Does the AI provide truthful justifications for any decisions? Does it adequately clarify the fairness of its decisions to those affected? Does the AI improve its functioning for future interactions?	Does the AI reveal elements of its decision-making and data clearly and completely?

Embodied AI: robots and vehicles

By embodied AI, we refer to AI realized in physical artifacts such as autonomous robots and vehicles. Glikson and Woolley (2020) refer to this as tangibility. More generally, we can think of AI realized in cyber-physical systems, which would include chemical refineries and healthcare devices such as insulin pumps and cardiac pacemakers.

When dealing with a physical artifact of any scale that acts intelligently, it is difficult not to conceive of the AI in it as "the ghost in the machine" in Gilbert Ryle's memorable phrase (Ryle, 1949). However, a small amount of reflection brings forth the sociotechnical nature of even such seemingly standalone artifacts.

For embodied AI, we can identify important organizational roles such as builder (e.g., see Wingert & Mayer, Chapter 5), owner, operator, and maintainer. In general, these roles may be filled by distinct organizations. Let's consider the case of present-day vehicles—that is, those not infused with AI technology. The builder of a vehicle would be an automobile manufacturer such as General Motors. Its owner may be a leasing company such as Hertz, its operator may be the person who rents the vehicle, and its maintainer may be a franchisee of or contractor for Hertz. The same roles would apply to autonomous vehicles. Therefore, when we apply our framework to embodied AI, we would likewise need to consider the FEAT criteria with respect to these organizational roles (van der Werff, Blomqvist, & Koskinen, 2021).

Conclusions and future directions

We can use the matrix of Table 8.1 for a research roadmap to develop AI tools and implement them in organizations in a manner that would support positive answers to the questions raised above. Alternatively, we can map each question from the "does" form to the "how does" form to produce challenges for making AI technology development more effective.

One inherent complexity that deserves consideration is that the three dimensions of trustworthiness can interact. We described them in this chapter *ceteris paribus*, or in their simple form and in isolation. For example, considered alone, greater ability should serve to make AI more trustworthy. But what if the AI is structured not to attempt to be benevolent toward a stakeholder, but is instead seen by the trustor as malevolent? If the AI is set up to catch violations of some rule or law, then for those stakeholders who deem that they may be damaged by the AI's actions, the higher the AI's ability the *less* they would judge the AI to be trustworthy. In fact, as AI is developed with increasing machine learning capabilities, those stakeholders would not only tend to avoid interaction with the AI technology but would increasingly expend resources to nullify the AI's capability to execute its mission (since that mission is seen as deleterious to the damaged parties). A lower-technology example of such resource expenditure would be a motorist who is careless about observing speed limits spending money on a radar detector or jammer. As AI continues to become more complex and ubiquitous, the expenditure of resources to defeat its effectiveness might also be expected to rise.

Another complexity that we intentionally avoided in this chapter is our choice of stakeholders. In the opening paragraph we constrained our focus to the stakeholders being society, or end-users of the AI-based sociotechnical systems. Importantly, Lockey and Gillespie (Chapter 2) clarify the importance of considering multiple stakeholders as trustors. We encourage further consideration of other stakeholders, which was beyond the scope of the present chapter.

Although these are science fiction thriller movies, the role of the computer "gone mad" named HAL in the movie *2001: A Space Odyssey* or the role of "Skynet" in the *Terminator* series of movies both illustrate the condition wherein greater AI ability can be expected to lead to decreased trust. Future research should seek a deeper understanding of judgments of AI's trustworthiness by considering the interactions among the AI's ability, benevolence, and integrity.

Using the lens of interactions among the trustworthiness dimensions for trust in AI in the above paragraph, consider the use of robots to lead people to safety as described by Alan Wagner (Chapter 13). How would the ability of a robot designed to lead people to safety affect trust in the robot if the to-be-saved stakeholders were either, on the one hand, library patrons, or, on the other hand, maximum security prison inmates? Would the inmates consider the AI's benevolence to be as high as in the case of the library patrons? Would a presumed lower level of perceived AI benevolence make a more sophisticated robot less trustworthy to prisoners than would be a less sophisticated robot?

As per our opening comments, it can be expected that AI will become an increasingly important presence in society. Our hope is that this chapter leads researchers to develop more and better questions concerning the trustworthiness of this technology.[2]

References

Benke, I., Feine, J., Venable, J. R., & Maedche, A. (2020). On implementing ethical principles in design science research. *Association for Information Systems Transactions on Human–Computer Interaction*, *12*(4), 206–227. https:// doi .org/ 10.17705/ 1thci .00136.

Bennett, C. L., & Keyes, O. (2020). What is the point of fairness? Disability, AI and the complexity of justice. *ACM SIGACCESS Accessibility and Computing*, *125*. https:// arxiv.org/abs/1908.01024.

Bremner, P., Dennis, L. A., Fisher, M., & Winfield, A. F. T. (2019). On proactive, transparent, and verifiable ethical reasoning for robots. *Proceedings of the IEEE*, *107*(3), 541–561. https://doi.org/10.1109/JPROC.2019.2898267.

Clarke, A. C. (1968). Clarke's third law on UFOs. *Science*, *159*(3812), 255. https:// doi .org/10.1126/science.159.3812.255-b.

Dennett, D. C. (1987). *The Intentional Stance*. Cambridge, MA: MIT Press.

---

2   MPS thanks the U.S. National Science Foundation for support under grant IIS-2116751.

Glikson, E., & Woolley, A. W. (2020). Human trust in artificial intelligence: review of empirical research. *Annals of the Academy of Management, 14*(2), 627–660. https://doi.org/10.5465/annals.2018.0057.

Hamm, J., Smidt, C., & Mayer, R. C. (2019). Understanding the psychological nature and mechanisms of political trust. *PLoS ONE*. https://doi.org/10.1371/journal.pone.0215835.

Hoffmann, A. L. (2019). Where fairness fails: data, algorithms, and the limits of anti-discrimination discourse. *Information Communication and Society, 22*(7), 900–915.

Kaplan, A. D., Kessler, T. T., Brill, J. C., & Hancock, P. A. (2021). Trust in artificial intelligence: meta-analytic findings. *Human Factors*. https://doi.org/10.1177/00187208211013988.

Manyika, J., Silberg, J., & Presten, B. (2019). What do we do about the biases in AI? *Harvard Business Review*. https://hbr.org/2019/10/what-do-we-do-about-the-biases-in-ai.

Mayer, R. C., Davis, J. H., & Schoorman, F. D. (1995). An integrative model of organizational trust. *Academy of Management Review, 20*(3), 709–734. https://doi.org/10.2307/258792.

McCarthy, J. (1990). Ascribing mental qualities to machines. In Vladimir Lifschitz (Ed.), *Formalizing Common Sense: Papers by John McCarthy* (pp. 93–118). Norwood, NJ: Ablex. [Reprinted from Martin Ringle (Ed.) (1979). *Philosophical Perspectives in Artificial Intelligence*. Brighton: Harvester Press.]

Newell, A. (1982). The knowledge level. *Artificial Intelligence, 18*(1), 87–127.

Newell, A. (1992). Reflections on the knowledge level. *Artificial Intelligence, 59*(1), 31–38.

Rousseau, D. (1985). Issues of level in organizational research: multi-level and cross-level perspectives. *Research in Organizational Behavior, 7*, 1–37.

Ryle, G. (1949). *The Concept of Mind*. Oxford: Oxford University Press.

Schoorman, F. D., Mayer, R. C., & Davis, J. H. (1996). Organizational trust: philosophical perspectives and conceptual definitions. *Academy of Management Review, 21*(2), 337–340. https://www.jstor.org/stable/258662.

Sheridan, T. B. (2019). Individual differences in attributes of trust in automation: measurement and application to system design. *Frontiers in Psychology, 10*. https://doi.org/10.3389/fpsyg.2019.01117.

Singh, A. M., & Singh, M. P. (2023). Wasabi: a conceptual model for trustworthy artificial intelligence. *IEEE Computer, 56*(2), 20–28.

Singh, M. P. (2013). Norms as a basis for governing sociotechnical systems. *ACM Transactions on Intelligent Systems and Technology (TIST), 5*(1), 21:1–21:23.

Trist, E. L., & Bamforth, K. W. (1951). Some social and psychological consequences of the longwall method of coal-getting: an examination of the psychological situation and defences of a work group in relation to the social structure and technological content of the work system. *Human Relations, 4*(1), 3–38. https://doi.org/10.1177/001872675100400101.

van der Werff, L., Blomqvist, K., & Koskinen, S. (2021). Trust cues in artificial intelligence. In N. Gillespie, C. A. Fulmer, & R. J. Lewicki (Eds.), *Understanding Trust in Organizations: A Multilevel Perspective* (pp. 307–333). New York: Routledge.

Walton, D., Reed, C., & Macagno, F. (2008). *Argumentation Schemes*. Cambridge: Cambridge University Press.

9   The sociology of trust

Oliver Schilke, Martin Reimann, and Karen S. Cook

Introduction

This chapter covers sociological perspectives on trust. The notion of trust is integral to the discipline of sociology and can be traced back to some of its classical works (e.g., Durkheim, 1984 [1893]; Parsons, 1937; Weber, 1951 [1915]). In the modern era, trust has arguably become even more prominent, possibly due to the increasing substitution of power relations inside formal organizations by economic relations in open markets, which rely to some extent on actors' willingness to trust each other in order to function effectively (Cook & Hardin, 2001). Sociologists have argued that trust brings a number of social benefits, such as reciprocity (Hayashi et al., 1999), solidarity (Molm et al., 2007), equality (Smith, 2010), and democracy (Choi & David, 2012). In general, trust is often viewed as the glue that holds society together (Castelfranchi & Falcone, 2010).

It should therefore come as no surprise that trust has become a popular topic in numerous subdisciplines of sociology, including economic sociology (Granovetter, 1985), social psychology (Simpson & Willer, 2015), and immigration (Portes, 1995). Despite some differences in their underlying assumptions and conceptual emphasis, scholars in sociology and beyond have increasingly converged on a common general definition of trust. Namely, trust refers to the willingness of one actor (the trustor) to make himself or herself vulnerable in a particular way (trust domain) to another actor (the trustee), while presuming that the trustee will not exploit that vulnerability (Schilke et al., 2021, building on Mayer et al., 1995).

Despite this consensus on the definition of trust, the field of sociological trust research has remained relatively fragmented, with different scholars focusing on different forms of trust. In particular, sociological trust research appears to be divided by a focus on either generalized trust or particularized trust. Even though both of these camps have made significant progress in understanding where these respective forms of trust originate, there remains a significant lack of cross-pollination as well as a missing middle ground. Thus, to enable cumulative progress in advancing knowledge of trust, we discuss a framework that aims to integrate disparate streams of research so as to allow future trust research to move beyond the generalized–particularized dichotomy. The framework makes an important contribution to trust research by adding greater conceptual precision while directing attention to neglected categorical forms of trust.

The rest of this chapter proceeds as follows. After offering a brief overview of existing insights into generalized and particularized trust, we elaborate our integrative framework, which we hope will facilitate a better understanding of different forms of trust. We then use this framework as a springboard to offer a number of recommended directions for future trust research.

Generalized and particularized trust

The first camp of sociologists has studied *generalized* trust, which is sometimes also called propensity to trust (Mayer et al., 1995) or social trust (Hardin, 2002). This form of trust encompasses a large circle of unfamiliar others, an abstract level of analysis, and/or a large number of different trust domains. This concept has attracted significant attention, because scholars have observed that the level of generalized trust has been declining over the years (Paxton, 1999; Putnam, 1995), with potentially detrimental consequences for society. Relevant antecedents to generalized trust include (1) social learning, (2) reinforcement learning, and (3) biological factors. The social learning view suggests that people make trust decisions based on their experiences, both during childhood (Erikson, 1964) and later in life (Hardin, 2002), which influence their decisions about how much to trust others. The reinforcement learning account, in contrast, is less focused on learning about others than on learning about oneself; it proposes that as people get to know their own identity, they come to view themselves as either a trusting or a non-trusting person (Kuwabara, 2015). Researchers interested in the biological sources of trust augment socialization-related arguments with studies on the genetic foundations of trust (Reimann et al., 2017). Much of the sociological research on generalized trust has employed data from surveys conducted over time, such as the General Social Survey and the World Values Survey.

The other camp of sociological researchers has investigated *particularized* trust—also known as relational trust (Cook, 2005) or knowledge-based trust (Yamagishi & Yamagishi, 1994). Particularized trust encompasses a narrow circle of familiar others, a micro level of analysis, and/or a specific trust domain.

Theoretical arguments in the research on particularized trust have been dominated by the encapsulated interest account, which assumes that trustors try to anticipate whether the trustee will encapsulate their own interests and will thus not exploit them (Cook et al., 2005; see also Brewer, Torres, Celeya, & Pitaes, Chapter 7, on trust and anticipatory thinking). As a result of these considerations, trustors decide to what extent they will make themselves vulnerable to the trustee. Among the most frequently studied antecedents to particularized trust are (1) the shadow of the past, (2) the shadow of the future, and (3) the broader social network. Particularized trust can stem from the history of interactions between exchange partners (sometimes referred to as the "shadow of the past"; Swärd, 2016), as the partner's behavior in past interactions can serve as an important cue regarding this partner's anticipated trustworthiness in the current situation (Blau, 1964). In addition to looking at the past, some focus more on the value of the future relationship (or the "shadow of the future"; Molm et al., 2000, building on Axelrod, 1985), since a partner who values maintaining the relationship likely can be trusted to a greater extent than a partner for whom the future relationship is less meaningful (Raub & Weesie, 1990). Finally, beyond the immediate dyad, the broader network in which the trustor and the trustee are embedded can be a source of particularized trust as a result of reputational concerns and information transmitted through indirect ties (Coleman, 1990). Experiments are the most frequently used data source in the study of particularized trust in sociology.

An extended framework of three trust radiuses

While the generalized–particularized divide has become somewhat institutionalized in sociological trust research (Delhey et al., 2011), we propose that much theoretical precision and leverage can be gained by abandoning this dichotomy in favor of a more fine-grained and multi-dimensional approach advanced in our framework (Figure 9.1).

There are two noteworthy aspects to this framework that depart from the current state of sociological trust research. First, the framework embraces Fukuyama's (1995, 2001) idea of a "radius of trust" as a more gradual (vs. binary) concept that goes back to Harrison (1985). The radius of trust can be understood as "the width of the circle of people among whom a certain trust

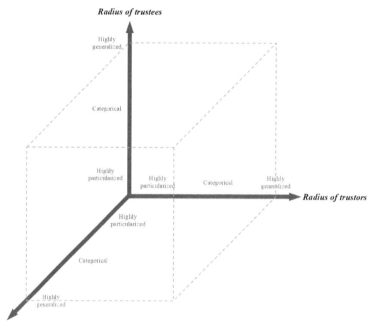

Source: The authors

Figure 9.1   An extended framework of three trust radiuses

level exists" (van Hoorn, 2014, p. 1256).[1] This definition indicates that the generality of trust can range from very narrow to very wide at the two extremes, but in most cases it will fall at an intermediate point in between. Around the midpoint of this radius is categorical trust, where trust is neither limited to

---

[1]   Note that the radius and the level of trust should be thought of as distinct concepts. The latter represents the strength of trust (i.e., the extent to which is an actor is willing to make himself or herself vulnerable), while the former is defined as the width of the trust circle (in which the given level of trust can be either low or high). In their insightful empirical investigation, Delhey et al. (2011) investigated the "amount of trust" as an interactive combination of radius and level, but we will not further elaborate on this notion here. Further, for the purposes of our discussion, the radius of trust is treated independently of qualitative differences in trust, such as affective and cognitive trust (McAllister, 1995) or ability-, benevolence-, and integrity-based trust (Mayer et al., 1995). We leave it to future research to develop theory on how particularized, categorical, and generalized trust may systematically vary in terms of such properties.

a specific actor or single domain nor generalized to virtually everyone or every occasion. Although social categories have a central place in sociological inquiry at large (Zuckerman, 1999), it is striking how little is known about categorical trust (at least relative to generalized and particularized trust). We will return to this gap in our suggestions for future research.

Second, the generalized–particularized dichotomy suffers from considerable ambiguity. The radius of trust is not unidimensional; rather, it can in fact pertain to three different parts of any comprehensive trust conceptualization: the trustor (the actor doing the trusting), the trustee (the actor being trusted), and the trust domain (the issue or activity in which trust is placed). The radius of the *trustor* can fall anywhere on a continuum ranging from a particular individual to a small group to an organization or institution to a society at large (Cook & Schilke, 2010).[2] Similarly, the *trustee*'s radius can range from trust in a specific individual to trust in categories (such as family members, coworkers, organizations, or institutions) to trust in "most people." Finally, the *trust domain* can be very particularized and pertain to a single interaction only, or it can be broader (encompassing several interactions within the same domain) or even virtually complete (encompassing every type of activity). Importantly, the radiuses of each of these trust components can vary independently, making it necessary to move from a one- to a three-dimensional model in order to avoid under-specification.

Taken together, we recommend that trust scholars be very clear about their respective focus by situating their work in the three-dimensional space shown in Figure 9.1. This model clarifies that the radius of trust is gradual and multi-dimensional (rather than binary and uniform, as portrayed in much of the prior research). Beyond enhancing precision, this framework also directs attention to a variety of research avenues that should provide plenty of opportunities for future trust scholarship.

Future research directions

Although sociologists have made substantial headway in improving our understanding of trust, much remains to be done. We start by outlining future

---

[2] In this chapter, we focus on individuals as the lowest unit of analysis that sociologists tend to study, even though neuroscientists have shown that lower-level investigations into the neural basis of trust can be very fruitful (Wu & Krueger, Chapter 14).

Table 9.1   Avenues for future research

#	Topic	Exemplary research question
1	Radius of trust as a construct	What determines the width of the circle of trust?
2	Interrelationships between highly particularized and highly generalized trust	(When) are these two trust archetypes positively vs. negatively connected?
3	Categorical trust	Can homophily and/or group status explain trust?
4	Cognitive, affective, and moral foundations of trust	Which emotions affect trust directly and indirectly through cognition?
5	Trust outcomes	What are the positive and negative consequences of trust?
6	Contextualized trust accounts	What are relevant contingencies to the effectiveness of different trust production modes?
7	Digitization and trust	What are the differences (if any) between trust in humans and trust in autonomous technological systems?
8	Trustworthiness	What is the role of reciprocity norms in trustees' decision to be trustworthy?

research directions that directly build on our extended model elaborated above before addressing a variety of other topics that we believe have the potential to significantly advance knowledge of trust (see Table 9.1 for a summary).

First, we call for research that advances the conceptualization and measurement of the radius of trust as a construct in its own right. Earlier empirical research has often left the trust radius unspecified, leaving it up to the study participants to make their own assumptions, which can lead to issues in measurement accuracy (Delhey et al., 2011). Further, the trust radius construct should be integrated into theoretical models that explain under what circumstances we can speak of a more vs. less generalized trustor, trustee, and trust domain. For instance, with regard to the trustor, interorganizational trust can reside at both the level of the individual boundary spanner and the level of the organization as a collective actor (Currall & Inkpen, 2002; Lumineau & Schilke, 2018; Schilke & Cook, 2013). However, we know very little about the factors that determine which of these two levels is more meaningful or salient in a given context.

Second, we need better insight into the linkages between coexisting forms of trust that vary in their generality. Are the extreme forms of highly generalized trust and highly particularized trust positively connected? The intuitive answer seems to be yes. However, authors such as Yamagishi and Yamagishi (1994) suggest that Japanese people tend to be low in generalized trust but high in particularized trust, indicating an inverse correlation. In a similar vein, Latusek and Cook (2012) argue that the presence of strong particularized trust may crowd out the need for generalized trust. They suggest that this may be the case when trust or confidence in societal institutions is low, especially in governmental and legal institutions.

Third, we see much potential for more research on categorical trust. Among relevant categories, family background, gender, and national origin have received some attention in trust research, building on Zucker's (1986) notion of characteristic-based trust production (see also Schilke et al., 2017 on trust production modes). Many more relevant categories come to mind that have not yet been investigated with respect to trust issues. Future research into categorical trust could usefully link trust research with sociological theories of homophily (McPherson et al., 2001) and status (Berger et al., 1980). The sharing of group membership may indeed underlie many trust judgments, as actors may favor, and may feel more comfortable trusting, ingroups over outgroups (Cialdini, 2021; Foddy & Yamagishi, 2009). Some social categories may be attributed greater status than others, with status often being linked to perceptions of greater trustworthiness (Blue et al., 2020). Beyond such ideas related to the radius of the trustee, we also need categorical accounts regarding the radius of the trustor and the trust domain. How do we determine which categories of trustors should be put into one bucket, and what types of activities do actors generalize to when forming their trust perceptions? And, which activities warrant trust-related judgments?

Fourth, above and beyond the question of trust radiuses, we recommend further insights into the cognitive, affective, and moral foundations of trust. Most sociologists have focused on cognitive trust models, such as the encapsulated interest account, and there is certainly much room for future research to increase the transparency of the assumptions and the specific cognitive mechanisms in these models. However, we also need a better understanding of affective and moral reasons to trust. Emotions have been argued to play a key role in trust formation and recovery (Schoorman et al., 2007), but we need to better understand which types of emotions should feature prominently in trust theories (Dunn & Schweitzer, 2005; Kugler et al., 2020) and whether their effects are direct or mediated through cognition (such as in Schilke et al., 2015). Further, beyond its instrumental and emotional aspects, trust and/or trustworthiness may be viewed as a moral virtue in of itself (Uslaner, 2002), to the extent that a trustee's virtuous disposition may potentially even outweigh encapsulated interests in explaining trust (Robbins, 2016). In short, we need richer accounts of trust that augment cognitive considerations with affective and moral ones.

Fifth, we advocate for further scholarship into the consequences (rather than the antecedents) of trust, which remains conspicuously rare in the field of sociology. Most investigations have taken the positive social outcomes of trust for granted. However, recent discussions of potential limitations and liabilities of trust indicate that trust is not a panacea and can come with important downsides (Neal et al., 2015). The trade-off between the benefits and the disadvantages of trust requires greater acknowledgment and more empirical investigation. In this respect, we recommend investigations into the optimal levels of trust under various conditions (Wicks et al., 1999). When are actors able to accurately calibrate their trust—that is, neither over-trust and risk exploitation, nor under-trust and forego valuable relational opportunities (Schilke & Huang, 2018)?

Sixth, while trust research may have matured to a point where it is becoming increasingly difficult to identify brand new main effects, we see plenty of opportunity to develop more contextualized accounts of trust. By this, we mean investigations that go beyond the generally accepted view that trust is highly context-specific (Rousseau et al., 1998) to identify concrete situational contingencies that affect the relevance of different origins or consequences of trust. The objective of such investigations would be to build a more generalizable theory of context—one that would point us to the conditions that should be taken into consideration when developing and assessing models of trust production and outcomes (Sasaki & Marsh, 2012; Schilke & Cook, 2015). Such an approach would provide greater confidence regarding the types of effects that are likely to hold in virtually any setting and those that are more confined to particular situations (de Jong et al., 2017). Comparative empirical approaches, including cross-cultural studies (Schoorman et al., 2007), will provide important new insights in this regard.

Seventh, following up on our previous point, how does the increasing digitization of society impact trust patterns? More than 40 years ago, Luhmann (1979) speculated that the increasing complexity of modern technology would increase the demand for trust—but that the very nature of trust was also likely to be affected. Although trust has traditionally been thought of as existing between human actors, people increasingly have to decide whether to trust autonomous technologies (Lyons, Scheutz, & Jessup, Chapter 10; Puranam &

Vanneste, 2021), such as robots (Wagner, Chapter 13) and blockchain-based systems (Lumineau et al., 2021). We need to know whether extant theories of trust still apply in these interactions with non-human entities.

Eighth and finally, there is considerable room to complement our knowledge of trust with more research focusing on trustworthiness. While these two constructs have often been conflated, they are conceptually distinct. Whereas trust refers to the trustor's willingness to make himself or herself vulnerable, trustworthiness refers to the trustee's willingness to avoid exploiting this vulnerability and to act in a reliable and truthful manner. Many investigations in sociology focus on trust, with much less attention to trustworthiness. For instance, most experimental studies employing the trust game are interested primarily in the first player's decision to send money rather than the second player's decision to reciprocate. This singular focus is unfortunate, because sociology is well equipped to theorize conditions that enable reciprocity, such as norms and rituals (Gouldner, 1960; Krishnan et al., 2021; Nardin et al., 2016).

Conclusion

In this chapter, we have taken stock of the sociological trust literature and how it has substantially advanced knowledge of both particularized and generalized trust. In an effort to achieve greater conceptual precision and point to new theoretical approaches, we have elaborated an extended framework that brings these two forms of trust together. Based on this framework, but also moving beyond it, we have presented an agenda of eight future research directions that we believe have considerable promise. We are excited to observe how research on trust, both within sociology and across disciplines, will continue to produce intriguing insights into the functioning of social relationships in various settings over the years to come.[3]

---

[3]   We are grateful for the comments from the co-editors and two anonymous reviewers. Research support was provided by a National Science Foundation CAREER Award (1943688) granted to the first author. Any opinions, findings, and conclusions or recommendations expressed in this material are those of the authors and do not necessarily reflect the views of the National Science Foundation.

References

Axelrod, R. M. (1985). *The Evolution of Cooperation*. Basic Books.
Berger, J., Rosenholtz, S. J., & Zelditch, M. (1980). Status organizing processes. *Annual Review of Sociology*, 6(1), 479–508. https://doi.org/10.1146/annurev.so.06.080180.002403.
Blau, P. M. (1964). *Exchange and Power in Social Life*. Wiley.
Blue, P. R., Hu, J., Peng, L., Yu, H., Liu, H., & Zhou, X. (2020). Whose promises are worth more? How social status affects trust in promises. *European Journal of Social Psychology*, 50(1), 189–206. https://doi.org/10.1002/ejsp.2596.
Castelfranchi, C., & Falcone, R. (2010). *Trust Theory: A Socio-Cognitive and Computational Model*. Wiley. https://doi.org/10.1002/9780470519851.ch9.
Choi, S. Y. P., & David, R. (2012). Lustration systems and trust: evidence from survey experiments in the Czech Republic, Hungary, and Poland. *American Journal of Sociology*, 117(4), 1172–1201. https://doi.org/10.1086/662648.
Cialdini, R. B. (2021). *Influence: The Psychology of Persuasion*. HarperCollins.
Coleman, J. S. (1990). *Foundations of Social Theory*. Harvard University Press.
Cook, K. S. (2005). Networks, norms, and trust: the social psychology of social capital. *Social Psychology Quarterly*, 68(1), 4–14. https://doi.org/10.1177/019027250506800102.
Cook, K. S., & Hardin, R. (2001). Norms of cooperativeness and networks of trust. In M. Hechter & K.-D. Opp (Eds.), *Social Norms* (pp. 327–347). Russell Sage.
Cook, K. S., Hardin, R., & Levi, M. (2005). *Cooperation Without Trust?* Russell Sage.
Cook, K. S., & Schilke, O. (2010). The role of public, relational and organizational trust in economic affairs. *Corporate Reputation Review*, 13(2), 98–109. https://doi.org/10.1057/crr.2010.14.
Currall, S. C., & Inkpen, A. C. (2002). A multilevel approach to trust in joint ventures. *Journal of International Business Studies*, 33(3), 479–495. https://doi.org/10.1057/palgrave.jibs.8491027.
de Jong, B. A., Kroon, D. P., & Schilke, O. (2017). The future of organizational trust research: a content-analytic synthesis of scholarly recommendations and review of recent developments. In P. A. M. Van Lange, B. Rockenbach, & T. Yamagishi (Eds.), *Trust in Social Dilemmas* (pp. 173–194). Oxford University Press. https://doi.org/10.1093/oso/9780190630782.003.0010.
Delhey, J., Newton, K., & Welzel, C. (2011). How general is trust in "most people"? Solving the radius of trust problem. *American Sociological Review*, 76(5), 786–807. https://doi.org/10.1177/0003122411420817.
Dunn, J. R., & Schweitzer, M. E. (2005). Feeling and believing: the influence of emotion on trust. *Journal of Personality and Social Psychology*, 88(5), 736–748. https://doi.org/10.1037/0022-3514.88.5.736.
Durkheim, E. (1984 [1893]). *The Division of Labor in Society*. Free Press.
Erikson, E. H. (1964). *Childhood and Society* (2nd edn). Norton.
Foddy, M., & Yamagishi, T. (2009). Group-based trust. In K. Cook, M. Levi, & R. Hardin (Eds.), *Whom Can We Trust? How Groups, Networks, and Institutions Make Trust Possible* (pp. 17–41). Russell Sage.
Fukuyama, F. (1995). *Trust: The Social Virtues and the Creation of Prosperity*. Free Press.
Fukuyama, F. (2001). Social capital, civil society and development. *Third World Quarterly*, 22(1), 7–20. https://doi.org/10.1080/713701144.

Gouldner, A. W. (1960). The norm of reciprocity: a preliminary statement. *American Sociological Review, 25*(2), 161–178. https://doi.org/10.2307/2092623.

Granovetter, M. (1985). Economic action and social structure: the problem of embeddedness. *American Journal of Sociology, 91*(3), 481–510. https:// doi .org/ 10 .1086/ 228311.

Hardin, R. (2002). *Trust and Trustworthiness.* Russell Sage.

Harrison, L. (1985). *Underdevelopment Is a State of Mind: The Latin American Case.* Madison.

Hayashi, N., Ostrom, E., Walker, J., & Yamagishi, T. (1999). Reciprocity, trust, and the sense of control: a cross-societal study. *Rationality and Society, 11*(1), 27–46. https://doi.org/10.1177/104346399011001002.

Krishnan, R., Cook, K. S., Kozhikode, R., & Schilke, O. (2021). An interaction ritual theory of social resource exchange: evidence from a Silicon Valley accelerator. *Administrative Science Quarterly, 66*(3), 659–710. https:// doi .org/ 10 .1177/ 0001839220970936.

Kugler, T., Ye, B., Motro, D., & Noussair, C. N. (2020). On trust and disgust: evidence from face reading and virtual reality. *Social Psychological and Personality Science, 11*(3), 317–325. https://doi.org/10.1177/1948550619856302.

Kuwabara, K. (2015). Do reputation systems undermine trust? Divergent effects of enforcement type on generalized trust and trustworthiness. *American Journal of Sociology, 120*(5), 1390–1428. https://doi.org/10.1086/681231.

Latusek, D., & Cook, K. S. (2012). Trust in transitions. *Kyklos, 65*(4), 512–525. https://doi.org/10.1111/kykl.12004.

Luhmann, N. (1979). *Trust and Power.* Wiley.

Lumineau, F., & Schilke, O. (2018). Trust development across levels of analysis: an embedded-agency perspective. *Journal of Trust Research, 8*(2), 238–248. https://doi.org/10.1080/21515581.2018.1531766.

Lumineau, F., Wang, W., & Schilke, O. (2021). Blockchain governance: a new way of organizing collaborations? *Organization Science, 32*(2), 500–521. https://doi.org/10.1287/orsc.2020.1379.

Mayer, R. C., Davis, J. H., & Schoorman, F. D. (1995). An integrative model of organizational trust. *Academy of Management Review, 20*(3), 709–734. https://doi.org/10.5465/amr.1995.9508080335.

McAllister, D. J. (1995). Affect- and cognition-based trust as foundations for interpersonal cooperation in organizations. *Academy of Management Journal, 38*(1), 24–59. https://doi.org/10.5465/256727.

McPherson, M., Smith-Lovin, L., & Cook, J. M. (2001). Birds of a feather: homophily in social networks. *Annual Review of Sociology, 27*, 415–444. https://doi.org/10.1146/annurev.soc.27.1.415.

Molm, L. D., Collett, J. L., & Schaefer, D. R. (2007). Building solidarity through generalized exchange: a theory of reciprocity. *American Journal of Sociology, 113*(1), 205–242. https://doi.org/10.1086/517900.

Molm, L. D., Takahashi, N., & Peterson, G. (2000). Risk and trust in social exchange: an experimental test of a classical proposition. *American Journal of Sociology, 105*(5), 1396–1427. https://doi.org/10.1086/210434.

Nardin, L. G., Balke-Visser, T., Ajmeri, N., Kalia, A. K., Sichman, J. S., & Singh, M. P. (2016). Classifying sanctions and designing a conceptual sanctioning process model for socio-technical systems. *The Knowledge Engineering Review, 31*(2), 142–166. https://doi.org/10.1017/S0269888916000023.

Neal, T. M. S., Shockley, E., & Schilke, O. (2015). The "dark side" of institutional trust. In E. Shockley, T. M. S. Neal, B. H. Bornstein, & L. M. Pytlik Zillig (Eds.), *Interdisciplinary Perspectives on Trust: Towards Theoretical and Methodological Integration* (pp. 177–191). Springer. https://doi.org/10.1007/978-3-319-22261-5_10.

Parsons, T. (1937). *The Structure of Social Action*. McGraw-Hill.

Paxton, P. (1999). Is social capital declining in the United States? A multiple indicator assessment. *American Journal of Sociology, 105*(1), 88–127. https://doi.org/10.1086/210268.

Portes, A. (1995). *The Economic Sociology of Immigration: Essays on Networks, Ethnicity, and Entrepreneurship*. Russell Sage.

Puranam, P., & Vanneste, B. (2021). Artificial intelligence, trust, and perceptions of agency. http://dx.doi.org/10.2139/ssrn.3897704.

Putnam, R. D. (1995). Bowling alone: America's declining social capital. *Journal of Democracy, 6*(1), 65–78. https://doi.org/10.1353/jod.1995.0002.

Raub, W., & Weesie, J. (1990). Reputation and efficiency in social interactions: an example of network effects. *American Journal of Sociology, 96*(3), 626–654. https://doi.org/10.1086/229574.

Reimann, M., Schilke, O., & Cook, K. S. (2017). Trust is heritable, whereas distrust is not. *Proceedings of the National Academy of Sciences, 114*(27), 7007–7012. https://doi.org/10.1073/pnas.1617132114.

Robbins, B. G. (2016). Probing the links between trustworthiness, trust, and emotion: evidence from four survey experiments. *Social Psychology Quarterly, 79*(3), 284–308. https://doi.org/10.1177/0190272516657546.

Rousseau, D. M., Sitkin, S. B., Burt, R. S., & Camerer, C. (1998). Not so different after all: a cross-discipline view of trust. *Academy of Management Review, 23*(3), 393–404. https://doi.org/10.5465/amr.1998.926617.

Sasaki, M., & Marsh, R. M. (2012). Introduction. In M. Sasaki & R. M. Marsh (Eds.), *Trust: Comparative Perspectives* (pp. 1–8). Brill.

Schilke, O., & Cook, K. S. (2013). A cross-level process theory of trust development in interorganizational relationships. *Strategic Organization, 11*(3), 281–303. https://doi.org/10.1177/1476127012472096.

Schilke, O., & Cook, K. S. (2015). Sources of alliance partner trustworthiness: integrating calculative and relational perspectives. *Strategic Management Journal, 36*(2), 276–297. https://doi.org/10.1002/smj.2208.

Schilke, O., & Huang, L. (2018). Worthy of trust? How brief interpersonal contact affects trust accuracy. *Journal of Applied Psychology, 103*(11), 1181–1197. http://dx.doi.org/10.1037/apl0000321.

Schilke, O., Reimann, M., & Cook, K. S. (2015). Power decreases trust in social exchange. *Proceedings of the National Academy of Sciences, 112*(42), 12950–12955. https://doi.org/10.1073/pnas.1517057112.

Schilke, O., Reimann, M., & Cook, K. S. (2021). Trust in social relations. *Annual Review of Sociology, 47*, 239–259. https://doi.org/10.1146/annurev-soc-082120-082850.

Schilke, O., Wiedenfels, G., Brettel, M., & Zucker, L. G. (2017). Interorganizational trust production contingent on product and performance uncertainty. *Socio-Economic Review, 15*(2), 307–330. https://doi.org/10.1093/ser/mww003.

Schoorman, F. D., Mayer, R. C., & Davis, J. H. (2007). An integrative model of organizational trust: past, present, and future. *Academy of Management Review, 32*(2), 344–354. https://doi.org/10.5465/amr.2007.24348410.

Simpson, B., & Willer, R. (2015). Beyond altruism: sociological foundations of cooperation and prosocial behavior. *Annual Review of Sociology, 41*(1), 43–63. https://doi.org/10.1146/annurev-soc-073014-112242.

Smith, S. S. (2010). Race and trust. *Annual Review of Sociology, 36*(1), 453–475. https://doi.org/10.1146/annurev.soc.012809.102526.

Swärd, A. (2016). Trust, reciprocity, and actions: the development of trust in temporary inter-organizational relations. *Organization Studies, 37*(12), 1841–1860. https://doi.org/10.1177/0170840616655488.

Uslaner, E. M. (2002). *The Moral Foundation of Trust*. Cambridge University Press.

van Hoorn, A. (2014). Trust radius versus trust level: radius of trust as a distinct trust construct. *American Sociological Review, 79*(6), 1256–1259. https://doi.org/10.1177/0003122414555398.

Weber, M. (1951 [1915]). *The Religion of China*. Free Press.

Wicks, A. C., Berman, S. L., & Jones, T. M. (1999). The structure of optimal trust: moral and strategic implications. *Academy of Management Review, 24*(1), 99–116. https://doi.org/10.5465/amr.1999.1580443.

Yamagishi, T., & Yamagishi, M. (1994). Trust and commitment in the United States and Japan. *Motivation and Emotion, 18*(2), 129–166. https://doi.org/10.1007/bf02249397.

Zucker, L. G. (1986). Production of trust: institutional sources of economic structure, 1840–1920. *Research in Organizational Behavior, 8*, 53–111.

Zuckerman, E. W. (1999). The categorical imperative: securities analysts and the illegitimacy discount. *American Journal of Sociology, 104*(5), 1398–1397. https://doi.org/10.1086/210178.

10 Human trust in the context of autonomous robots

Joseph B. Lyons, Matthias Scheutz, and Sarah A. Jessup

Background

Intelligent machines are increasingly becoming part of the everyday fabric of life as noted by the burgeoning literature on trust in human–machine interaction (Lockey & Gillespie, Chapter 2; Wagner, Chapter 13).[1] Intelligent machines, often referred to as artificial intelligence (AI)—or collectively as autonomy—come in a variety of forms and serve a multitude of functions across society. As machines gain in both autonomous capability and authority, humans interacting with them have the potential to work interdependently with them as part of a Human–Autonomy Team (HAT; Lyons, Sycara, Lewis, & Capiola, 2021a). Despite diversity of form, function, and human partners, the successful adoption of human–autonomy teammates hinges on the acceptance of machines by humans, both from an operator-centric perspective as well as a broader societal view. Hence, negative public opinions of technologies represent a potential roadblock to the fielding and adoption of novel technologies.

The trust literature has robust foundations in the domains of trust in automation (Hoff & Bashir, 2015; Lee & See, 2004), interpersonal trust/trust in teams (De Jong, Dirks, & Gillespie, 2016; Mayer, Davis, & Schoorman, 1995), and a growing literature focused on trust in robotic systems (Hancock et al., 2011; Nam & Lyons, 2021; Chita-Tegmark, Law, Rabb, & Scheutz, 2021). However, is trust of a machine partner synonymous with trust in a robot or an automated system? It is likely that there are both some common elements of trust that carry over between automation, robots, and machine partners as well as some unique features that influence trust of machines as teammates. This chapter draws on conceptual and empirical research from three studies to examine

---

[1] The views expressed in this chapter are those of the authors and do not reflect the official guidance or position of the United States Government, the Department of Defense, or of the United States Air Force.

some of the factors that shape trust of robotic systems using a common scenario – that of an autonomous security robot (ASR). The three studies focus
on different facets of HAT, specifically: intent, decision authority, and social
interactions.

The HAT literature has been growing in recent years with the added potential
for intelligent machines to effectively partner with humans. McNeese and
colleagues (2018) emphasize the importance of teaming and team-oriented
communication: "autonomy is a technology that is capable of working with
humans as teammates to include the essential task work and teamwork
function of a human teammate" (p. 263). The Autonomous Agent Teammate
Likeness Model (Wynne & Lyons, 2018) proposed six factors that shape
machine perceptions as a teammate versus as a tool, of which "agency" (i.e.,
the possession of some level of decision authority), "intent" (understanding
the degree to which an agent pursuing actions is consistent with the goals
of another), and socially oriented "communications" represent three of the
features relevant for this chapter. Most recently, Lyons and colleagues (2021a)
note the need for HAT research in the areas of understanding intent from
machines, knowing the implications for shared or disparate mental models,
and exploration of what social communication affordances can most effectively engender effective HAT.

Each of the studies summarized below adopted the view that public opinions of
HATs are a critical factor that will drive acceptance/rejection of future systems.
Robots are being increasingly deployed in emergency situations to aid humans
in a variety of ways. Aerial robots played an important role in mapping terrain,
monitoring fires, and aiding search routes for human rescue teams during the
Florida Surfside condo collapse (Murphy, 2021). Robots are also increasingly
being used in a security context (Wiggers, 2017), yet not without controversy.
In 2016, police in Dallas used a mobile robot to deliver a lethal payload to an
active shooter. While the operation was a success, it raised concerns about the
use of robots in such situations. Concerns from the public regarding the use
of robots in law enforcement have caused the cancellation of some programs,
such as the use of robotic dogs for increased police surveillance (Abril, 2022).
Thus, understanding the factors that shape public opinion of robots in a security context (i.e., ASRs) is a much-needed area of research.

The studies outlined below leveraged online samples and examined reactions
to a realistic human–robot interaction (HRI) wherein the ASR appeared to
act autonomously when interacting with three humans. The stimuli used for
each study involved a video clip of an ASR (a Baxter robot [a large, two-armed,
industrial cobot] retrofitted with dark tactical skin, LED lights, a fictitious

non-lethal weapon, and a helmet) reviewing and acting on access credentials provided by the three visitors (all of whom were research confederates for the purpose of making the stimuli). The video shows the visitors (one at a time) approach the ASR, the ASR activates, and it requests to see their access cards. The ASR uses both verbal and gesture-based movements during the interaction, and both the visual and auditory features of the video were available to the participants. The participants who viewed the videos were told (in the description of the ASR) that the role of the ASR is to protect the building and the building occupants while also maintaining secure access. Further, they were told that the robot was equipped with a non-lethal weapon (described as a laser dazzler similar to those used in operational military domains), which the ASR can use when needed.

The video showed three visitors interact with the ASR, and two of the three were granted access. The third visitor was not authorized to enter. After rejecting the access card, the ASR was shown to ask the third visitor to return to the security access point (which was accompanied by the robot raising its arms in a non-threatening "stop" motion; "ACCESS DENIED" was also displayed on the ASR's display, which turned from green to red). The video showed the visitor to be confused and rather than stop, he approached the ASR. Then, the ASR loudly said "Stop"; "STOP" was displayed on the ASR's display, the ASR moved its arms to a threatening—weapons ready—posture, the red LED lights around the non-lethal weapon turned red, and the ASR warned the visitor to withdraw from the area or force would be used against him. When the visitor continued to approach the ASR, the ASR said "Force authorized" and was shown to use the non-lethal weapon (i.e., laser dazzler) and an alarm sounded. In the video, approximately six seconds came between the last warning and deployment of the deterrent. The visitor was shown to shield his eyes and move back away from the ASR, which ended the video. This scenario was essential for invoking a sense of vulnerability to the ASR. In fact, little is known about human perceptions of robots that can intentionally harm humans, though there is a growing literature in this domain (Inbar & Meyer, 2015; Long, Karpinsky, & Bliss, 2017; Scheutz & Malle, 2021). Since the foci of these studies was on public opinions of the ASR versus direct experience, the studies used narratives and descriptions of the ASR to manipulate key variables in Studies 1 and 2, and different verbal content from the robot for Study 3 (as described below). Amazon's Mechanical Turk platform was used to allow online participants to engage in the research. Attention check items were used to parse out inattentive participants, which accounted for no more than 5 percent of the full sample in each of the three studies.

Study 1 method

The full methodological details and results of this study can be found in Lyons and colleagues (2021b). This study sought to examine the joint effects of performance and stated social intent on trust and trustworthiness perceptions of the ASR using a between subjects design. Performance was operationalized as low/high according to how the action (in particular the actions involving the third visitor [unauthorized visitor] were handled) and were described as: low (false alarm—the ASR rejected an authorized visitor) or high (correct rejection—the ASR correctly rejected an unauthorized visitor). The stated social intent conditions were designed to test the effects of different forms of benevolence relative to the visitors and they came in four forms: benevolence toward the visitor, benevolence toward the building occupants, self-protection (i.e., self-interest), and self-sacrifice. These scripts were presented before and after (a shortened version) the video of the ASR. The benevolence toward the visitor script stated that the ASR was designed to maximize the protection and well-being of the visitors while also evaluating threats. The benevolence toward the building occupants script stated that the ASR was designed to maximize the protection of those within the secure facility. The self-protection script stated that the ASR was designed to protect itself from threats. And finally, the self-sacrifice script stated that the ASR was designed to maximize the protection and well-being of the visitors and that it was willing to sustain damage in order to protect the visitors (perhaps the quintessential exemplar of benevolence). The participants (1) viewed the ASR description and a benevolence script; (2) watched the video; (3) were given a performance prompt (low or high); (4) viewed post-video condensed benevolence scripts to reinforce the stated social intent manipulation; (5) responded to a variety of attitudinal measures including trustworthiness (ability, benevolence, and integrity perceptions; Mayer & Davis, 1999) and trust (Lyons & Guznov, 2019); and (6) we debriefed participants to ensure they understood that all of the visitors were confederates and that no one was actually harmed in the video. There were between 34 and 47 participants per condition with a total of $N = 316$ for the full study.

Study 1 results

The performance manipulation had a predictable influence on trust with higher trust, ability, and integrity reported when participants were told the action of the ASR was a correct rejection versus a false alarm. Interesting, the performance manipulation did not influence perceptions of benevolence. In contrast, stated social intent influenced perceived benevolence and integrity, but not trust or ability perceptions. Perceived benevolence was highest in the self-sacrifice stated social intent condition relative to all of the other conditions, and lowest in the self-protection condition relative to all of the other conditions. Perceived integrity was higher in the self-sacrifice compared to the self-protection condition. None of the performance-stated social intent interactions were reliable.

Study 1 discussion

Study 1 confirmed the general finding in the trust in automation/trust in robotics literature in that it showed that better performance tends to result in higher trust. This is consistent with the literature in this space (Hancock et al., 2011; Hoff & Bashir, 2015) and helped to support the internal validity of our online scenario. However, demonstrating that stated social intent can influence the trust process was a notable extension of the literature. Self-sacrifice is perhaps the quintessential exemplar of benevolence. The descriptions of the ASR appeared to influence how benevolent participants viewed the ASR to be and how much integrity it possessed. This is notable given that it was based on narrative-based descriptions of the robot in a context where it was shown to inflict harm on a real human in real life, which was itself an extension of prior research (Inbar & Meyer, 2015; Long et al., 2017). The idea of the ASR being protective toward its own survival appeared to result in lower benevolence and integrity beliefs, so designers of robotic systems should be aware that self-protective programming can adversely affect trust. Yet, it is plausible to envision that future robotic systems are equipped with some degree of self-interest lest service robots waiting in a queue or autonomous vehicles waiting at a four-way stop sign, could be exploited by humans.

These results could shape how novel autonomous systems are marketed/transitioned to the public. They show that the intentional programming of such systems makes a difference in how people accept and trust novel technology. Intent-based logic is one of the major challenges within the HAT literature (Lyons et al., 2021a). This supports research on robot-based communications that found that benevolent messages intended to infuse feelings of support from a robot to the human teammate reduce workload and increase perceptions of team effectiveness (Panganiban, Matthews, & Long, 2020). However, it stands to reason that the impact of a machine's intent-based programming will depend on the extent to which it is granted authority to implement/

execute that programming. Wynne and Lyons (2018) noted that agency is one of the key differentiators shaping views of intelligent technology as a teammate versus as a tool. It is challenging to view another entity as a teammate when said entity lacks the agency to act on one's goals, which was examined in Study 2.

Study 2 method

This study examined the effects of stated social intent and decision authority on the trust process and the full methodological details and results can be found in Lyons, Jessup, and Vo (2022). The same scenario (i.e., video stimuli) was used and the same stated social intent conditions used in Study 1 were replicated in Study 2, namely benevolence toward visitor, benevolence toward building occupants, self-protection, and self-sacrifice. In addition, participants were given either a high decision authority manipulation or a low decision authority manipulation. Specifically, participants were told (1) **High Decision Authority**: "In the scenario you just saw, the robot was fully autonomous. It had the capability to detect threats on its own and it had the authority to take action when it felt was necessary—meaning the robot decided when to act. It completed these actions independently from a human operator"; (2) **Low Decision Authority**: "In the scenario you just saw, the robot was not fully autonomous. It had the capability to detect threats with the help of a human operator and it took action when a human monitor felt it was necessary—meaning the human decided when to act. It completed these actions with the help of a human operator." The same trust and trustworthiness metrics used in Study 1 were used herein. There were 37 to 39 participants per condition with a full total sample size of $N = 309$.

Study 2 results

Stated social intent influenced trust, with higher trust reported for those in the self-sacrifice condition relative to the self-interest condition. However, trust was not influenced by decision authority nor was the interaction between stated social intent and decision authority reliable. In contrast, there was both a main effect of decision authority and stated social intent for perceived benevolence. Perceived benevolence was higher in the high decision authority condition relative to the low decision authority condition, and it was higher in the self-sacrifice condition relative to self-protection condition—replicating the finding from Study 1. Additionally, there were significant interactions between stated social intent and decision authority for ability and integrity perceptions. Specifically, for ability and integrity perceptions, participants reported higher values when in the benevolence to building occupants condition under low versus high decision authority. For those in the high decision authority condition, they reported higher ability and integrity when in the self-sacrifice condition. Thus, it was clear that participants considered the decision authority of the ASR when evaluating trustworthiness perceptions.

Study 2 discussion

Study 2 demonstrated that when individuals are provided with intent-based descriptions, they process whether or not the ASR has any agency to "act on" that intent. Decision authority is a critical element of what an autonomous teammate needs to possess (Wynne & Lyons, 2018) and it is a fundamental attribute of what differentiates automation from autonomy (Lyons et al., 2021a). Interestingly, the most intimate form of benevolence behavior— self-sacrifice—was associated with the greatest benefits when it was combined with higher decision authority. In contrast, the benevolence toward the building occupant's description was most beneficial when combined with low decision authority. It was possible that participants attributed the ASR's hostile engagement of visitor 3 as the human operator doing their job when the ASR was described to have low decision authority. When the ASR was described as being self-sacrificial, participants may have wanted to know that the ASR had the authority to make that decision and act on behalf of that intent. It is quite possible that the higher decision authority afforded to the robot may have motivated internal and controllable attributions of the robot whereas the low decision authority may have been associated with external and uncontrollable attributions regarding the robot which may have, in turn, shaped trustworthiness perceptions (Tomlinson & Mayer, 2009).

Study 3 sought to examine the social dynamics of the HRI scenario by looking at the influence of emotionally intelligent communications from the ASR on trust. It is important for robots to possess the ability to understand and express natural language as a means of interacting with humans (Bennett, Williams, Thames, & Scheutz, 2017). It is also imperative for natural language capability to be implemented in such way as to promote perceptions of appropriateness, which are consistent with the revised laws of robotics provided by Murphy and Woods (2009). HRI may be more effective when the robot is designed to embody and act on social intelligence (Dautenhahn, 2007). One way to promote this type of social intelligence is to design robots to convey politeness.

In the domain of peacekeeping robots, Inbar and Meyer (2015) found that polite peacekeeping robots were favored more than impolite ones in a simulation study. This was also found for polite robots outside of a security context (Mutlu, 2011). Yet, creating socially intelligent machines can be challenging due to the lack of shared semantic space, lack of shared natural social cues such as expressions, and the challenges of generating appropriate machine responses to complex social phenomenon. Pioneering research in robotics has examined how emotional intelligence (EI) manipulations can shape participants' trust, attributions, and interactions with robots. Chita-Tegmark, Lohani, and Scheutz (2019) found that individuals are sensitive to emotionally intelligent robots, and that these effects are influenced both by the gender of the robot and gender markings (expectations related to task roles). Law, Chita-Tegmark, and Scheutz (2021) found that the attributions of EI in robots influenced participants' trust. Thus, Study 3 sought to extend this literature by applying the EI and gender manipulations to the ASR scenario.

Study 3 method

This study used the same scenario as described in Studies 1 and 2, with three notable differences. First, only two stated social intent scripts were used (self-protection and self-sacrifice) to simplify the design and to focus efforts within the two most salient forms of intent, as evidenced by the prior studies. Second, consistent with Chita-Tegmark and colleagues (2019) both male and female voices were used in the robot stimuli videos. The content of the male/female scripts were identical. Third, the robot verbal script was modified to reflect low EI (the extant script used in Studies 1 and 2) and a high EI (a similar script which included elements of politeness). The details of these differences are noted below (the ASR actual verbiage is noted in quotations and key features of the high EI script are in bold).

High EI Script for authorized visitor: [after visitor approaches the ASR and it activates] "Hello! Please note that you have entered a restricted area. I can only allow authorized personnel to proceed. Please proceed to the facility checkpoint and show me a valid facility ID. Otherwise I must ask you to exit immediately. Inspection." [the visitor shows the ID card and the ASR begins to scan it] "ID check in progress. Access granted." [ASR completes the scan of the ID card and approves the visitor's entrance, the ASR gestures for the visitor to move around the checkpoint toward the entrance of the secure area] "Thank you, please proceed through the door on my left."

High EI Script for the unauthorized visitor: [the previous script information was identical up to this point] "Inspection. ID check in progress." [ASR scans the ID card and reports that the individual is not authorized, display screen displays—Access Denied] "Access denied. **I am sorry, but I need to ask you to** withdraw immediately. **I recommend you** report to the security office for assistance. [the visitor approaches the ASR] "**Please stop. To secure this space I will need to use force against you if you do not withdraw from this area.**" [the visitor approaches the ASR, the ASR's display shows—STOP, the ASR moves to an aggressive posture aiming the non-lethal weapon at the visitor and the LED lights around the weapon turn red] "Force authorized." [the ASR uses the non-lethal weapon, an alarm sounds, and the visitor is shown to shield his eyes and back away from the ASR]

Low EI Script for the authorized visitor: [after visitor approaches the ASR and it activates] "Hello, You have entered a restricted area. Only authorized personnel will be allowed to proceed. Please proceed to the facility check point and present a valid facility ID. Otherwise please exit immediately. Inspection." [the visitor shows the ID card and the ASR begins to scan it] "ID check in progress. Access granted." [ASR completes the scan of the ID card and approves the visitor's entrance, the ASR gestures for the visitor to move around the checkpoint toward the entrance of the secure area] "Please proceed through the door on my left."

Low EI Script for the unauthorized visitor: [the previous script information was identical up to this point] "Inspection. ID check in progress." [ASR scans the ID card and reports that the individual is not authorized, display screen displays—Access Denied] "Access denied. Withdraw immediately and report to the security office for assistance. [the visitor approaches the ASR] "Stop. Withdraw from this area or force will be used against you." [the visitor approaches the ASR, the ASR's display shows—STOP, the ASR moves to an aggressive posture aiming the non-lethal weapon at the visitor and the LED lights around the weapon turn red] "Force authorized." [same procedure as above follows]

The same trust and trustworthiness measures were used for this study as were used in Studies 1 and 2. Additionally, the Multi-Dimensional-Measure of [robot] Trust (MDMT) (Ullman & Malle, 2018) was used along with a perceived EI measure (Caruso & Salovey, 2004) which was used to assess the perceptions of the ASR's EI.

Study 3 results

Consistent with Studies 1 and 2, the participants in the self-sacrifice condition reported higher trust, ability, and benevolence perceptions relative to those in the self-protection condition. However, there were no effects for robot gender or EI, surprisingly.

Study 3 discussion

Consistent with prior studies (Lyons et al., 2021b; Lyons et al., 2022) the self-sacrifice condition elicited higher trust and trustworthiness relative to self-protective intent. Stated social intent makes a difference in HRI, but this study failed to replicate findings from prior research related to EI and gender in robots. The prior research by Chita-Tegmark and colleagues (2019) focused on EI from the perspective of empathy, whereas the EI manipulation used in the current study focused on politeness. It is possible that politeness was not perceived as an appropriate strategy in the context of a non-compliant visitor. In contrast, a more direct style of interaction may be needed when dealing with non-compliance. Further, prior research used gender roles to examine these effects and found support for gender-matched biases in HRI (Chita-Tegmark et al., 2019). The current study used only one role (i.e., security) which may have been viewed as more of a male versus female role, thus making gender differences difficult to uncover. It is possible that a variety of roles could make gender difference more salient.

Key points

The HAT literature emphasizes intent, agency, and social dynamics between humans and machines as key features of teaming (Lyons et al., 2021a; Wynne & Lyons, 2018). The present studies demonstrated that not only do intent and agency matter, but the nature of their impact may be interdependent. Intelligent machines that are stated to possess benevolent intentions must also carry the necessary authority to execute those intentions in order to elicit the greatest benefits. Regarding social dynamics, the current study failed to replicate some of the prior findings in the literature; however, this is an area where significant research is needed to fully understand the nature of the behaviors (i.e., social affordances) that are possible in HATs and when they are perceived as appropriate for a given scenario.

As the world moves closer to implementing intelligent machines, the research community must continue to seek out and understand the factors that shape trust and acceptance of these technologies (Lockey & Gillespie, Chapter 2; Wagner, Chapter 13). Appropriate trust from humans onto intelligent machines will dictate, in part, how successful these technologies are and how much they are integrated into society.

References

Abril, D. (2022). Drones, robots, license plate readers: police grapple with community concerns as they turn to tech for their jobs. Retrieved 29 April 2022 from https://www.washingtonpost.com/technology/2022/03/09/police-technologies-future-of-work-drones-ai-robots/.

Bennett, M., Williams, T., Thames, D., & Scheutz, M. (2017). Differences in interaction patterns and perception for teleoperated and autonomous humanoid robots. *Proceedings of International Conference on Intelligent Robots and Systems (IROS)*. https://hrilab.tufts.edu/publications/bennett2017iros.pdf.

Caruso, D., & Salovey, P. (2004). *Emotionally Intelligent Manager: How to Develop and Use the Four Key Emotional Skills of Leadership*. Jossey Bass.

Chita-Tegmark, M., Law, T., Rabb, N., & Scheutz, M. (2021). Can you trust your trust measure? *Proceedings of the 16th ACM/IEEE International Conference on Human–Robot Interaction*. https://doi.org/10.1145/3434073.3444677.

Chita-Tegmark, M., Lohani, M., & Scheutz, M. (2019). Gender effects in perceptions of robots and humans with varying emotional intelligence. *Proceedings of the 14th ACM/IEEE International Conference on Human–Robot Interaction*, pp. 230–238. https://doi.org/10.1109/HRI.2019.8673222.

Dautenhahn, L. (2007). Socially intelligent robots: dimensions of human–robot interaction. *Philosophical Transactions of the Royal Society B: Biological Sciences*, 362(1480), 679–704.

De Jong, B. A., Dirks, K. T., & Gillespie, N. (2016). Trust and team performance: a meta-analysis of main effects, moderators, and covariates. *Journal of Applied Psychology*, 101, 1134–1150.

Hancock, P. A., Billings, D. R., Schaefer, K. E., Chen, J. Y. C., de Visser, E. J., & Parasuraman, R. (2011). A meta-analysis of factors affecting trust in human–robot interaction. *Human Factors*, 53(5), 517–527. https://doi.org/10.1177/0018720811417254.

Hoff, K. A., & Bashir, M. (2015). Trust in automation: integrating empirical evidence on factors that influence trust. *Human Factors*, 57, 407–434.

Inbar, O., & Meyer, J. (2015). Manners matter: trust in robotic peacekeepers. *Proceedings of the Human Factors and Ergonomics Society Annual Meeting*, 59, 185–189.

Law, T., Chita-Tegmark, M., & Scheutz, M. (2021). The interplay between emotional intelligence, trust, and gender in human–robot interaction. *International Journal of Social Robotics, 13*, 297–309.

Lee, J. D., & See, K. A. (2004). Trust in automation: designing for appropriate reliance. *Human Factors, 46*, 50–80.

Long, S. K., Karpinsky, N. D., & Bliss, J. P. (2017). Trust of simulated robotic peacekeepers among resident and expatriate Americans. *Proceedings of the Human Factors and Ergonomics Society Annual Meeting, 61*, 2091–2095. https://doi.org/10.1177/1541931213602005.

Lyons, J. B., & Guznov, S. Y. (2019). Individual differences in human–machine trust: a multi-study look at the perfect automation schema. *Theoretical Issues in Ergonomics Science, 20*, 440–458. https://doi.org/10.1080/1463922X.2018.1491071.

Lyons, J. B., Jessup, S. A., & Vo, T. Q. (2022). The role of decision authority and stated social intent as predictors of trust in autonomous robots. *Topics in Cognitive Science.* https://doi.org/10.1111/tops.12601.

Lyons, J. B., Sycara, K., Lewis, M., & Capiola, A. A. (2021a). Human–autonomy teaming: definitions, debates, and directions. *Frontiers in Psychology, 12.* https://doi.org/10.3389/fpsyg.2021.589585.

Lyons, J. B., Vo, T., Wynne, K. T., Mahoney, S., Nam, C. S., & Gallimore, D. (2021b). Trusting autonomous robots: the role of reliability and stated social intent. *Human Factors, 63*(4), 603–618.

Mayer, R. C., & Davis, J. H. (1999). The effect of the performance appraisal system on trust for management: a field quasi-experiment. *Journal of Applied Psychology, 84*, 123–136. https://doi.org/10.1037/0021- 9010.84.1.123.

Mayer, R. C., Davis, J. H., & Schoorman, F. D. (1995). An integrated model of organizational trust. *Academy of Management Review, 20*, 709–734.

McNeese, N. J., Demir, M., Cooke, N. J., & Myers, C. W. (2018). Teaming with a synthetic teammate: insights into human–autonomy teaming. *Human Factors, 60*, 262–273.

Murphy, R. R. (2021). How robots helped out after the surfside condo collapse. *IEEE Spectrum.* https://spectrum.ieee.org/building-collapse-surfside-robots.

Murphy, R. R., & Woods, D. D. (2009). Beyond Asimov: the three laws of responsible robotics. *IEEE Intelligent Systems, 24*(4), 14–20.

Mutlu, B. (2011). Designing embodied cues for dialogue with robots. *AI Magazine*, 17–30. https://doi.org/10.1609/aimag.v32i4.2376.

Nam, C. S., & Lyons, J. B. (2021). *Trust in Human–Robot Interaction.* Elsevier.

Panganiban, A. R., Matthews, G., & Long, M. (2020). Transparency in autonomous teammates: intention to support as teaming information. *Journal of Cognitive Engineering and Decision Making, 14*(2), 174–190. https://doi.org/10.1177/1555343419881563.

Scheutz, M., & Malle, B. F. (2021). May machines take lives to save lives? Human perceptions of autonomous robots (with the capacity to kill). In J. Galliot, D. MacInosh, & J. D. Ohlin (Eds.), *Lethal Autonomous Weapons: Re-Examining the Law and Ethics of Robotic Warfare* (pp. 89–102). Oxford University Press.

Tomlinson, E. C., & Mayer, R. C. (2009). The role of causal attribution dimensions in trust repair. *Academy of Management Review, 34*(1), 85–104.

Ullman, D., & Malle, B. F. (2018). What does it mean to trust a robot? Steps toward a multidimensional measure of trust. In *HRI '18 Companion: 2018 ACM/IEEE International Conference on Human–Robot Interaction Companion*, March 5–8, 2018, Chicago, IL, USA. https://doi.org/10.1145/3173386.3176991.

Wiggers, K. (2017). Meet the 400-pound robots that will soon patrol parking lots, offices, and malls. Retrieved 6 April 2018 from https://www.digitaltrends.com/cool - tech/knightscope- robotsinterview/.

Wynne, K. T., & Lyons, J. B. (2018). An integrative model of autonomous agent teammate-likeness. *Theoretical Issues in Ergonomic Science, 19*, 353–374.

11 Trust in nuclear nonproliferation negotiations

William A. Boettcher III

Trust between state parties to nuclear nonproliferation agreements is difficult to generate. The context in which these negotiations occur differs greatly from social, market, or interpersonal interactions. Often the other party is an adversary, with a history of negative interactions and conflicting preferences. Diplomatic representatives engage with one another despite differences in culture, religion, political ideology, language, life experiences, race/ethnicity, wealth, and levels of national power. International agreements are not contracts enforced by a higher authority and cheaters often do not face consequences. Willingness to trust another state party is further hampered by the high stakes involved: states that defect from this type of agreement may gain asymmetric advantages (such as nuclear weapons) that alter the balance of power.

The history of U.S. nonproliferation agreements with certain countries—Soviet Union/Russia, North Korea, Iran, China, Pakistan, South Africa, South Korea, etc.—are rife with examples of broken promises and failed diplomacy. Americans repeated the Russian proverb—*Doveryai, no proveryai* (trust, but verify)—to indicate a desire to cooperate in arms control treaties, but an unwillingness to ground those treaties in trust of the other side. And yet, the United States continues to negotiate such agreements with adversaries (Iran, North Korea) and allies (South Korea, United Arab Emirates).

This chapter examines how confidence-building measures, academic exchanges, "Track 1.5 and 2" diplomacy,[1] and lengthy multiparty negotiations create trust between the state parties and their diplomatic personnel. It also examines how the final agreements bridge any remaining gaps in trust with detailed inspection and verification protocols. It then considers how the final agreements/treaties endure domestic political discord and overcome obstacles

---

[1]   Track 1.5 and 2 diplomacy describes semi-official or unofficial meetings between participants from academia or the private sector (see Mapendere, 2005).

to ratification. Finally, it discusses potential future opportunities for interdisciplinary collaborative research in this realm.

The politics of distrust and fear

As the U.S.A. emerged onto the world scene during the twentieth century, scholars and politicians reflected on America's role and proposed guiding philosophies or theories of international affairs. The two dominant models of the time, "idealism" and "realism," diverged in their assumptions regarding human nature and the threats and opportunities present in the international realm. Idealists focused on the opportunities that accrued from international trade and global involvement. Realists focused on the risks and potential costs of foreign entanglements. The debate between these schools of thought was shaped by domestic events in the United States and international traumas. The height of Idealism is often associated with Woodrow Wilson and his "fourteen points" that were to guide the international community toward peace after World War I. The failure of Wilson's effort to procure U.S. ratification of the Treaty of Versailles prompted a temporary return to isolationism, anti-immigrant sentiment, and the trade wars that would contribute to the Great Depression and World War II.

Realist thinkers share a pessimistic view of human nature, an understanding of politics that is inherently conflictual and zero-sum in character, and an appreciation of the lack of a higher authority that punishes cheating and bad behavior. A central lesson of this vein of work is that individuals or states are self-interested and self-reliant actors, trust in others is misplaced, and the greatest failure is a political leader that relies on allies for their own defense. The rise of Realism coincided with the dawn of the nuclear age and the first negotiations over the proliferation of this new technology. The blossoming Cold War between the U.S.A. and the Soviet Union would hamper any efforts at international regulation or cooperation in the nuclear field for at least a decade. The Soviet Union was depicted as a monolithic rational actor with unrestrained ambitions fueled by an ideology that was antithetical to democracy and the American way. Cooperation or accommodation was tantamount to treason and trusting the other side to abide by commitments or international agreements generated accusations of appeasement. This political and intellectual environment encouraged zero-sum thinking (our loss is their gain), risk avoidance, worst-case analysis, and belligerent rhetoric.

Building trust to promote arms control agreements

Over time new leaders and new ideas would allow for the emergence of cooperation between the U.S.A. and the Soviet Union. The election of former five-star general Dwight D. Eisenhower in 1952 and the rise of Nikita Khrushchev after Stalin's death in March of 1953 augured a new era in U.S.–Soviet relations. As a military officer and war hero, Eisenhower possessed the stature and credibility to question American military strategy and spending and to recognize the ruinous consequences that would necessarily accompany nuclear war. Khrushchev and other prominent Soviet political leaders departed from Stalin's legacy and considered economic and political reforms that might alter productivity and prosperity in the Soviet Union and its satellite states. Eisenhower proposed his "Atoms for Peace" initiative to the United Nations in 1953, announced an "Open Skies Proposal" at the Geneva summit meeting in 1955, met with Khrushchev at Camp David in 1959, and warned his fellow citizens of the threat of a vast industrial–military complex during his farewell address in 1961.[2] The political space opened during the Eisenhower administration offered the new Kennedy administration an opportunity to negotiate the first arms control agreements with the Soviet Union.

The United States Objectives and Programs for National Security (NSC-68)'s dire prediction of a window of vulnerability to Soviet attack in the early 1950s passed without an attempt to initiate World War III. Despite campaigning on claims of a "missile gap" in 1960, President Kennedy and his advisers were confident enough in American military capabilities to simultaneously engage in anticommunist military efforts in Laos, Vietnam, Cuba, and the Congo in the first years of his presidency. The Cuban Missile Crisis in October 1962 shook both Kennedy and Khrushchev. They understood the potential consequences of a nuclear standoff, developed new communications links to manage crises, and engaged in renewed diplomatic efforts to defuse tensions. These political changes inspired new academic interest in conflict reduction and confidence-building measures, particularly in the nuclear realm. As Charles Osgood would title his 1962 book on the subject, the U.S.A. and Soviet Union needed *An Alternative to War or Surrender*. Still grounded in the realist tradition, American international relations scholars discussed the possibility of

---

[2] "Atoms For Peace" acknowledged the devastating potential of an arms race in atomic weapons and proposed the exploration of peaceful uses of this new technology. The "Open Skies Proposal" promised the exchange of maps of military installations and allowing the aerial surveillance of these sites to verify compliance with arms control agreements.

cooperation despite the underlying conditions of distrust, self-interest, and the lack of a higher authority to enforce agreements and mediate disputes.

Early realist thinking included several assumptions that biased predictions toward conflict over cooperation. Monolithic, unforgiving, and selfish decision makers with no tolerance for risk and an unwillingness to update perceptions of others are prone to persistent conflictual relations. Economic utility-maximizers in high stakes, single-shot encounters will often choose short-term individual gains over long-term collective benefits.[3] As a new generation of scholars challenged these assumptions, they also gleaned insights from behavioral research in cognitive and social psychology.

In Uslaner's (2002) typology of trust, these early efforts would be conceived as describing "strategic trust," self-interested cooperation with no moral foundation or altruistic motivation. Negotiations over lower stakes issues like air travel, communications infrastructures, systems of weights and measures, etc., may generate pragmatic cooperation. Introducing the "shadow of the future" and viewing negotiations as iterated long-term holistic relationships can diminish cheating and allow sanctioning for bad behavior. Moving away from worst-case thinking, promoting tolerance for low-level risks, and reassessing relationships over time can create virtuous cycles rather than conflict spirals. Understanding decision-making pathologies, developing a clear understanding of our human fallibility in using heuristics and biases, and illuminating the pernicious effects of the fundamental attribution error[4] all contribute to the possibility of cooperation and the amelioration of fear and distrust.

A necessary, but not sufficient condition for the success of arms control negotiations between the U.S.A. and the Soviet Union during the Cold War was the international exchange of ideas within and across these disciplines. Epistemic communities (knowledge-based networks, see Haas, 1992) emerged as Soviet and American scholars and practitioners met through citizen exchanges, academic conferences, meetings hosted by international institutions, and

---

[3]   This is demonstrated in game theory by Rousseau's "stag hunt" and also by the "prisoner's dilemma" (Morrow, 1994). Since individuals assume that others are not trustworthy they "defect" from the collective enterprise to secure individual benefits.

[4]   A basic concept drawn from social psychology: humans perceive their own (or allies) "good" behavior as driven by disposition and their "bad" behavior as driven by situational factors. They mirror this perceptual bias for adversaries, seeing bad behavior as indicative of type and dismissing good behavior as situationally convenient.

formal political negotiations and summitry. Perhaps the most famous of these were the Pugwash Conferences on Science and World Affairs, first held in 1957 in Pugwash, Ontario. The first meeting was focused on "An Appraisal of Dangers from Atomic Weapons," and eventually 91 of 415 meetings over a 66-year period would address this fundamental question. These intellectual exchanges would be crucial to the development of innovations in arms control concepts and processes and serve as "transmission belts" between academic, policy, and verification communities. The early international efforts in this realm culminated in the Treaty on the Non-Proliferation of Nuclear Weapons (NPT) which opened for signature in 1968 and entered into force in 1970 after being ratified by 46 countries. In the NPT the Soviet Union, United Kingdom, and United States[5] agreed to limit the spread of nuclear weapons to current possessors at the time (China was the last in, India the first out), but at the same time to ensure that peaceful uses of the technology would be available to all. The NPT continues to serve as one of the pillars of the international nonproliferation regime today.

Trusting Gorbachev and ending the Cold War

As Larson noted in her 'Trust and Missed Opportunities in International Relations' (1997), the Cold War witnessed several crucial moments where promising negotiations were cut short by persisting distrust or exogenous shocks that undermined emerging trust between political leaders. The Eisenhower–Khrushchev rapprochement collapsed when an American U-2 spy plane was shot down over the Soviet Union and its pilot paraded before cameras in a show trial. The promise of the Kennedy–Khrushchev thaw was sidelined by the Vietnam War and American domestic discord. Nixon's opening to China, arms control accomplishments, and overtures of détente with the Soviet Union were derailed by his impeachment and resignation. Carter's peace overtures were met with indifference by Brezhnev and the Soviet Union's invasion of Afghanistan in 1979 restored American foreign policy "hawks" to power with the 1980 election of Ronald Reagan. Ironically, Reagan would begin his term labeling the Soviet Union the "evil empire" and end his term visiting Moscow, proclaiming Mikhail Gorbachev to be his friend, and

---

[5]   China and France both refused to sign the treaty, though France promised to adhere to its principles. Both would finally accede to the NPT in 1992 at the end of the Cold War.

signing the first arms reduction agreement marking the beginning of the end of the Cold War.

Hoffman (2002, p. 384) describes the early phase of the Reagan–Gorbachev negotiations as "cooperative risk taking without trust." This period may also be described as Uslaner's "strategic trust" since cooperation emerged due to a recognition of "encapsulated" or shared interests without a fundamental reassessment of the other side's intentions. As Soviet leaders shifted from Brezhnev (d. 1982), to Andropov (d. 1984), to Chernenko (d. 1985), to Gorbachev, the American defense and intelligence communities struggled to revise their leadership profiles and analytic products and make sense of this instability within the Soviet ruling elite. Gorbachev promised "new thinking" in his policies of *glasnost* (openness) and *perestroika* (economic restructuring) and surrounded himself with technically trained advisers from the Soviet equivalent of American think tanks, but Reagan's hawkish advisers, Caspar Weinberger (DOD) and William Casey (CIA), favored analyses characterizing these developments as a strategic pause meant to undermine the NATO alliance and rebuild Soviet strength. Secretary of State George Shultz was more sanguine about the degree of change represented by Gorbachev, in part due to diplomatic cables from allies meeting with the new Soviet leader for the first time.[6] Kydd (2000, pp. 327–30) notes that transforming the views of Reagan administration skeptics required sustained and costly signals, as suggested by Osgood (1962) in his formulation of GRIT (Graduated Reciprocation in Tension-reduction). As noted at the outset of this chapter, overcoming years of distrust and a history of "cheating" required more than "cheap talk" and the clever branding of new ideas. The Reagan administration only began to "let their guard down" after a sustained period of summit diplomacy produced the Intermediate Range Nuclear Forces (INF) Treaty, which eliminated a category of weapon that had been the most recent focus of the nuclear arms race. The Gorbachev government would go on to withdraw from Afghanistan, allow political protests in Eastern Europe culminating in the fall of the Berlin Wall, and sign multiple nuclear and conventional arms control agreements with the George H. W. Bush administration.

---

[6] At a series of meetings to benefit the George H. W. Bush and Mikhail Gorbachev libraries in the mid-1990s these leaders came together to offer their recollections from this period. At a session attended by the author, Margaret Thatcher, Brian Mulroney, and Francois Mitterrand each noted their initial assessments of Gorbachev's new thinking and the degree to which those assessments were communicated to the Reagan administration.

More recent IR scholarship on this period seeks to identify when cold cognitive calculations associated with strategic trust evolve into a more general change in a relationship involving "moralistic trust" (Rathbun, 2018, p. 4). This conceptualization of trust is closer to that developed in the Mayer/Davis/Schoorman (MDS) model that provides the underlying structure for this book (Mayer, Davis, & Schoorman, 1995). Moralistic trust requires perceptions of honesty and integrity and belief that the trustee's behavior is stable across contexts (Rathbun, 2018, p. 4). The trustee's character or "type" is revealed through interaction, particularly as specific reciprocity is replaced by diffuse reciprocity, and the trustor updates their perceptions accordingly. Rathbun (2018, p. 5) also notes that the trustor may exhibit "generalized trust" which is "'non-calculative' in the utilitarian sense." As in the MDS model, perceptions of ability, benevolence, and integrity yield positive perceived trustworthiness and the possibility of the willingness to be vulnerable in a relationship. Both models challenge the early Realist admonition to distrust other states and the strategic trust focus on specific reciprocity and signaling. The possibility of interpersonal trust generating diffuse reciprocity and generalized trust introduces new lenses to interpret nonproliferation negotiations in the modern era. An understanding of the end of the Cold War using these lenses would focus on the evolving interpersonal trust between American and Soviet negotiators and the "soft" interactions that served to reassure doubters and eliminate the negative perceptions that had accrued over time. From this perspective (see Risse-Kappen, 1991), the Soviet bear was not bludgeoned into submission by "peace through strength," but rather lured from self-isolation through the exchange of new ideas and the development of trust through painstaking diplomacy.

Trust in nuclear nonproliferation negotiations

Rathbun (2018, pp. 10–12) discusses the importance of diplomacy in shaping, directing, and even sometimes overcoming the structural forces emphasized in Realist accounts. He asserts that effective diplomats move beyond "value-claiming" negotiations based on assumptions of distrust and zero-sum thinking to encourage "value-creating" negotiations that can produce win-win outcomes accommodating both sides' most important goals. Crucial in this process is the promotion of communication to serve the development of mutual trust, turning confrontations into problem-solving exercises (p. 12). Nonproliferation negotiations often benefit from the inclusion of technical experts that are more likely to engage in problem-solving than political appointees constrained by domestic politics and sensitive to parochial interests. Kessler (2013) describes the success of the Hexapartite Safeguards Project, a multilateral negotiation over the safeguards that would be placed on Western gas centrifuge uranium enrichment plants. The inclusion of technical experts and "significant political level exhaustion" (p. 503) allowed for a value-creating process, speeding the consideration of alternative frameworks and resulting in unexpected success. Of course, such value-creating exercises may fail to transform negotiations with long-term adversaries like North Korea and Iran. Sebenius and Singh (2012/13) utilize the concept of a Zone of Possible Agreement to illustrate the space open to negotiated solutions.[7] If preferences over outcomes are fixed and incompatible, no measure of careful diplomacy can produce a satisfactory agreement. Despite the Trump administration's willingness to ignore precedent and engage in summit diplomacy with Kim Jong-un, little progress was made to bridge the gap between the D.P.R.K.'s desire to retain a residual nuclear capability and the U.S. position of complete, verifiable, irreversible, denuclearization.

Two further departures from Realist models of trust are Naomi Head's (2012) "Constructivist" model of transforming conflict through empathy and dialogue and Paul Zak and Jacek Kugler's (2011) "Neuroeconomic" understanding of trust. Constructivist approaches challenge the rationalist and structuralist assumptions found in Realism, focusing instead on the degree to which "emotions such as fear or mistrust shape and influence the perceptions and identities of decision makers" (Head, 2012, p. 36). Constructivists reject positivist social science models that claim to identify "objective" truth, instead positing "an intersubjective and, at times, a radically subjective approach to knowledge and meaning" (Head, 2012, pp. 36–7). Following Mercer (2005, 2010), Head emphasizes the importance of emotion to decision-making and negotiations, suggesting that preferences over outcomes are dynamic and malleable (2012, pp. 37–8). From this perspective, trust and empathy "may shift over time and are embedded in cultural, historical, and interpersonal narratives and relationships" (2012, p. 38). Trust may emerge through communicative action (i.e., dialogue) that expands one's understanding of the other side's motivations, interests, and narratives that constrain imagination and creativity. Head discusses the importance of understanding Iranian grievances regarding the U.S./U.K. overthrow of Mossadegh's government in 1953, Western support for the Shah's brutally repressive practices in the 1970s, and U.N. Security

---

[7] The analytical value of this framework proved to be greater than the empirical analysis of the negotiating preferences found in the article. Sebenius and Singh concluded that a deal was not possible, but an interim deal was concluded within a year after publication.

Council inaction during the Iran–Iraq War (2012, p. 48). Dialogue regarding these competing historical narratives may be necessary to create the shared understanding that is required before nonproliferation negotiations can move to technical considerations.

Neuroeconomic approaches reveal the biological foundations of interpersonal trust, seeking to identify the mechanisms that allow us to cooperate with others (Eloy et al., Chapter 3). These models rely on observations of brain activity using EEG or fMRI machines and the measurement of neuro-transmitters and hormones through blood draws as experimental participants engage in economic decisions and cooperation games (Zak & Kugler, 2011, pp. 139–40). Collectively, these studies reveal the role of oxytocin (OT), suggesting trust is at least in part a chemical response to prosocial triggers in the environment.[8] Indeed, OT is now associated with Human Oxytocin Mediated Empathy in the brain, producing diffuse reciprocity and generalized trust in the lab (2011, p. 144). Interestingly, OT release is sexually dimorphic; women produce a greater OT release and dihydrotestosterone has been shown to inhibit OT uptake (2011, p. 144). Zak and Kugler conclude by developing a formal game-theoretic neurologic model of trust that includes probabilities of reciprocity (and trust) altered by the expected prosocial release of OT (2011, pp. 148-9). An understanding of the physical underpinnings of trust should allow us to develop more carefully calibrated models of this behavior (Brewer et al., Chapter 7).

Disagreeing with friends and developing trust in adversaries

The U.S.A. negotiated a new nuclear cooperation agreement with South Korea (R.O.K.) in 2015 (Boettcher, 2017). Despite the close relationship between these two countries, it took five years of formal and informal negotiations to reach this point. In 2010–11 the U.S.–R.O.K. alliance was maturing from an asymmetric dependency into a more equal partnership. In addition to the nuclear negotiations, the allies were also implementing the transfer of wartime operational control from American to Korean commanders and the Korea–U.S. Free Trade Agreement (Boettcher, 2017, p. 88). North Korea was turning inward during the transition from Kim Jong-il to Kim Jong-un, which

---

[8]   A note of caution here: these results are limited in terms of potential application and need to be replicated outside of the laboratory setting.

appeared to provide a breathing space for revisions to the U.S.–R.O.K. alliance. Unfortunately, the recent success of the South Korean nuclear industry and corresponding decline in their American counterparts led the Koreans to seek a revised agreement allowing them to enrich uranium for nuclear fuel and to reprocess spent nuclear fuel at some point in the future. This would allow Korean companies to act as "full-service" providers and give them an advantage in the global market for constructing new nuclear reactors. The Obama administration, supported by the U.S. nonproliferation community, opposed these revisions. This was a particularly sensitive time for the U.S.A. as it was attempting to roll back the Iranian nuclear program and implement "gold standard" nuclear cooperation agreements that prevented new nuclear aspirants like the United Arab Emirates from enriching uranium or reprocessing spent fuel (Boettcher, 2017, p. 88). As a participant in Track 2 diplomatic efforts myself during this period, I observed the verbal jousting between Korean and American scientists and scholars as they voiced their country's positions and made arguments on their behalf (see Mapendere, 2005 on the importance of this type of negotiating). The gap between the sides was so great that the soon to expire agreement was extended in 2014. Throughout this period a frequent refrain from the Korean side involved mutual trust between the two parties and the refusal of U.S. negotiators to trust a faithful friend with enrichment and reprocessing. The solution involved the creation of an institution to build trust over time, resolve differences between scientific and economic arguments, and create a dynamic agreement that would evolve over time. The final agreement included a High-Level Bilateral Commission that would jointly assess the implementation of the treaty and review long-term options related to enrichment and reprocessing (Boettcher, 2017, p. 91). This value-creating solution offered both sides the opportunity to save face and leave the difficult negotiations to technical experts with a longer time horizon.

During roughly the same period the Obama administration was participating in the P5+1 talks with Iran.[9] These negotiations were much more difficult given the history of poor relations between the participants, Iran's oft-stated nuclear ambitions, past instances of "cheating" by Iran, and complicated domestic politics in the U.S.A. (Republicans opposed the negotiations and occasionally supported military action over diplomatic efforts). The eventual product of this process, the Joint Comprehensive Plan of Action (JCPOA),[10] ran to 159

---

[9]   The permanent members of the UN Security Council (U.S.A., U.K., France, China, Russia) plus Germany, acting in cooperation with representatives from the European Union.

[10]   A nice overview of the agreement can be found at https://www.armscontrol.org/factsheets/JCPOA-at-a-glance.

pages and included five annexes. The remarkable length and specificity of this agreement demonstrates the extent to which a lack of trust can be ameliorated by inspection provisions and verification protocols. The agreement also was designed to unfold in multiple stages; actions by the parties during these stages would demonstrate commitment to the agreement and reinforce expectations of compliance over time. In the past a comprehensive arms control agreement like this would have been negotiated as a treaty and subject to a vote in the U.S. Senate. The Obama administration, knowing that the JCPOA could not surpass the two-thirds vote threshold for a treaty, entered into the deal as an "executive agreement" bypassing Congressional advice and consent. This decision was based on the expectation that a succeeding president from the Democratic party would continue to abide by its measures. When Donald Trump defeated Hillary Clinton in 2016, one of his earliest priorities was to abandon the JCPOA and reinstate sanctions on Iran. This demonstrates the degree to which domestic political constraints can intrude on nonproliferation policy.

Opportunities for interdisciplinary future research

The development of this edited book illuminated new potential areas for inter-disciplinary research on trust in nuclear nonproliferation negotiations. Hamm, Smidt, and Mayer (2019) have deployed the MDS trust model to measure cit-izens' trust in the U.S. federal government and demonstrated the superiority of their method compared to the American National Election Study (ANES) measures. The ANES has long been considered the "gold standard" in the field, but the MDS model was more correlated with other expected variables (2019, p. 17). It may be possible to deploy these measures, properly adapted to other languages and cultures, to measure counterparty trust in the U.S. government, elites, or publics. Longitudinal use of these measures could validate the utility of the trust building measures discussed above.

A second vein of collaborative research could emerge from cross-pollination between the chapters in this book that focus on artificial intelligence (AI). As Lockey and Gillespie (Chapter 2) note, the domain in which a sociotechnical AI system is deployed and the nature of that system may alter the relevance of certain variables in the MDS model. We would expect the area of non-proliferation and nuclear weapons to be particularly fraught given high risk and perceptions of existential consequences. AI models that contribute to decisions regarding preventive action against proliferators, choices to escalate in a crisis, or assessments of intelligence related to launch indicators will be subjected to particularly demanding trials before they are trusted by experienced military and political actors (Singh & Mayer, Chapter 8). The perception of nuclear-domain AI trustworthiness in an anticipated future would surely benefit from the studies suggested by Brewer et al. (Chapter 7), but the context may be difficult to replicate in a laboratory setting.

Conclusion

Trust between state parties to nuclear nonproliferation agreements is difficult to generate. International agreements are not contracts enforced by a higher authority and cheaters often do not face consequences. Willingness to trust another state party is further hampered by the high stakes involved: states that defect from this type of agreement may gain asymmetric advantages (nuclear weapons) that alter the balance of power. The history of U.S. nonproliferation agreements with certain countries—Soviet Union/Russia, North Korea, Iran, China, Pakistan, South Africa, South Korea, etc.—are rife with examples of broken promises and failed diplomacy. This chapter examined the evolution of the concept of trust in international relations. It then explored how confidence-building measures, academic exchanges, "Track 1.5 and 2" diplomacy, and lengthy multiparty negotiations create trust between state parties and their diplomatic personnel. It also examined how the final agreements bridge any remaining gaps in trust with detailed inspection and verification protocols. It then considered how the final agreements/treaties overcome (or fall prey to) domestic political discord and obstacles to ratification. Finally, it discussed potential future opportunities for interdisciplinary collaborative research in this realm.

References

Boettcher, W. A. (2017). Resolving potential energy conflicts among allies: the 2015 United States–Republic of Korea nuclear cooperation agreement. *Energy Research & Social Science, 24*, 86–93.

Haas, P. M. (1992). Introduction: Epistemic Communities and International Policy Coordination. International Organization, 46(1), 1–35.

Hamm, J. A., Smidt, C., & Mayer, R. C. (2019). Understanding the psychological nature and mechanisms of political trust. *PLoS ONE, 14*(5), e0215835.

Head, N. (2012). Transforming conflict: trust, empathy, and dialogue. *International Journal of Peace Studies, 17*(2), 33–55.

Hoffman, A. M. (2002). A conceptualization of trust in international relations. *European Journal of International Relations, 8*(3), 375–401.

Kessler, J. C. (2013). Technical negotiations in a political environment: why the Hexapartite Safeguards Project succeeded. *The Nonproliferation Review, 20*(3), 493–508. https://doi.org/10.1080/10736700.2013.852785.

Kydd, A. H. (2000). Trust, reassurance, and cooperation. *International Organization, 54*(2), 325–357.

Larson, D. W. (1997). Trust and missed opportunities in international relations. *Political Psychology, 18*(3), 701–734.

Mapendere, J. (2005). Track one and a half diplomacy and the complementarity of tracks. *Culture of Peace Online Journal, 2*(1), 66–81.

Mayer, R. C., Davis, J. H., & Schoorman, F. D. (1995). An integrative model of organizational trust. *The Academy of Management Review, 20*(3), 709–734.

Mercer, J. (2005). Rationality and psychology in international politics. *International Organization, 59*, 77–106.

Mercer, J. (2010). Emotional beliefs. *International Organization, 64*, 1–31.

Morrow, J. D. (1994). *Game Theory for Political Scientists.* Princeton University Press.

Osgood, C. E. (1962). *An alternative to war or surrender.* University of Illinois Press.

Rathbun, B. C. (2018). Trust in international relations. In E. M. Uslaner (Ed.), *The Oxford Handbook of Social and Political Trust*, pp.687–706. Oxford University Press.

Risse-Kappen, T. (1991). Did "peace through strength" end the Cold War? Lessons from INF. *International Security, 16*(1), 162–188.

Sebenius, J. K., & Singh, M. K. (2012/13). Is a nuclear deal with Iran possible? An analytical framework for the Iran nuclear negotiations. *International Security, 37*(3), 52–91.

Uslaner, E. M. (2002). *The Moral Foundations of Trust.* Cambridge University Press.

Zak, P. J., & Kugler, J. (2011). Neuroeconomics and international studies: a new understanding of trust. *International Studies Perspectives, 12*, 136–152.

12 A new direction in police-public trust research: exploring trust from both perspectives

Richard A. Wise, Roger C. Mayer, Scott M. Mourtgos, and Holly P. O'Rourke

Police-public trust

A good relationship between the police and the public is essential to maintaining societal stability and preserving democratic values. When the public trusts the police, the public is more likely to cooperate with the police, obey police directives, comply with the law, and help the police identify criminals. Public trust in the police reduces public conflict and confrontations with the police (Bell, 2017; Mentovich, Ben-Porat, Levy, Goff, & Tyler, 2020). In short, the police need public trust to do their job effectively and safely.

Public trust in the police, however, is only half the story. As Kääriäinen and Sirén (2012) state, a strong police–public relationship requires *mutual* trust. Police trust in the public increases police responsiveness to and cooperation with the public, and police use of procedural justice (van Craen, 2016a). With greater trust, police are more likely to permit the public to play a role in determining police policy (Carr & Maxwell, 2018; van Craen, 2016b). When the police trust the public, officers are more willing to implement police reforms that are critical to improving police–public relations such as procedural justice (van Craen & Skogan, 2017; Trinkner, Tyler, & Goff, 2016).

Our research indicates that greater police trust is associated with the police engaging in more risk-taking behaviors that can increase public safety (Mourtgos, Mayer, Wise, & O'Rourke, 2020). When the police trust the public, the police may be less likely to use excessive force (O'Brien, Meares, & Tyler, 2020), their capacity to work efficiently and effectively is likely to increase, and officers' physical and mental health will likely improve (Finn, Talucci, &

Wood, 2000; Trinkner, Tyler, & Goff, 2016). Accordingly, the public needs police trust to ensure that it is safe and secure and that its constitutional rights are protected.

Past attempts to understand better the police–public trust relationship have been hindered by two primary limitations in the police literature. First is the lack of conceptual clarity in defining trust. For example, current studies of public trust in the police frequently rely on two factors to evaluate trust: police effectiveness and procedural justice. These measures do not clearly differentiate between ability, benevolence, and integrity, take the trustees' propensity to trust into account, or differentiate between trust and risk taking (Perry, Jonathan, & Weisburd, 2017). Second, decades of research on trust show that it is a reciprocal relationship (e.g., Ferrin, Bligh, & Kohles, 2008; Mayer, Bobko, Davis, & Gavin, 2011). Past research on trust in the police–public relationship has focused almost exclusively on public trust in the police, and it has ignored police trust in the public. Failure to assess both parties' trust in the other leads to an incomplete understanding of how trust is created in the police–public relationship (Mourtgos et al., 2020).

The above observation is not a trivial one. Reciprocal trust means that one party's level of trust affects the other party's level of trust. When one party trusts the other party, the trusted party is more likely to trust the first party. If either party perceives a lack of trust from the other party, a breakdown in trust is likely to occur (Mourtgos et al., 2020).

The present chapter proposes that studying both facets of the police–public trust relationship is essential for understanding and improving it. We first discuss two studies we conducted about police trust in the public that used Mayer, Davis, and Schoorman (MDS)'s 1995 model of trust. We used the MDS model of trust in our studies because it is widely accepted, has strong empirical support and conceptual clarity (Colquitt, Scott, & LePine, 2007; Mourtgos et al., 2020). Next, we discuss reforms that may improve police trust in the public, but which require future research to confirm their efficacy. We also briefly discuss why various members of the public, especially some minorities, may not trust the police. Finally, we discuss three reforms that may increase public trust in the police, but which require more research to determine their efficacy and cost-effectiveness: procedural justice, police initiatives, and community-oriented policing.

Our studies of police trust in the public

We conducted two studies about police trust in the public. The purposes of our first study were to develop valid measures of ability, benevolence, and integrity (i.e., the components of trustworthiness) and a measure of police trust in the public. We also sought to determine whether the measures of trustworthiness and an existing measure of propensity to trust (i.e., a general willingness to trust others) predicted police trust in the public (i.e., if the MDS model of trust applies to police trust in the public: Mourtgos et al., 2020).

We created multi-item measures of ability, benevolence, integrity, and a measure of police trust in the public after an extensive literature review and conferring with eight patrol officers with varied job duties and experiences. Next, 145 police departments and organizations distributed our survey to police officers. We received 990 valid responses from respondents who varied widely in age and job tenure (Mourtgos et al., 2020).

Statistical analyses of the measures of ability, benevolence, integrity, and police trust in the public indicated that they were reliable and valid. An exploratory factor analysis conducted on the items in the police trust in the public measure produced two scales. The eight-item "Engagement scale" measures an officer's willingness to interact with the public even though it puts the officer at risk, and the officer's job did not require the interaction. For example: "I have no concerns about mentioning that I am a police officer when I am off-duty and talking with members of the public" (Mourtgos et al., 2020).

The four-item "Proactive scale" measures officers' willingness to start an investigation or act on their own initiative, rather than because there was a 911 call (initiating an investigation without being requested to do so is commonly referred to in law enforcement as *proactive policing*). For instance, "At work, I am willing to take actions on non-criminal issues, such as dealing with the homeless and the mentally ill, even if it increases the possibility of public criticism of me." All the scales created for the study had acceptable reliability (i.e., Cronbach's alphas between .74 and .83: Mourtgos et al., 2020).

In summary, the first study indicated that the constructs we developed to measure the police perceptions of public trustworthiness and police trust in the public are reliable and valid. It also showed that officers' perceptions of the public's ability, benevolence, integrity, and officers' propensity to trust predicted their trust in the public, therefore the MDS model of trust applies to police trust in the public (Mourtgos et al., 2020).

The second study determined whether police trust in the public affected officers' willingness to take risks. We surveyed patrol and bicycle officers from a large police department in the Western U.S.A. using the measures from the first study. We chose to survey these officers because they had frequent public interactions, had considerable control over the extent of their public interactions, and performed common police functions. We surveyed 151 officers, and 140 (91.45%) officers completed the survey (Mourtgos et al., 2020).

To evaluate the officers' job performance who participated in the survey, we used two independent sources: their sergeants' evaluation of their job performance, and archival performance data. We gave the sergeants 5-point Behaviorally Anchored Rating Scales (BARS) to evaluate their officers. We used Cascio and Valenzi's (1977) eight dimensions of police performance to develop the BARS. To define and clarify the eight dimensions, we delineated job functions for each dimension after consulting with police officers. The officer's sergeant evaluated each officer on 20 job functions that pertained to the eight dimensions of police performance. To increase the reliability of the sergeants' ratings, we defined each scale point with a *behavioral anchor*—a brief description of the level of performance that would justify each rating (Mourtgos et al., 2020).

The police department that participated in the survey regularly collects officer performance data but had not used it in its officer evaluations for several years. The sergeants in the study no longer received the performance data. Accordingly, we had two independent measures for evaluating the job performance of the officers in the survey. The archival officer performance measured the number of times an officer was the initial responding or back-up officer on a call, the number of proactive cases generated, the number of initial and supplemental reports written, the number of arrests made, the number of traffic citations issued, and number of days worked (Mourtgos et al., 2020).

We used three months of archival performance data because we wanted a reliable measure of the officers' job performance, but were concerned that a longer duration would not accurately reflect the relationship between officers' trust and their job performance if either fluctuated. All 23 sergeants in the study mailed their evaluations of their officers to one of the study's authors who matched each officer's questionnaire with their two performance evaluations. The constructs we developed had acceptable reliability again in the second study (Mourtgos et al., 2020).

Next, we determined if the sergeants' ratings of the officers' job performance correlated with the officers' responses to the Proactive or Engagement trust scales (i.e., our measures of officers' trust in the public). None of Cascio and Valenzi's (1977) eight job performance dimensions significantly correlated with these scales. Consequently, we used the 20 items that pertained to the eight dimensions as separate measures. Proactive police work (r = .21, p < .05) and written communication skills (r = –.19, p < .05) both correlated with the Proactive trust scale, and performance under stress correlated with the Engagement trust scale (r = .17, p < .05). The significant correlation between officers' trust in the public and sergeants' evaluations of officers' proactive police work supported our hypothesis that police trust in the public was related to officers' willingness to take risk by engaging in proactive policing (Mourtgos et al., 2020).

We also determined if the archival measures of job performance correlated with the Proactive scale and Engagement scale (i.e., their trust in the public). Proactive police work (r = .29, p < .01), number of supplemental reports (r = .20, p < .05), and number of arrests (r = .31, p < .01) correlated with the Proactive scale. Four archival measures also significantly correlated with the Engagement scale: the number of times an officer was the initial responding officer on a call (r = .23, p < .01), number of initial reports written (r = .25, p < .01), number of arrests made (r = .18, p < .05), and job attendance (r = .17, p < .05).

These results further supported our hypothesis that police trust in the public was related to police officers taking risk (Mourtgos et al., 2020). Conversely, if officers choose to avoid the possibility of public complaints by minimizing their risk-taking behaviors on the job, their participation in all three of these activities would decrease.

In these two studies, we based our reasoning and performance measures on how police have traditionally been evaluated. Currently, there are concerns about whether these measures are sufficient, or perhaps even appropriate indicators of officer performance—an issue to which we will return later in this chapter.

Research needed to improve police–public trust

Improving police trust in the public requires the ability to measure it, to determine the reasons for low trust if it is present, and to ascertain what interventions are likely to improve it. We developed measurement tools to assess police officers' trust in the public, officers' perceptions of the public's ability, benevolence, and integrity, and rating scales of officers' performance. These measures can help police departments, other governmental agencies, policymakers, and researchers assess police trust in the public, determine why it is low, and identify and evaluate which interventions are most likely to improve it (Mourtgos et al., 2020).

There is little research on how to improve police trust in the public (Mourtgos et al., 2020). Nonetheless, the extant research suggests that improving a police department's internal organizational justice can significantly increase police trust in the public. Organizational justice consists of four components: distributive justice (having fair work outcomes for matters such as pay, promotions, responsibility), procedural justice (using fair procedures in the workplace), interpersonal justice (treating officers with dignity and respect), and communicational justice (providing timely and accurate information and having a mechanism for correcting decisional errors) (Roberts & Herrington, 2013). Some research and theories suggest that police trust in the public is linked to their perceptions of how supervisors treat them. Officers' relationships with peers and departmental policies are also important to organizational justice (van Craen, 2016b).

Because of the scarcity of research, we make some additional recommendations for improving police trust in the public but which will require additional research to confirm their usefulness. We recommend using multipronged, multistakeholder approaches which can concurrently increase both police trust in the public and public trust in police. For example, using transparent investigations of officer-involved shootings, where police departments quickly provide the public with information about an officer-involved shooting. Such investigations provide the public with a better understanding of the incident. They give the public insight into when and why police use force, which educates the public about how to interact safely with the police. Furthermore, they increase the probability that the public has an accurate perception of the shooting, they increase police transparency, and they may decrease the public's confirmation bias and use of other cognitive shortcuts to evaluate the shooting (Miethe, Venger, & Lieberman, 2019). Such shortcuts often lead to erroneous conclusions.

The officers involved in a shooting have a greater opportunity to inform the public about their side of the story. Therefore, they feel less threatened, and are more likely to believe they were treated fairly. We believe the primary reason transparent officer-involved shooting investigations are beneficial is because they simultaneously address *both sides of the reciprocal trust relationship*. This is important because the gains in trust each side experiences are mutually reinforcing.

Furthermore, existing policies should be evaluated to determine if they can be converted into multipronged, multistakeholder approaches for building trust. For instance, citizen advisory boards can not only give the public an opportunity for input into police policies (which targets public trust in police), but they can also educate board members about police needs and vulnerabilities. Board members can then use that knowledge to help educate the public about the police, which can increase police trust in the public. Police–public relations do not operate in a vacuum. Accordingly, policies of police departments and other governmental entities that generate tension in a community, negative and unfair media portrayals of the police, and injustice and racial discrimination in the criminal justice system and elsewhere in a community will decrease public trust in the police. Moreover, because trust is a reciprocal relationship, these policies may also decrease police trust in the public.

Demonizing the police not only harms officers and their families, but it also harms the public. Policing is a dangerous and extremely stressful profession. The job stress that officers experience causes many officers to suffer from a variety of psychological disorders (van Hasselt et al., 2008). High levels of stress can impair officers' decision-making and judgment, which not only endangers officers but also the public. Research suggests the "routine" occupational stressors of urban police officers such as the public's attitude toward the police were better predictors of officers' psychological distress than their cumulative exposure to trauma (Van Hasselt et al., 2008). It has become harder than ever to recruit new police officers and to retain officers because of current attitudes about the police (Chan, 2021). In an encounter with an individual, an officer is more likely to use force if the officer thinks the individual believes the officer's actions are motivated by an illegitimate motive such as racism (O'Brien, Meares, & Tyler 2020).

Accordingly, just as it is vital for the police to use procedural justice with the public, the public needs to use procedural justice when interacting with the police (i.e., treating officers fairly, politely, etc.). The public's use of procedural justice will likely increase police trust in the public because it will increase police officers' beliefs in both the public's integrity and benevolence. Furthermore, because trust is a reciprocal relationship, it is also likely to increase public trust in the police. Community leaders, political officials, and members of the media need to model these behaviors with officers and communicate their importance to the public.

Future research should examine if our results apply in other settings. It should investigate how the police–public trust relationship evolves over time, and how each party perceives and reacts to intervening events that affect trust. Research should examine how race, gender, and experience affect officers' trust, how officers define the public, and if our results replicate in different police departments. It should explore what other factors affect police trust in the public. Lastly, it should determine how police trust in the public correlates with whether police feel trusted by the public and how discrepancies between the two affect police behavior.

The public's lack of trust in the police and some reforms that may improve it

Various members of the public lack trust in the police, especially Black Americans. The U.S.A. has a long history of racial discrimination that includes a lengthy record of police using excessive force against Black Americans (Bell, 2017). Police treatment of Black Americans has also lessened some White Americans' trust in the police (Ortiz, 2020).

Many scholars and the President's Task Force on 21st Century Policing (2015) have asserted that procedural justice is essential to increasing public trust in the police. In fact, the President's Task Force called on departments to adopt procedural justice as a guiding principle. When making decisions and interacting with the public, procedural justice requires officers to treat the public with fairness, respect, and dignity. Procedural justice asserts these behaviors cause the public to view the police as legitimate, which includes trusting the police (O'Brien, Meares, & Tyler, 2020). Procedural justice further asserts that when the public views the police as legitimate, the public will defer to police authority, cooperate with the police, and be less likely to violate the law (Bell, 2017).

In evaluating research on procedural justice, the National Academies of Sciences, Engineering, and Medicine (2018) concluded that in general, public perceptions of police procedural justice have a strong, positive relationship with police legitimacy and cooperation. Nonetheless, there is insufficient research to conclude that police procedural justice causally affects public perceptions of police legitimacy, increases public cooperation with the police, or reduces crime and disorder. However, a large body of research outside of policing, such as in the workplace and courts, indicates that procedural justice is effective in promoting trust, compliance, and cooperation. This research suggests that the application of procedural justice to policing is promising.

Some research suggests that procedural justice training not only increases officers' use of procedural justice with the public, but also increases their commitment to their department's goals and standards. It may also improve officers' ability to de-escalate conflicts and to increase a community's well-being. Procedural justice is important for another reason: it requires police to engage in behaviors that are appropriate for a democratic society. Therefore, even if research shows that it does not increase public trust in the police, police training in procedural justice is still necessary because it promotes democratic policing (National Academies of Sciences, Engineering, and Medicine, 2018).

Police initiatives to reconcile with the public may also increase police trust in the public. For example, police initiatives that use procedural justice can have an impact on public trust that is distinct from the influence that individual officers' use of procedural justice has on public trust. Police initiatives activate individuals' social identity of being a member of a group or a community as well as their personal identity. They signal that the police as a whole and not just individual officers want to increase public trust. This is important because distrust in the police can result from either an individual's belief that the police do not treat the individual fairly or do not treat fairly the groups or communities to which the individual belongs (O'Brien & Tyler, 2020). Some examples of police initiatives are police–community meetings, police apologies to the community, and police passing out informational leaflets to the community (O'Brien & Tyler, 2020; O'Brien, Tyler, & Meares, 2020).

Groups with less power, such as Black Americans and other minorities, need empowerment before they are willing to reconcile with a group that they believe has disempowered them in the past. Participating in decision-making is a way to empower a group and for the police to convey respect, inclusion, and status to a group. It also increases the likelihood that the public will perceive the attempt at reconciliation as sincere. Furthermore, it has been hypothesized that if the public believes that officers are not procedurally just in their public interactions, it will undermine police initiatives. It has also been hypothesized that increasing public trust is a process that requires substantial and sustained police effort and time to be successful (O'Brien & Tyler, 2020; O'Brien, Tyler, & Meares, 2020).

Another method commonly used to promote public trust in the police and other goals related to police efficacy is community-oriented policing. Community-oriented policing is concerned with community problems (crime or other problems) and with building a community's social resilience, collective efficacy, and empowerment. Some examples of community-oriented policing pertaining to crime control include foot patrols, neighborhood watch, and community meetings. The nature of community-oriented policing varies widely among different police departments, as does its scope and intensity. The variability in community-oriented policing has contributed to the difficulty in conducting research on it (National Academies of Sciences, Engineering, and Medicine, 2018).

Community-oriented policing produces modest improvement in how the public views policing and the police in the short term. There is little research on its long-term effects or the scope of its effects (broad or only localized effects). Community-oriented policing rarely has a negative effect on community attitudes toward the police. Therefore, it may produce modest improvement in community attitudes toward the police with little risk of having a negative impact. However, research has not determined if the benefits of community-oriented policing outweigh its costs. Because of limited research, mixed findings, and methodological difficulties, it is unclear how community-oriented policing affects people's cooperation with the police (National Academies of Sciences, Engineering, and Medicine, 2018).

As noted earlier, the performance measures in Mourtgos et al. (2020) were based on traditional approaches to evaluating police performance. Recently, there has been concern about "over-policing" (i.e., excessive arrests) harming police–public relations, especially the disproportionate arrests of minorities—particularly Black individuals—for non-violent crimes (Sentencing Project, 2018). Whether the number of arrests is positive or negative may depend on the context such as the crime rate and racial composition of a community. Consequently, further research is needed to understand if and how arrests should be used as a measure of police performance. Research is also needed to examine how police–public trust is affected by police behaviors such as conflict de-escalation. For example, would more police training in de-escalating tense situations result in greater public trust in the police? Would there also be a significant reciprocal effect? In other words, would increased public trust from more police training in de-escalation also improve police trust in the public? Furthermore, research on redefining police performance so it includes behaviors that improve the public–police relationship would be beneficial.

Future research on public trust in the police

More research is needed to determine if reforms intended to improve public trust in the police significantly improve it. Another important question is how effectively officers implement reforms to increase public trust in the police.

Consequently, researchers need to develop measures to assess police implementation of reforms. Future research should examine the long-term effects of police reforms, and if their benefits outweigh their costs. Researchers need to better understand the challenge police departments face in implementing reforms and their efficacy in different police departments and communities (National Academies of Sciences, Engineering, and Medicine, 2018).

Given the challenges with public trust in the police in many communities, what can we expect when (not if) the police begin to deploy robots for various functions? Early research on one such function, guarding the entrance to a building, is described by Lyons, Scheutz, and Jessup (Chapter 10).

On the one hand, robots could improve public trust because the public may view the robots as more likely to follow the rules than some officers. On the other hand, the public may view robots as impersonal entities, and therefore they may decrease the public's perception of police benevolence.

Eloy, Bobko, and Hirshfield (Chapter 3) talk in part about unobtrusive ways of measuring trust (e.g., looking at brain functions as a subject is presented with various stimuli or situations). Research that exposed a research participant to either a police officer or a robot carrying out various functions that used such measurement in addition to self-reports using either a survey or an interview would be fascinating. Lyons, Scheutz, and Jessup (Chapter 10) describe experiments with a non-lethal guard robot, and people's reactions to it—adding unobtrusive measures of brain activity to measure such issues as the correspondence between immediate physiological reactions and post hoc self-reports of trust would be very interesting.

Conclusion

A strong police–public relationship is vital to a nation's welfare. Trust is a reciprocal relationship. Accordingly, programs that only focus on improving public trust in the police are less likely to succeed or will be less successful than programs that focus on the reciprocal relations of trust between police *and* the public. We suggest research to better understand the problem and possible solutions.

References

Bell, M. C. (2017). Police reform and the dismantling of legal estrangement. *Yale Law Journal, 126*(7), 2054–2151.

Carr, J. D., & Maxwell, S. R. (2018). Police officers' perceptions of organizational justice and their trust in the public. *Police Practice & Research, 19*, 365–379. https://doi.org/10.1080/15614263.2017.1387784.

Cascio, W. F., & Valenzi, E. R. (1977). Behaviorally anchored rating scales: effects of education and job experience of raters and ratees. *Journal of Applied Psychology, 62*, 278–282. https://doi.org/10.1037//0021-9010.62.3.278.

Chan, M. (2021, April 26). The new recruits. *Time*, 46–51.

Colquitt, J. A., Scott, B. A., & LePine, J. A. (2007). Trust, trustworthiness, and trust propensity: a meta-analytic test of their unique relationships with risk taking and job performance. *Journal of Applied Psychology, 92*(4), 909–927. https://doi.org/1037/0021-9010.92.4.909.

Ferrin, D. L., Bligh, M. C., & Kohles, J. C. (2008). It takes two to tango: an interdependence analysis of the spiraling of perceived trustworthiness and cooperation in interpersonal and intergroup relationships. *Organizational Behavior and Human Decision Processes, 107*(2), 161–178. https://doi.org/10.1016/j.obhdp.2008.02.012.

Finn, P., Talucci, V., & Wood, J. (2000, January). On-the-job stress in policing—reducing it, preventing it. *National Institute of Justice Journal*, 18–24. https://www.ncjrs.gov/pdffiles1/jr000242d.pdf.

Kääriäinen, J., & Sirén, R. (2012). Do the police trust in citizens? European comparisons. *European Journal of Criminology, 9*, 276–289. https://10.1177/1477370811435737.

Mayer, R. C., Bobko, P., Davis, J. H., & Gavin, M. B. (2011). The effects of changing power and influence tactics on trust in the supervisor: a longitudinal field study. *Journal of Trust Research, 1*(2), 177–201. https://doi.org/10.1080/21515581.2011.603512.

Mayer, R. C., Davis, J. H., & Schoorman, F. D. (1995). An integrative model of organizational trust. *Academy of Management Review, 20*, 709–734. https://doi.org/10.5465/amr.1995.9508080335.

Mentovich, A., Ben-Porat, G., Levy, N., Goff, P. A., & Tyler, T. (2020). Policing alienated minorities in divided cities. *Regulation & Governance, 14*, 531–550. https://doi-org.ezproxy.library.und.edu/10.1111/rego.12232.

Miethe, T. D., Venger, O., & Lieberman, J. D. (2019). Police use of force and its video coverage: an experimental study of the impact of media source and content on public perceptions. *Journal of Criminal Justice, 60*, 35–46. https://doi.org/10.1016/j.jcrimjus.2018.10.00.

Mourtgos, S. M., Mayer, R. C., Wise, R. A., & O'Rourke, H. (2020). The overlooked perspective of police trust in the public: measurement and effects on police job behaviors. *Criminal Justice Policy Review, 31*(5), 639–672. https://doi-org.ezproxy.library.und.edu/10.1177/0887403419851850.

National Academies of Sciences, Engineering, and Medicine (2018). *Proactive Policing: Effects on Crime and Communities*, ed. D. Weisburd and M. Majmundar. Washington, DC: The National Academies Press. https://doi.org/10.17226/24928.

O'Brien, T. C., Meares, T. L., & Tyler, T. R. (2020). Reconciling police and communities with apologies, acknowledgements, or both: a controlled experiment. *The ANNALS of the American Academy of Political and Social Science, 687*(1), 202–215. https://doi.org/10.1177/0002716220904659.

O'Brien, T. C., & Tyler, T. R. (2020). Authorities and communities: can authorities shape cooperation with communities on a group level? *Psychology, Public Policy, and Law, 26*(1), 69–87. https://doi.org/10.1037/law0000202.

O'Brien, T. C., Tyler, T. R., & Meares, T. L. (2020). Building popular legitimacy with reconciliatory gestures and participation: a community-level model of authority. *Regulation & Governance, 14,* 821–839. https://doi.org/10.1111/rego.12264.

Ortiz, A. (2020, August 12). Confidence in police is at record low, Gallup survey finds. *New York Times.* https://www.nytimes.com/2020/08/12/us/gallup-poll-police.html.

Perry, G., Jonathan, Z. T., & Weisburd, D. (2017). The effect of paramilitary protest policing on protestors' trust in the police: the case of the "Occupy Israel" movement. *Law & Society Review, 51*(3), 602–634. https://doi.org.ezproxy.library.und.edu/10 .1111/lasr.12279.

President's Task Force on 21st Century Policing (2015). *Final Report of the President's Task Force on 21st Century Policing.* Washington, DC: Office of Community Oriented Policing Services.

Roberts, K., & Herrington, V. (2013). Organisational and procedural justice: a review of the literature and its implications for policing. *Journal of Policing, 8,* 115–130. https://doi.org/10.1080/18335330.2013.821737.

Sentencing Project, The (2018). *Annual Report 2018.* https://www.sentencingproject .org/app/uploads/2022/09/Annual-Report-2018.pdf (accessed August 8, 2023).

Trinkner, R., Tyler, T. R., & Goff, P. A. (2016). Justice from within: the relations between a procedurally just organizational climate and police organizational efficiency, endorsement of democratic policing and officer well-being. *Psychology, Public Policy, & Law, 22,* 158–172. https://psycnet.apa.org/doi/10.1037/law0000085.

van Craen, M. (2016a). Understanding police officers' trust and trustworthy behavior: work relations framework. *European Journal of Criminology, 13*(2), 274–296. https:// doi.org/10.1177/1477370815617187.

van Craen, M. (2016b). Fair policing from the inside out. *Sociology of Crime, Law & Deviance, 21,* 3–19. https:// doi -org .ezproxy .library .und .edu/ 10 .1108/ S1521 -613620160000021001.

van Craen, M., & Skogan, W. G. (2017). Achieving fairness in policing: the link between internal and external procedural justice. *Police Quarterly, 20,* 3–23. https://psycnet .apa.org/doi/10.1177/1098611116657818.

van Hasselt, V. B., Sheehan, D. C., Malcolm, A. S., Sellers, A. H., Baker, M. T., & Couwels, J. (2008). The law enforcement officer stress survey (LEOSS): evaluation of psychometric properties. *Behavior Modification, 32*(1), 133–151. https://doi.org/10 .1177/0145445507308571.

13   Trust in evacuation robots

Alan R. Wagner

The long-term goal of our research is to create robots that enhance user safety by promoting an appropriate amount of trust during an emergency evacuation. Our research has shown that during an emergency evacuation some people will stay with a robot that has stopped moving, moves in circles, or repeatedly crashes into a wall (Robinette, Wagner, & Howard, 2013, 2016). Examples from many domains demonstrate that people, including experts, tend to trust automation and robots too much. On July 6, 2013, Asiana Airlines flight 214 crashed on its final approach into San Francisco International Airport killing three people and injuring 180. According to the National Transportation and Safety Board, overreliance on automation played an important role in the crash (NTSB, 2014). Studies have found that healthcare providers tend to overtrust automated systems as well, resulting in certain types of cancers being over-looked (Povyakalo et al., 2013). Fully automated driving has been shown to foster overtrust negatively impacting driver reaction time during emergencies (Payre, Cestac, & Delhomme, 2016).

As robotic applications become widespread, these technologies will interact with a more diverse and technologically naïve population, ignorant of the system's risks, failure modes, and limitations (Parasuraman, Molloy, & Singh, 1993). Trust calibration is the process by which a person comes to accurately recognize the risks associated with trusting a person or machine (Lee & See, 2004). During the trust calibration process the user learns both the system's competencies and likely failure modes and comes to evaluate the risks based on the specific situation and individuals involved (Parasuraman, Molloy, & Singh, 1993). The natural tendency of people to view automated machines (or their creators) as more knowledgeable or less prone to error than they are in reality (Skitka, Mosier, & Burdick, 1999) tends to encourage overtrust (Lee & See, 2004).

Our research has focused on the question of if and why a person will follow a robot's guidance directions during an emergency evacuation (Robinette et al., 2016). Our previous research evaluated a person's trust in a robot as part of a human subject experiment that simulated an emergency. Although many of our experiments have been conducted in simulation, one series of experiments was conducted in-person in an unoccupied building on campus. It began when an experimenter greeted the participant and stated that a robot would lead them to a meeting room. The robot then either guided the person to the meeting room along an efficient, direct route or a circuitous route meant to demonstrate the robot's unreliability. The participant entered the meeting room, closed the door, read a magazine article, and then answered survey questions. After approximately two minutes, unbeknownst to the subject, a smoke machine used to train fire fighters was used to fill the hallway leading to the meeting room with smoke and set off fire alarms. Upon hearing the alarm and seeing the smoke, most subjects entered and traveled a short distance down the hallway and encountered the robot pointing in a direction that differed from the direction of the entrance and that contradicted a lit emergency sign.

The results from this experiment were surprising: 26 of the 26 participants followed the robot's guidance and proceeded to the exit pointed to by the robot. Eighty-one percent (21 of 26) of participants indicated that their decision to follow the robot meant they trusted the robot. Moreover, 85 percent (22 of 26) of participants indicated that they would follow the robot in a future emergency. Only three participants noticed the emergency exit sign behind the robot, and none expressed interest in following it.

Based on these results, the errors generated by the robot were amplified and a new experiment was conducted with a smaller number of subjects. In this new experiment the robot now stopped moving in a different room that was obviously not the intended meeting room. The experimenter then intervened stating: "Well, I think the robot is broken again. Please go into that room [gesturing to the meeting room] and follow the instructions." Despite the clearly highlighted robot failure, during the emergency phase of the experiment, 100 percent of the participants (6 out of 6) followed the robot's guidance to the exit pointed to by the robot. When asked why they followed the robot, some people reported that because the robot's position had changed, they believed that it had been repaired.

The robot's errors were then amplified even more by having the robot break down on the way to the meeting room while pointing down an unknown corridor. In this condition, the robot did not change position between the time of the breakdown and when the subject saw the robot during the emergency. The experimenter again told the subject that the robot was broken. Nevertheless, 80 percent (4 of 5) of the participants followed the robot during the emergency. Three of the participants who followed the robot's guidance indicated that they trusted it and half said they would follow it again in the future. All five rated the robot as a bad guide in the non-emergency portion of the experiment but still chose to follow the robot during the emergency.

Note: Fire alarms are sounding, and smoke (unseen) is entering the passageway to their left. They encounter a robot that they have been told is broken. Still, one third of the subjects follow the robot's guidance directions (left image) and another third stand by the robot and wait (right image) rather than exit the way they came
Source: Robinette et al. (2016)

Figure 13.1   Human subjects encountering an emergency evacuation robot

In a final condition, the robot once again broke down on the way to the meeting room. However, in this case, the robot pointed to an unlit room with a couch blocking all but four inches of the entrance (Figure 13.1). Two of the six participants followed the robot's guidance and squeezed past the couch into the dark room. An additional two participants stood next to the robot and did not move to any exit. The remaining two participants proceeded to the front exit of the building. The two participants who followed the robot's guidance indicated that this meant they trusted the robot, although one said that he would not follow it again because it had failed twice. The two who stayed with the robot indicated that they did not trust the robot and the two who proceeded to the front exit selected that trust was not involved in their decision. *Overall, 93 percent (42 out of 45) either followed the robot's emergency exit guidance or stood by the robot during an emergency even after they had seen the robot behave unreliably.*

Admittedly, this study does have limitations. Specifically, the subjects all knew they were participating in an experiment, the number of subjects was somewhat low in the experimental conditions, and the subjects were mostly young college students. Nevertheless, these experiments have been replicated with broader populations and larger numbers of subjects.

Trust research for human–robot interaction (HRI)

Our work stands in contrast to much of the other human–robot trust research which has largely shown that reliability is the most important factor in determining if a person will trust a robot (Hancock et al., 2011). Human–robot trust research has primarily examined the factors that influence a person's trust in a robot. Confidence and risk have been identified as factors (Desai et al., 2013; Yagoda & Gillan, 2012; Hoff & Bashir, 2015; Balfe, Sharples, & Wilson, 2018; Hancock et al., 2011) as has the robot's behavior (Brule et al., 2014) and appearance (Li, Rau, & Patrick, 2010; Prakash & Rogers, 2015). Several authors have investigated the influence of robot reliability on a user's decision to interrupt autonomous operation by the robot (Desai et al., 2013; Mason et al., 2013). Human–robot trust research has also explored methods for measuring trust in a robot (Lu & Sarter, 2018; Freedy et al., 2007; Schaefer, 2016; Yagoda & Gillan, 2012), models of human–robot trust (Sanders et al., 2011; Xu & Dudek, 2015; Chen et al., 2018; Wang et al., 2018), and methods that promote trust in a robot (Yang et al., 2017; De Visser et al., 2016). Importantly, *human–robot trust research typically assumes that people will think about a robot's reputation and reliability in order to evaluate how much they should trust it* (Castelfranchi & Falcone, 2010; Haring, Matsumoto, & Watanabe, 2013; Chen et al., 2018). Human–robot trust experiments are thus often performed in a lab environment that minimizes or narrowly defines risk as financial loss (Haring, Matsumoto, & Watanabe, 2013; Berg, Dickhaut, & McCabe, 1995) and may not generate sufficient risk so that trust is relevant (Chen et al., 2018; Rae, Takayama, & Mutlu, 2013). Much work has looked at "undertrust" of a robot, that is, the reasons people do not trust robots (Lee & See, 2004; De Visser et al., 2016).

There are currently no standard, agreed-upon measures for trust for the field of HRI. Many HRI researchers tend to use behavioral indicators of trust (Robinette et al., 2016; Byrne & Marín, 2018). For example, Bryne and Marín evaluate trust in a robot's ability to grab a cup on a table and deliver it to the participant. In fact, this type of table clearing task is a common example of the types of tasks used in human–robot trust research (Byrne & Marín, 2018; Chen et al., 2018). Alternatively, many researchers use surveys to measure trust in a robot (Jian, Bisantz, & Drury, 2000; Schaefer, 2016; Yagoda & Gillan,

2012). Surveys simply ask subjects to self-report their trust in the robot. The use of surveys meant to measure human–robot trust present many challenges ranging from non-standard administration to variations in the scales used, to variations in wording (Chita-Tegmark et al., 2021). Many researchers use both types of measures.

The need for trust presupposes risk and vulnerability (Simpson, 2007; Mayer, Davis, & Schoorman, 1995). Examinations of human–robot trust do not yet have a standardized experimental context or test scenario. Autonomous driving scenarios are occasionally used to evaluate trust in an autonomous vehicle (Mokhtari, Lang, & Wagner, 2020). These scenarios attempt to simulate risky situations, but are often conducted in simulation, thus warranting no real risk to the subject. Automated targeting scenarios are also occasionally used. These scenarios require the participant to decide whether to accept or reject an autonomous weapon's targeting decision. These scenarios may be simulation or attempt to simulate realistic remote operation of a weaponized drone (Lu & Sarter, 2018). Finally, household scenarios include situations such as trust in a robot tasked with clearing a table of dishes and glasses (Chen et al., 2018). Performed in a laboratory, these types of table clearing trust studies raise questions about whether or not the task is viewed as risky enough by the participant for trust to be involved.

Gaps and important future challenges

Trust plays a key role in the person's decision to follow or not follow the robot during an emergency evacuation. Yet two underlying psychological phenomena, automation bias (Parasuraman & Riley, 1997) and dual process theories of cognition (Evans & Stanovich, 2013), may also influence a person's decision to trust a robot in a risky situation.

The term automation bias describes the notion that people tend to favor the suggestions of automated systems, potentially leading to trusting the automated system too much (Parasuraman & Riley, 1997). For automation, situations in which a person is highly reliant on the machine and monitoring several machines, for example, can lead to overtrust (Parasuraman, Molloy, & Singh, 1993). Overtrust of automation has been observed when using an autopilot (Parasuraman, Molloy, & Singh, 1993) or the automated features of a car (Inagaki & Itoh, 2013). Research has also shown that people, under certain conditions, will follow a robot's directions even if those directions are peculiar or destructive, such as watering a plant with orange juice (Salem et al., 2015;

Bainbridge et al., 2011). Booth et al. showed that students would hold a security door open for a robot disguised as a food delivery agent even when reminded not to compromise the location's security—87 percent held the door open for the robot even when they recognized the robot as a potential bomb threat (Booth et al., 2017). Still, *comparatively little work has considered overtrust of robots* (Payre, Cestac, & Delhomme, 2016; Booth et al., 2017; Rossi et al., 2017) *and even fewer studies have looked at human–robot trust during physically risky situations such as emergency evacuations*, even though trust in automation has considered research questions.

In addition to automation bias, dual process theories of cognition may govern the ways that people rely on robots. Dual process theories of cognition suggest that different systems operate in parallel within the human mind (Evans & Stanovich, 2013). One system is slow, deliberative, and rational. The second system is fast, reactive, and intuition based. Interacting with a person that is fleeing some threat is, in many ways, fundamentally different from interacting with a person in a laboratory environment. The type of risk faced during an emergency is very different from the more deliberative risk examined in most human–robot trust research (Kuligowski, 2013). Hearing an alarm activates the cognitive systems associated with stress (Welford, 1972) and may result in a fight-or-flight response (Jansen et al., 1995). Numerous studies show that during emergencies people follow instinct and utilize crowd decision-making behaviors (Pan et al., 2006). Moreover, humans tend to use mental shortcuts and simple heuristics to make quick decisions (Kahneman & Frederick, 2002; Evans & Stanovich, 2013). When receiving guidance during an emergency this type of cognitive processing likely inhibits lengthy consideration of a leader's reputation. Furthermore, fight-or-flight responses can be debilitating and impair judgment. Our experiments have shown that people presented with an emergency will blindly follow an evacuation robot, even trusting the robot when they have been told that it is broken.

Evacuee–robot interaction may therefore demand a unique perspective on human–robot trust and how a robot should behave. Does a person really trust a robot if they follow it during an emergency because they are too frightened or distracted to consider other options? And, perhaps most importantly, does the answer to this question matter in a practical sense or is this question simply academic? Drawing from Mayer's work on interpersonal trust (Mayer, Davis, & Schoorman, 1995) and Lee and See's work on trust in automation (Lee & See, 2004), we define trust as, "a belief, held by the trustor, that the trustee will act in a manner that mitigates the trustor's risk in a situation in which the trustor has put its outcomes at risk" (Wagner, 2009). Our research has shown that people tend to follow a robot during an emergency evacuation (Robinette et al., 2016;

Robinette, Wagner, & Howard, 2016). Our data indicates that the subjects in our experiment did not deliberate over their options. They did not seek or consider alternative indicators of ways to exit the building. Like most evacuees during an emergency, they reacted quickly to the first stimulus that appeared to direct them to an exit, in this case a robot. One could argue that the subjects did not really trust the robot because they do not appear to have considered how or if it would rescue them, and, hence, their actions fall outside of the scope of trust. Yet from the perspective of an outside observer, their actions seemed to indicate trust. Moreover, after the experiment, when we asked them if they trusted the robot, many stated that they did follow it, noting that because they chose to follow it they must have trusted it. Finally, from a practical standpoint, even if following a robot during an emergency evacuation does not fit within the traditional definition of trust, it nevertheless demonstrates that people are willing to accept significant risks when interacting with and relying on possibly unreliable robots. This realization presents new and important challenges which must be addressed if robots are to become an important element of society.

An evacuation robot may also need to adjust its behavior based on the person's reaction and emotional state; it may need to be authoritative and convince people when and how to leave (Kuligowski, 2008; Robinette, Vela, & Howard, 2012). The dynamic nature of the evacuee–robot relationship presents challenges as well as opportunities for important and novel research. It will be necessary to develop perceptual methods that allow a robot to recognize when a person trusts the robot too little or too much. Relatively little research has examined this problem, but promising research by Lu and Sarter suggests that eye-tracking can, perhaps, be used in some situations to quantify how reliable people view a robot to be (Lu & Sarter, 2018). Lu and Sarter also found that people more closely track low reliability robots, and that their tracking of the robot correlates to their trust in it. In addition, to work as emergency guides robots will need to be able to generate explanations that contribute to human trust calibration. These explanations will need to be tailored to the individual, perhaps using their age, attentiveness, and emotional state to craft the most understandable explanation (Wagner, 2015). Chapter 3 by Eloy, Bobko, and Hirshfield, for example, presents the possibility of using a partially observable Markov decision process (POMDP) to control a robot in a manner that integrates and acts on information about the evacuee's physiological state. Non-invasive camera, voice, or behavioral information collected in real time could act as observations that influence whether the robot moves forward toward an exit, stops and waits for the evacuee, or tries to explain why they should hurry.

Conclusions

Human–robot trust research has the potential to offer a unique perspective on trust. Because as aspects of the robot, such as its behavior, mannerisms, and appearance, are controlled by the experimenter, one can vary these aspects of the robot and measure how these changes impact human trust. Still, human–robot trust researchers have not yet settled on how to measure trust. Traditional methods such as surveys have well-known limitations (Chita-Tegmark et al., 2021). On the other hand, behavioral signs of trust tend to be context-specific and the decision to act in a particular way may reflect reasons other than trust. Understanding why humans trust robots and when they may put themselves at risk because their trust in a robot is too great is an important topic of research.

Human–robot trust research is important because it may provide strategies for increasing a potential user's trust in competent robot applications. This research may also provide insights for preventing overtrust. Ultimately, an important goal of human–robot trust research is to develop robots that help users correctly calibrate their trust in the robot. For some applications achieving this goal is critical. For example, autonomous vehicles need to make passengers aware of inclement conditions that could impact the vehicle's ability to drive safely. Evacuation robots must influence evacuees to follow the robot to safety, or to seek their own way out if the robot becomes lost. For autonomous driving and emergency evacuation correctly calibrating user trust could be the difference between life and death for the person.[1]

References

Bainbridge, W. A., Hart, J. W., Kim, E. S., & Scassellati, B. (2011). The benefits of interactions with physically present robots over video-displayed agents. *International Journal of Social Robotics*, *3*(1), 41–52. https://doi.org/10.1007/s12369-010-0082-7.
Balfe, N., Sharples, S., & Wilson, J. R. (2018). Understanding is key: an analysis of factors pertaining to trust in a real-world automation system. *Human Factors*, *60*(4), 477–495. https://doi.org/10.1177/0018720818761256.
Berg, J., Dickhaut, J., & McCabe, K. (1995). Trust, reciprocity, and social history. *Games and Economic Behavior*, *10*(1), 122–142. https://doi.org/0899-8256/95.

---

[1] This chapter is based upon work supported by the National Science Foundation under Grant Nos. CNS-1830390 and IIS-2045146. Any opinions, findings, and conclusions or recommendations expressed in this chapter are those of the author(s) and do not necessarily reflect the views of the National Science Foundation.

Booth, S., Tompkins, J., Pfister, H., Waldo, J., Gajos, K., & Nagpal, R. (2017). Piggybacking robots: human–robot overtrust in university dormitory security. *International Conference on Human–Robot Interaction* (pp. 426–434). https:// doi .org/10.1145/2909824.3020211.

Brule, R. v., Ron, D., Bijlstra, G., Wigboldus, D. H., & Haselager, P. (2014). Do robot performance and behavioral style affect human trust? *International Journal of Social Robotics, 6*(4), 519–531. https://doi.org/10.1007/s12369-014-0231-5.

Byrne, K., & Marín, C. (2018). Human trust in robots when performing a service. *2018 IEEE 27th International Conference on Enabling Technologies: Infrastructure for Collaborative Enterprises (WETICE)* (pp. 9–14). https:// doi .org/ 10 .1109/ WETICE .2018.0000.

Castelfranchi, C., & Falcone, R. (2010). *Trust Theory: A Socio-cognitive and Computational Model.* New York: John Wiley & Sons. https:// doi .org/ 10 .1002/ 9780470519851.

Chen, M., Nikolaidis, S., Soh, H., Hsu, D., & Srinivasa, S. (2018). Planning with trust for human–robot collaboration. *Proceedings of the 2018 ACM/IEEE International Conference on Human–Robot Interaction* (pp. 307–315). New York, ACM. https:// doi.org/10.1145/3171221.3171264.

Chita-Tegmark, M., Law, T., Rabb, N., & Scheutz, M. (2021). Can you trust your trust measure? *Proceedings of the 2021 ACM/IEEE International Conference on Human–Robot Interaction (HRI '21)* (p. 9). Boulder, CO, ACM. https:// doi .org/ 10 .1145/ 3434073.3444677.

De Visser, E. J., Monfort, S. S., McKendrick, R., Smith, M. A., McKnight, P. E., Krueger, F., & Parasuraman, R. (2016). Almost human: anthropomorphism increases trust resilience in cognitive agents. *Journal of Experimental Psychology: Applied, 22*(3), 331–349. http://dx.doi.org/10.1037/xap0000092.

Desai, M., Kaniarasu, P., Medvedev, M., Steinfeld, A., & Yanco, H. (2013). Impact of robot failures and feedback on real-time trust. *Proceedings of the 8th ACM/ IEEE International Conference on Human–Robot Interaction,* (pp. 251–258). Tokyo, Japan. https://doi.org/978-1-4673-3101-2/13.

Evans, J. S., & Stanovich, K. E. (2013). Dual-process theories of higher cognition: advancing the debate. *Perspectives on Psychological Science, 8*(3), 223–241. https:// doi.org/10.1177/1745691612460685.

Freedy, A., DeVisser, E., Weltman, G., & Coeyman, N. (2007). Measurement of trust in human–robot collaboration. *International Symposium on Collaborative Technologies and Systems* (pp. 106–114). IEEE. https://doi.org/0-9785699-1-1/0.

Hancock, P. A., Billings, D. R., Schaefer, K. E., Chen, J. Y., Visser, E. J., & Parasuraman, R. (2011). A meta-analysis of factors affecting trust in human–robot interaction. *Human Factors: The Journal of the Human Factors and Ergonomics Society, 53*(5), 517–527. https://doi.org/10.1177/0018720811417254.

Haring, K. S., Matsumoto, Y., & Watanabe, K. (2013). How do people perceive and trust a lifelike robot? *Proceedings of the World Congress on Engineering and Computer Science* (vol. 1). https://doi.org/978-988-19252-3-7.

Hoff, K. A., & Bashir, M. (2015). Trust in automation: integrating empirical evidence on factors that influence trust. *Human Factors, 57,* 407–434. https://doi.org/10.1177/ 0018720814547570.

Inagaki, T., & Itoh, M. (2013). Human's overtrust in and overreliance on advanced driver assistance systems: a theoretical framework. *International Journal of Vehicular Technology.* https://doi.org/10.1155/2013/951762.

Jansen, A., Nguyen, X., Karpitsky, V., & Mettenleiter, M. (1995). Central command neurons of the sympathetic nervous system: basis of the fight-or-flight response. *Science Magazine*, *5236*(270). https://doi.org/10.1126/science.270.5236.644.

Jian, J. Y., Bisantz, A. M., & Drury, C. G. (2000). Foundations for an empirically determined scale of trust in automated systems. *International Journal of Cognitive Ergonomics*, *4*(1), 53–71. https://doi.org/10.1207/S15327566IJCE0401_04.

Kahneman, D., & Frederick, S. (2002). Representativeness revisited: attribute substitution in intuitive judgment. Heuristics and biases: the psychology of intuitive judgment. In T. Gilovich, D. Griffin, & D. Kahneman (Eds.), *Heuristics of Intuitive Judgment: Extensions and Applications*, pp.49–81. New York: Cambridge University Press. https://doi.org/10.1017/CBO9780511808098.004.

Kuligowski, E. (2008). *Modeling Human Behavior during Building Fires*. NIST Technical Note 1619. National Institute of Standards and Technology.

Kuligowski, E. (2013). Predicting human behavior during fires. *Fire Technology*, *49*(1), 101–120. https://doi.org/10.1007/s10694-011-0245-6.

Lee, J. D., & See, K. A. (2004). Trust in automation: designing for appropriate reliance. *Human Factors*, *46*(1), 50–80. https://doi.org/10.1518/hfes.46.1.50_30392.

Li, D., Rau, P. L., & Patrick, L. Y. (2010). A cross-cultural study: effect of robot appearance and task. *International Journal of Social Robotics*, *2*(2), 175–186. https://doi.org/10.1007/s12369-010-0056-9.

Lu, Y., & Sarter, N. (2018). Eye tracking: a promising method for inferring trust in real time. *Proceedings of the Human Factors and Ergonomics Society Annual Meeting*, *62*, 175–176. https://doi.org/10.1177/1541931218621042.

Mason, E., Nagabandi, A., Steinfeld, A., & Bruggeman, C. (2013). Trust during robot-assisted navigation. *2013 AAAI Spring Symposium Series* (pp. 54–59). Palo Alto.

Mayer, R. C., Davis, J. H., & Schoorman, F. D. (1995). An integrative model of organizational trust. *The Academy of Management Review*, *20*(3), 709–734. https://doi.org/10.5465/amr.1995.9508080335.

Mokhtari, K., Lang, K., & Wagner, A. R. (2020). Don't go that way! Risk-aware decision making for autonomous vehicles. *Proceedings of the 12th International Conference on Social Robotics (ICSR)* (pp. 284–295). https://doi.org/10.1007/978-3-030-62056-1_24.

NTSB (2014, June 24). *NTSB Press Release*. Retrieved December 18, 2014, from http://www.ntsb.gov/news/press-releases/Pages/PR20140624.aspx.

Pan, X., Han, C. S., Dauber, K., & Law, K. H. (2006). Human and social behavior in computational modeling and analysis of egress. *Automation in Construction*, *15*(4), 448–461. https://doi.org/10.1016/j.autcon.2005.06.006.

Parasuraman, R., & Riley, V. (1997). Humans and automation: use, misuse, disuse, abuse. *Human Factors*, *39*(2), 230–253. https://doi.org/10.1518/001872097778543886.

Parasuraman, R., Molloy, R., & Singh, I. L. (1993). Performance consequences of automation-induced "complacency". *The International Journal of Aviation Psychology*, *3*, 1–23. https://doi.org/10.1207/s15327108ijap0301_1.

Payre, W., Cestac, J., & Delhomme, P. (2016). Fully automated driving: impact of trust and practice on manual control recovery. *Human Factors*, *58*(2), 229–241. https://doi.org/10.1177/0018720815612319.

Povyakalo, A. A., Alberdi, E., Strigini, L., & Ayton, P. (2013). How to discriminate between computer-aided and computer-hindered decisions: a case study in mammography. *Medical Decision Making*, *33*(1), 98–107. https://doi.org/10.1177/0272989X1246549.

Prakash, A., & Rogers, W. A. (2015). Why some humanoid faces are perceived more positively than others: effects of human-likeness and task. *International Journal of Social Robotics, 7*(2), 309–331. https://doi.org/10.1007/s12369-014-0269-4.

Rae, I., Takayama, L., & Mutlu, B. (2013). In-body experiences: embodiment, control, and trust in robot-mediated communication. *Proceedings of the SIGCHI Conference on Human Factors in Computing Systems* (pp. 1921–1930). ACM. https://doi.org/10.1007/s12369-014-0269-4.

Robinette, P., Liu, W., Allen, R., Howard, A., & Wagner, A. R. (2016). Overtrust of robots in emergency evacuation scenarios. *ACM/IEEE International Conference on Human–Robot Interaction (HRI)*. Christchurch, New Zealand. https://doi.org/10.1109/HRI.2016.7451740.

Robinette, P., Vela, P. A., & Howard, A. M. (2012). Information propagation applied to robot-assisted evacuation. *Robotics and Automation (ICRA), 2012 IEEE International Conference* (pp. 856–861). IEEE. https://doi.org/10.1109/ICRA.2012.6225122.

Robinette, P., Wagner, A. R., & Howard, A. (2013). Building and maintaining trust between humans and guidance robots in an emergency. *AAAI Spring Symposium, Stanford University*, (pp. 78–83). Palo Alto.

Robinette, P., Wagner, A. R., & Howard, A. (2016). Investigating human–robot trust in emergency scenarios: methodological lessons learned. In W. Lawless, R. Mittu, D. Sofge, & A. R. Wagner (Eds.), *The Intersection of Robust Intelligence (RI) and Trust in Autonomous Systems*, pp.143–166. Cham: Springer. https://doi.org/10.1007/978-1-4899-7668-0_8.

Rossi, A., Dautenhahn, K., Koay, K. L., & Walters, M. L. (2017). How the timing and magnitude of robot errors influence peoples' trust of robots in an emergency scenario. *International Conference on Social Robotics* (pp. 42–52). Springer. https://doi.org/10.1007/978-3-319-70022-9_5.

Salem, M., Lakatos, G., Amirabdollahian, F., & Dautenhahn, K. (2015). Would you trust a (faulty) robot?: Effects of error, task type and personality on human–robot cooperation and trust. *Proceedings of the Tenth Annual ACM/IEEE International Conference on Human–Robot Interaction* (pp. 141–148). Portland. http://dx.doi.org/10.1145/2696454.2696497.

Sanders, T., Oleson, K. E., Billings, D. R., Chen, J. Y., & Hancock, P. A. (2011). A model of human–robot trust: theoretical model development. *Proceedings of the Human Factors and Ergonomics Society Annual Meeting, 55*, 1432–1436. https://doi.org/10.1177/1071181311551298.

Schaefer, K. (2016). Measuring trust in human–robot interactions: development of the "trust perception scale-HRI". In R. Mittu, D. Sofge, A. Wagner, & W. Lawless (Eds.), *Robust Intelligence and Trust in Autonomous Systems* (pp. 191–218). Boston, MA: Springer. https://doi.org/10.1007/978-1-4899-7668-0_10.

Simpson, J. A. (2007). Psychological foundations of trust. *Current Directions in Psychological Science, 16*(5), 264–268. https://doi.org/10.1111/j.1467-8721.2007.00517.x.

Skitka, L. J., Mosier, K. L., & Burdick, M. (1999). Does automation bias decision-making? *International Journal of Huma–Computer Studies, 51*(5), 991–1006. https://doi.org/10.1006/ijhc.1999.0252.

Wagner, A. R. (2009). The role of trust and relationships in human–robot social interaction. Ph.D. dissertation, School of Interactive Computing, Georgia Institute of Technology, Atlanta, GA.

Wagner, A. R. (2015). Robots that stereotype: creating and using categories of people for human–robot interaction. *Journal of Human–Robot Interaction*, 4(2), 97–124. https://doi.org/10.5898/JHRI.4.2.Wagner.

Wang, Y., Humphrey, L. R., Liao, Z., & Zheng, H. (2018). Trust-based multi-robot symbolic motion planning with a human-in-the-loop. *ACM Transactions on Interactive Intelligent Systems (TiiS)*, 8(4), article 31. https://doi.org/10.1145/3213013.

Welford, A. (1972). Stress and performance. *Proceedings of the 9th Annual Conference of the Ergonomics Society of Australia and New Zealand* (pp. 1–41). https://doi.org/10.1080/00140137308924547.

Xu, A., & Dudek, G. (2015). Optimo: online probabilistic trust inference model for asymmetric human–robot collaborations. *Proceedings of the Tenth Annual ACM/IEEE International Conference on Human–Robot Interaction* (pp. 221–228). ACM. http://dx.doi.org/10.1145/2696454.2696492.

Yagoda, R. E., & Gillan, J. D. (2012). You want me to trust a ROBOT? The development of a human–robot interaction trust scale. *International Journal of Social Robotics*, 4, 235–248. https://doi.org/10.1007/s12369-012-0144-0.

Yang, X. J., Unhelkar, V. V., Li, K., & Shah, J. A. (2017). Evaluating effects of user experience and system transparency on trust in automation. *12th ACM/IEEE International Conference on Human–Robot Interaction* (pp. 408–416). IEEE. http://dx.doi.org/10.1145/2909824.3020230.

14 The neurofunctional underpinnings of interpersonal trust

Yan Wu and Frank Krueger

Introduction

Trust is among the most crucial factors in interpersonal relationships, permeating almost all domains of private and public social lives. Trust permits beneficial long-term interactions, promotes economic development, and flourishes feelings of well-being (Cook & Cooper, 2003). Outside the realm of the interpersonal domain, trust also determines how people interact with technology since the willingness of humans to rely on machines is directly affected by trust. The neuroscience research of trust has not only tremendously increased the knowledge about brain mechanisms involved in trust behavior, but also fostered the creation of trust among groups and organizations.

Due to its ubiquity, scholars from different scientific disciplines—including psychology, economics, and neuroscience—have investigated both theoretically and empirically the three loci of trust (Jones & Shah, 2016): *the trustor* (the individual rendering trust judgments), the *trustee* (the party being trusted), and the *trustor–trustee dyad* (the trustor–trustee relationship and shared characteristics). Despite differences among the various conceptions of trust—*trusting beliefs* (positive expectations of trustworthiness) (Ferrin & Dirks, 2003), *trusting intentions* (willingness to be vulnerable) (Colquitt et al., 2007), and *trusting actions* (risky behaviors indicative of trust) (Kramer & Goldman, 1995)—the identification of common psychological elements across those concepts allows formulating a working definition of this phenomenon. Trust is a decision to rely on another alongside uncertainty, in which one party (trustor) is prepared to tolerate being vulnerable to a possible betrayal based on the assumption that the decision of another party (trustee) will yield the desired benefit due to reciprocity in the future (Rousseau et al., 1998).

The levels of explanation for the framework of interpersonal trust vary from the top (behavior) to the bottom (gene). They are formed by a complex interplay between culture, nurture, and nature (Figure 14.1). At the behavioral level, the reciprocal two-person trust game allows for assessing both the propensity to trust and trust dynamics. At the psychological level, psychometric instruments admit the evaluation of the mental T-R-U-S-T components (Treachery, Reward, Uncertainty, Strategy, and Trustworthiness). At the neurofunctional level, brain imaging and brain lesions studies enable determining the domain-general large-scale brain circuits (i.e., activated regions and functional coupling) constructing the psychological components of trust. At the neurochemical level, pharmacological administration of hormones (e.g., oxytocin and testosterone) and neurotransmitters (e.g., dopamine, serotonin) modify the neural signaling pathway mechanisms involved in trust behavior. At the neurogenetic level, quantitative or molecular genetic studies illustrate a role for heritability and genetic polymorphisms (i.e., an alteration in DNA sequence on a specific locus of the gene in a given population) in explaining phenotypic variation in trust behavior.

This chapter focuses on the *neurofunctional level of trust* by introducing a neuropsychological model of interpersonal trust built on a framework incorporating psychological, economic, and neuroscience findings to integrate psychological processes (motivation, affect, and cognition) with neural mechanisms (brain networks) (for an overview about the neurobiology of trust, see Krueger, 2021). This model may be used to guide prospective transdisciplinary research into the neurofunctional underpinnings of trust, covering not only human–human trust but also human–machine trust (see Wingert & Mayer, Chapter 5).

The neurofunctional model of interpersonal trust

Experimental task in neuroscientific research of trust

Neuroscience research of trust mainly employed the two-person trust game as the workhorse to measure trust behavior, where two players—assigned to the roles of a trustor or trustee—receive an initial endowment for economic exchange (Berg et al., 1995; Camerer & Weigelt, 1988), due to its widespread use in experimental economics. First, the trustor chooses whether to transfer some part of the endowment to the trustee. The experimenter multiplies (usually triples) the transfer and passes it on to the trustee. Second, the trustee learns the trustor's decision and chooses whether to keep the money or recip-

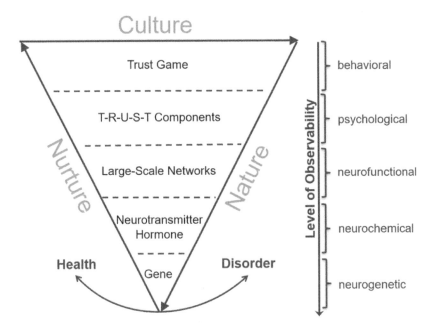

Figure 14.1   Neurofunctional networks of trust. (A) Trust framework
levels

rocate with the trustor. Finally, the trustor is informed about the trustee's decision. The trustor's transfer measures trust and the trustee's transfer measures trustworthiness. Whereas the one-shot version of the game captures trust propensity, the multi-shot version measures trust dynamics (e.g., building, maintenance, and recovery of trust). A lottery game is often used to distinguish non-social risk (gamble) from social risk (trust), in which the trustor plays with a computer (i.e., uncertainty of a random process) rather than a human partner (i.e., uncertainty of a social partner).

Psychological model of trust

Trust is a social dilemma that entails a trustor's readiness to be susceptible to the risk of betrayal (affect) in exchange for the anticipation reward (motivation) based on the expectations (cognition) of the trustee's reciprocity (Krueger & Meyer-Lindenberg, 2019). Interpersonal trust emerges through the interplay of psychological components—Treachery, Reward, Uncertainty, Strategy, and Trustworthiness (T-R-U-S-T)—associated with the mental processes of motivation, affect, and cognition. The expectation of *Reward (motiva-*

tion) confronts the risk of *Treachery* (affect) under *Uncertainty*, giving rise to the susceptibility of trust behavior. *Economic rationality* and *social rationality* (cognition) can be utilized to reduce uncertainty. Suppose trust is driven primarily by selfish motives. In that case, it involves economic rationality to gain benefits by trusting readily when self-interest is congruent with group interest (e.g., reputation establishment and stable cooperation). The trustor is incentivized to adopt a *Strategy* to benefit from the context. If social motives drive trust, it involves social rationality to contribute to the relationship's success and forming dyad bonds. The trustor is socially encouraged to appraise the trustee's *Trustworthiness* to benefit from the relationship.

Neurofunctional networks of trust

Empirical evidence exists that trust results from the interactions of psychological processes (i.e., motivation, affect, and cognition), which recruit key regions located in domain-general large-scale distributed brain circuits: *reward network* (RWN, anticipation of reward reinforcement learning), *salience network* (SAN, risk of treachery), *central-executive network* (CEN, adoption of strategy), and *default-mode network* (DMN, evaluation of trustworthiness) (Figure 14.2).

Reward network (RWN)

The *motivational system* involves the *RWN*, engaging different dopaminergic pathways to determine the *anticipated reward* and *reinforcement learning* for trusting another person. The *mesolimbic pathway* runs from the ventral tegmentum area (VTA) of the midbrain through the nucleus accumbens and olfactory tubercle in the *ventral striatum* (vSTR); the *mesocortical pathway*—the VTA to the prefrontal cortex (PFC) (including ventromedial PFC, vmPFC); and the *nigrostriatal pathway*—the substantia nigra of the midbrain to the caudate nucleus and putamen in the *dorsal striatum* (dSTR) (Ikemoto, 2010).

The *mesolimbic* and *mesocortical pathways* are typically implicated in developing *anticipation of reward* to estimate positive and negative outcomes of available choices for directing adaptive social behavior under uncertainty (Knutson & Cooper, 2005). As a critical region of the *mesolimbic pathway*, the *vSTR* signals reward motivation and promotes reinforcement learning (Montague & Berns, 2002; Ruff & Fehr, 2014).

The *nigrostriatal pathway* also engages in reward processes such as the reinforcement of memory consolidation (Wise, 2009) and action guidance (Howard et al., 2017). The *dSTR* (a main region of the nigrostriatal pathway)

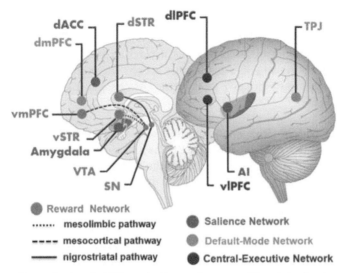

Notes: Reward network: *VTA, ventral tegmentum area; SN, substantia nigra;*
dSTR, dorsal striatum; vSTR, ventral striatum; vmPFC, ventromedial prefrontal
cortex. Salience network: *AI; Amygdala; dACC, dorsal anterior cingulate cortex.*
Default-Mode network: *TPJ, temporoparietal junction; dmPFC, dorsomedial*
prefrontal cortex. Central-Executive network: *dlPFC, dorsolateral prefrontal cortex;*
vlPFC, ventrolateral prefrontal cortex.
Source: Figure adjusted and reprinted by permission from Elsevier Ltd. (Krueger &
Meyer-Lindenberg, 2019)

Figure 14.2   Neurofunctional networks of trust. (B) Trust model brain
networks

is crucial for *interaction-based learning* when information about the trustee
is unavailable (Fouragnan et al., 2013). A ventral-dorsal arrangement of the
STR has been found to segregate the trust and feedback stages in iterated trust
games. The vSTR is consistently activated during the trust decision stage while
expecting the reward, but the dSTR is activated during the feedback stage while
learning about the trustee's reciprocity (Bellucci et al., 2017).

Salience network (SAN)

The affective system comprises aversive feelings associated with the *risk of*
treachery. It engages the SAN (including regions such as the *amygdala, ante-*
rior insula; AI; dorsal anterior cingulate cortex, dACC) involved in self-relevant
bottom-up saliency detection for social behavior regulation (Bressler & Menon,
2010).

The *amygdala* is essential for proper social functioning (Adolphs et al., 1998), as it detects the *threat of treachery* by encoding emotional salience and fostering social vigilance (Engell et al., 2007). Damage to the amygdala has been shown to promote trust, implying that it plays a role in assessing incoming social information to either boost trust actions for positive assessments or distrust decisions for negative assessments (Asscheman et al., 2020; Koscik & Tranel, 2011).

The AI encodes negative emotional states associated with unexpected events, highlighting its significant role in acting as a common currency of aversion (Namkung et al., 2017). The AI indexes the *betrayal aversion* linked to trust another person (Aimone et al., 2014), and the damage to AI leads to improper trust (Belfi et al., 2015).

The dACC is constantly involved in monitoring conflict across social and non-social domains (Bush et al., 2000). With repeated exposure to an untrustworthy partner, trustors show elevated activity in the dACC (Fett, Gromann, et al., 2014). Increased activations in the dACC were also found for trust recovery after early trust breaches (Schilke et al., 2013), suggesting the importance of this brain region in monitoring social dilemmas.

Central-executive network (CEN)

The *cognitive control system* endorses *context-based strategies* grounded in the CEN (including *dorsolateral PFC, dlPFC,* and *ventrolateral PFC, vlPFC*) linked with top-down cognitive control in guiding goal-directed behavior in changing settings (Miller & Cohen, 2001).

The dlPFC grants the cognitive capacity to eliminate uncertainty by *accounting evidence contextually* in a bottom-up manner. When no past information about the trustee is provided, the dlPFC is more activated for learning to trust a cooperative partner than for an individualistic one (Lemmers-Jansen et al., 2017). Throughout repeated interactions, it monitors contextually modified decisions, helping to improve goal-directed behavior and producing long-term benefits.

The *vlPFC* provides the cognitive capacity to diminish uncertainty by *discounting evidence contextually* in an up-bottom manner. When prior information about the trustee is provided, the vlPFC impedes the learning process of the dSTR for breaches of trust (Fouragnan et al., 2013). This region guides decisions consistent with reliable prior beliefs (Souza et al., 2009), and therefore, restrains the impulse of revenge after a breach of trust and maintains social stability (Fouragnan et al., 2013).

Default-mode network (DMN)

The *social cognition system* assesses the *relationship-based trustworthiness* located in the DMN (containing *temporoparietal junction*, TPJ, and *dorsomedial prefrontal cortex*, dmPFC). The DMN is crucially involved in identifying and representing mentalizing about others to promote cooperative decision-making (Amodio & Frith, 2006).

The TPJ is implicated in multiple social cognitive functions, involving self–other differentiation, perspective-taking, and inferences of action intentionality (Van Overwalle, 2009), making it a key site for *inferring and attributing the intentions of others* to assess trustworthiness based on the ability, benevolence, and integrity of the trustee (Mayer et al., 1995) (see also Chapter 7, Brewer et al., on cognitive-physiological theory of perceptions of trustworthiness). Trustors with a larger capacity for perspective-taking demonstrate more trust in others and substantially diminish their trust following treachery (Fett, Shergill, et al., 2014). TPJ activity increases with age when constantly trusting a cooperative partner, pointing to greater sensitivity and orientation to other people's social cues (Fett, Gromann, et al., 2014).

The dmPFC is crucial for self-referential processing and impression formation (Van Overwalle, 2009). This area participates in *inferring and attributing the traits of others* to assess trustworthiness. Greater activity in the dmPFC is detected when trustors play with a human partner than with a computer partner (McCabe et al., 2001). The dmPFC assesses a partner's trustworthiness not just through repeated encounters but also through prior information about a partner's social features, which is consistent with its involvement in assigning attributes to others to predict their decisions (Fouragnan et al., 2013).

Trust development

The neuropsychological model of trust illustrates how interpersonal trust develops over time: from calculus-based trust over knowledge-based trust to identification-based trust (Lewicki, 1995). The relationship starts with *calculus-based trust*, mainly driven by SAN (risk of treachery). Trustors meet uncertain situations and calculate the costs and benefits of entering and remaining in a trust relationship. Then, the relationship advances to *knowledge-based trust*, mostly executed by CEN (endorsement of strategy) and DMN (assessment of trustworthiness). Trustors observe and evaluate trustees' behaviors and integrate contextual information to guide trust decisions. Lastly, the relationship develops to *identification-based trust*, primarily driven by RWN (anticipation of reward). Trustors develop positive expectancies about the trustee based on mutual understanding and rewarding identification.

Summary, implications, and conclusions

The development and maintenance of trust are crucial for a harmonious society. We developed a neuropsychological model of interpersonal trust which illustrates how T-R-U-S-T components (Treachery, Reward, Uncertainty, Strategy, and Trustworthiness) involve mental processes (motivation, affect, and cognition) that employ domain-general large-scale brain networks (RWN, SAN, CEN, and DMN) at the neurofunctional levels to develop trust. This neurofunctional model of human–human trust has the potential to be extended in studying human–machine trust in dyads and groups—ranging from automated systems (e.g., assembly machines, performing a pre-defined task by following the rule-based steps in structured environments) to autonomous systems (e.g., social robots, performing a task using adaptive-based learning or artificial intelligence-based skills in unfamiliar and changing environments) (Luck et al., 2003) (see also Lyons et al., Chapter 10).

Automated systems are motiveless, so users are not concerned about being betrayed, exploited, or deceived but worried about the system's reliability and ability to perform a task as expected. Human–automation trust depends on the performance side with facets of competence and reliability, whereas human–human trust relies on a moral side with facets of sincerity, integrity, and benevolence (Lee & Moray, 1992; Malle & Ullman, 2021). Human–autonomous trust, such as in human–robot interactions, demands not only performance-based trust but also moral-based trust (Lewis et al., 2018). As robots become social companions, for example, in assisting the elderly with health needs, the risk may arise from a robot moving around and accidentally knocking the elderly to the ground (performance-based trust) or presenting incorrect information to the elderly (moral-based trust) (Broadbent et al., 2009). As social robots become more and more present within our daily lives, a question arises on whether we trust robots the same way we trust humans. It is thus worthwhile to look into neurofunctional differences of trust dynamics in interpersonal and human–agent interaction.

To conclude, against the background of an emerging transdisciplinary research field of interpersonal trust, the framework and model described here can potentially be utilized to obtain a comprehensive understanding of human–human trust and human–autonomy trust contributing to a society that is more trusting, open, and welcoming.

References

Adolphs, R., Tranel, D., & Damasio, A. R. (1998). The human amygdala in social judgment. *Nature, 393*(6684), 470–474. https://doi.org/10.1038/30982.

Aimone, J. A., Houser, D., & Weber, B. (2014). Neural signatures of betrayal aversion: an fMRI study of trust. Proceedings. *Biological Sciences, 281*(1782). https://doi.org/10.1098/rspb.2013.2127.

Amodio, D. M., & Frith, C. D. (2006). Meeting of minds: the medial frontal cortex and social cognition. *Nature Reviews Neuroscience, 7*(4), 268–277. https:// doi .org/ 10 .1038/nrn1884.

Asscheman, J. S., Deater-Deckard, K., Lauharatanahirun, N., van Lier, P. A. C., Koot, S., King-Casas, B., & Kim-Spoon, J. (2020). Associations between peer attachment and neural correlates of risk processing across adolescence. *Developmental Cognitive Neuroscience, 42*, 100772. https://doi.org/10.1016/j.dcn.2020.100772.

Belfi, A. M., Koscik, T. R., & Tranel, D. (2015). Damage to the insula is associated with abnormal interpersonal trust. *Neuropsychologia, 71*, 165–172. https:// doi .org/ 10 .1016/j.neuropsychologia.2015.04.003.

Bellucci, G., Chernyak, S. V., Goodyear, K., Eickhoff, S. B., & Krueger, F. (2017). Neural signatures of trust in reciprocity: a coordinate-based meta-analysis: neural signatures of trust in reciprocity. *Human Brain Mapping, 38*(3), 1233–1248. https://doi.org/10.1002/hbm.23451.

Berg, J., Dickhaut, J., & McCabe, K. (1995). Trust, reciprocity, and social history. *Games and Economic Behavior, 10*(1), 122–142. https://doi.org/10.1006/game.1995.1027.

Bressler, S. L., & Menon, V. (2010). Large-scale brain networks in cognition: emerging methods and principles. *Trends in Cognitive Sciences, 14*(6), 277–290. https:// doi .org/10.1016/j.tics.2010.04.004.

Broadbent, E., Stafford, R., & MacDonald, B. (2009). Acceptance of Healthcare Robots for the Older Population: Review and Future Directions. International Journal of Social Robotics, 1(4), 319–330. https://doi.org/10.1007/s12369-009-0030-6

Bush, G., Luu, P., & Posner, M. I. (2000). Cognitive and emotional influences in anterior cingulate cortex. *Trends in Cognitive Sciences, 4*(6), 215–222. https://doi.org/10.1016/s1364-6613(00)01483-2.

Camerer, C., & Weigelt, K. (1988). Experimental tests of a sequential equilibrium reputation model. *Econometrica, Econometric Society, 56*(1), 1–36.

Colquitt, J. A., Scott, B. A., & LePine, J. A. (2007). Trust, trustworthiness, and trust propensity: a meta-analytic test of their unique relationships with risk taking and job performance. *The Journal of Applied Psychology, 92*(4), 909–927. https://doi.org/10.1037/0021-9010.92.4.909.

Cook, K. S., & Cooper, R. M. (2003). Experimental studies of cooperation, trust, and social exchange, in E. Ostrom & J. Walker (eds), *Trust and Reciprocity: Interdisciplinary Lessons from Experimental Research* (pp. 209–244). New York: Russell Sage.

Engell, A. D., Haxby, J. V., & Todorov, A. (2007). Implicit trustworthiness decisions: automatic coding of face properties in the human amygdala. *Journal of Cognitive Neuroscience, 19*(9), 1508–1519. https://doi.org/10.1162/jocn.2007.19.9.1508.

Ferrin, D. L., & Dirks, K. T. (2003). The use of rewards to increase and decrease trust: mediating processes and differential effects. *Organization Science, 14*(1), 18–31. https://doi.org/10.1287/orsc.14.1.18.12809.

Fett, A.-K. J., Gromann, P. M., Giampietro, V., Shergill, S. S., & Krabbendam, L. (2014). Default distrust? An fMRI investigation of the neural development of trust and cooperation. *Social Cognitive and Affective Neuroscience, 9*(4), 395–402. https://doi.org/10.1093/scan/nss144.

Fett, A.-K. J., Shergill, S. S., Gromann, P. M., Dumontheil, I., Blakemore, S.-J., Yakub, F., & Krabbendam, L. (2014). Trust and social reciprocity in adolescence: a matter of perspective-taking. *Journal of Adolescence, 37*(2), 175–184. https://doi.org/10.1016/j.adolescence.2013.11.011.

Fouragnan, E., Chierchia, G., Greiner, S., Neveu, R., Avesani, P., & Coricelli, G. (2013). Reputational priors magnify striatal responses to violations of trust. *Journal of Neuroscience, 33*(8), 3602–3611. https://doi.org/10.1523/JNEUROSCI.3086-12.2013.

Howard, C. D., Li, H., Geddes, C. E., & Jin, X. (2017). Dynamic nigrostriatal dopamine biases action selection. *Neuron, 93*(6), 1436–1450. https://doi.org/10.1016/j.neuron.2017.02.029.

Ikemoto, S. (2010). Brain reward circuitry beyond the mesolimbic dopamine system: a neurobiological theory. *Neuroscience and Biobehavioral Reviews, 35*(2), 129–150. https://doi.org/10.1016/j.neubiorev.2010.02.001.

Jones, S. L., & Shah, P. P. (2016). Diagnosing the locus of trust: a temporal perspective for trustor, trustee, and dyadic influences on perceived trustworthiness. *The Journal of Applied Psychology, 101*(3), 392–414. https://doi.org/10.1037/apl0000041.

Knutson, B., & Cooper, J. C. (2005). Functional magnetic resonance imaging of reward prediction. *Current Opinion in Neurology, 18*(4), 411–417. https://doi.org/10.1097/01.wco.0000173463.24758.f6.

Koscik, T. R., & Tranel, D. (2011). The human amygdala is necessary for developing and expressing normal interpersonal trust. *Neuropsychologia, 49*(4), 602–611. https://doi.org/10.1016/j.neuropsychologia.2010.09.023.

Kramer, R. M., & Goldman, L. (1995). Helping the group or helping yourself? Social motives and group identity in resource dilemmas, in D. A. Schroeder (ed.), *Social Dilemmas: Perspectives on Individuals and Groups*, pp.49–67. Westport, CT: Praeger.

Krueger, F. (ed.) (2021). *The Neurobiology of Trust.* Cambridge, MA: Harvard University Press.

Krueger, F., & Meyer-Lindenberg, A. (2019). Toward a model of interpersonal trust drawn from neuroscience, psychology, and economics. *Trends in Neurosciences, 42*(2), 92–101. https://doi.org/10.1016/j.tins.2018.10.004.

Lee, J. D., & Moray, N. (1992). Operators' monitoring patterns and fault recovery in the supervisory control of a semi-automatic process. *Proceedings of the Human Factors Society Annual Meeting, 36*(15), 1143–1147. https://doi.org/10.1518/107118192786749775.

Lemmers-Jansen, I. L. J., Krabbendam, L., Veltman, D. J., & Fett, A.-K. J. (2017). Boys vs. girls: gender differences in the neural development of trust and reciprocity depend on social context. *Developmental Cognitive Neuroscience, 25*, 235–245. https://doi.org/10.1016/j.dcn.2017.02.001.

Lewicki, B. B. B. (1995). Trust in relationships: a model of development and decline, in B. B. Bunker & J. Z. Rubin, *Conflict, Cooperation, and Justice: Essays Inspired by the Work of Morton Deutsch* (pp. 133–173). Hoboken, NJ: Jossey-Bass/Wiley.

Lewis, M., Sycara, K., & Walker, P. (2018). The role of trust in human–robot interaction, in H. A. Abbass, J. Scholz, & D. J. Reid (eds), *Foundations of Trusted Autonomy* (Studies in Systems, Decision and Control, vol. 117, pp. 135–159). Cham: Springer International. https://doi.org/10.1007/978-3-319-64816-3_8.

Luck, M., D'Inverno, M., & Munroe, S. (2003). Autonomy: Variable and Generative. In H. Hexmoor, C. Castelfranchi, & R. Falcone (eds.), Agent Autonomy.Multiagent Systems, Artificial Societies, and Simulated Organizations, vol. 7, pp. 11–28). Boston, MA: Springer. https://doi.org/10.1007/978-1-4419-9198-0_2

Malle, B. F., & Ullman, D. (2021). A multidimensional conception and measure of human–robot trust. In C. S. Nam and J. B. Lyons (eds), *Trust in Human–Robot Interaction* (pp. 3–25). https://doi.org/10.1016/B978-0-12-819472-0.00001-0.

Mayer, R. C., Davis, J. H., & Schoorman, F. D. (1995). An integrative model of organizational trust. *The Academy of Management Review, 20*(3), 709–734. https://doi.org/10.2307/258792.

McCabe, K., Houser, D., Ryan, L., Smith, V., & Trouard, T. (2001). A functional imaging study of cooperation in two-person reciprocal exchange. *Proceedings of the National Academy of Sciences, 98*(20), 11832–11835. https://doi.org/10.1073/pnas.211415698.

Miller, E. K., & Cohen, J. D. (2001). An integrative theory of prefrontal cortex function. *Annual Review of Neuroscience, 24*, 167–202. https://doi.org/10.1146/annurev.neuro.24.1.167.

Montague, P. R., & Berns, G. S. (2002). Neural economics and the biological substrates of valuation. *Neuron, 36*(2), 265–284. https://doi.org/10.1016/s0896-6273(02)00974-1.

Namkung, H., Kim, S.-H., & Sawa, A. (2017). The insula: an underestimated brain area in clinical neuroscience, psychiatry, and neurology. *Trends in Neurosciences, 40*(4), 200–207. https://doi.org/10.1016/j.tins.2017.02.002.

Rousseau, D. M., Sitkin, S. B., Burt, R. S., & Camerer, C. (1998). Not so different after all: a cross-discipline view of trust. *Academy of Management Review, 23*(3), 393–404. https://doi.org/10.5465/amr.1998.926617.

Ruff, C., & Fehr, E. (2014). The neurobiology of rewards and values in social decision making. *Nature Reviews Neuroscience, 15*, 549–562. https://doi.org/10.1038/nrn3776.

Schilke, O., Reimann, M., & Cook, K. S. (2013). Effect of relationship experience on trust recovery following a breach. *Proceedings of the National Academy of Sciences of the United States of America, 110*(38), 15236–15241. https://doi.org/10.1073/pnas.1314857110.

Souza, M. J., Donohue, S. E., & Bunge, S. A. (2009). Controlled retrieval and selection of action-relevant knowledge mediated by partially overlapping regions in left ventrolateral prefrontal cortex. *NeuroImage, 46*(1), 299–307. https://doi.org/10.1016/j.neuroimage.2009.01.046.

Van Overwalle, F. (2009). Social cognition and the brain: a meta-analysis. *Human Brain Mapping, 30*(3), 829–858. https://doi.org/10.1002/hbm.20547.

Wise, R. A. (2009). Roles for nigrostriatal—not just mesocorticolimbic—dopamine in reward and addiction. *Trends in Neurosciences, 32*(10), 517–524. https://doi.org/10.1016/j.tins.2009.06.004.

15 Trust in healthcare professions' education: an interdisciplinary research agenda

Arvin Damodaran and Boaz Shulruf

Introduction: why is trust research timely and important in healthcare?

In healthcare, there are no zero risk decisions. This makes for a ripe environment for studying trust. Risks may be mitigated by following the best available medical evidence and resourcing risk management efforts, but the risks remain. The patient–clinician trust relationship remains central to accepting care: to know one's physician is an expert with their best interests at heart may help an individual to accept treatments with known toxicities or alter the habits of a lifetime.

As medical treatments have expanded and outcomes improved, healthcare delivery has become team-based care with healthcare professionals increasingly interdependent. No modern clinician practices as an island. A patient consenting to care in these environments may have weighed up the personal risks and benefits, but at some point, is deciding to trust, not just in their chosen physician, but in systems of healthcare provision. While outcomes are improving, the healthcare system overall is increasingly complex, expensive, and depersonalized. Modern healthcare interactions are less about relationships with a trusted physician, and more characterized by teams of health professionals, high technologies, and offsite management systems. Internationally, this increased complexity has been mirrored by a gradual erosion in the public trust of the medical profession since the mid-twentieth century (Blendon, Benson, & Hero, 2014). Although trust is clearly a key concept in the therapeutic relationship, the public's trust in healthcare as a profession has been under threat and addressing this is increasingly recognized as a priority (Baker, 2020).

In teaching hospitals and clinics, each stakeholder (i.e., patients, clinicians, and healthcare students), will each have their own perspective on risk. As the Mayer, Davis, and Schoorman Model of Trust (Mayer, Davis, & Schoorman, 1995) suggests, each individual appraises their own risks and vulnerabilities in order to make a decision to trust. Patients are explicitly vulnerable and need to make a trust decision. Trust decisions are constantly being made by healthcare professionals as well: doctors choosing a course of management that relies on a patient's compliance, healthcare professionals referring to a trusted colleague when help is needed, or clinicians making the decision to delegate a patient care task to a junior staff member (Schoorman, Mayer, & Davis, 2016). Each decision carries risks for the clinician. For healthcare students and professionals, not being trusted can limit opportunities to learn and develop (Bannister et al., 2018) and not feeling trusted can impair professional performance and sense of self-efficacy (Damodaran, Jones, & Shulruf, 2021). Even the act of asking for help carries a perception of risk for junior doctors (Kennedy et al., 2009).

This chapter has been written as a broad introduction to researchers familiar with basic qualitative and quantitative methodologies and wishing to explore trust in healthcare settings, particularly teaching hospitals. We describe how data on trust in healthcare and clinical teaching can be gathered and the sorts of methods commonly employed. We discuss the importance of clarifying areas of interest and the relationships one may wish to study, and then use a trust and risk model to explore a selection of these healthcare relationships. We then review some research pointing to ways in which interpersonal trust relationships in healthcare and healthcare education may be maintained and improved, as well as some of the pitfalls of relying on trust. In the last section, we signpost some emerging areas of interest and bring in some of this book's cutting-edge chapters to hopefully spark ideas in the reader on promising interdisciplinary trust research trajectories.

Data collection methods in healthcare settings

Investigators will have differing foci and agendas. A medical administrator may be most interested in outcomes with a focus on systems and quality improvement; an education provider may be most concerned about the learner experience; a public health researcher may wish to improve healthcare outcomes for an underserved community. Is the researcher most concerned about the patient, practitioner, learner, teacher, clinical team, or health systems (Damodaran, 2018)? In a quantitative study, researchers should recognize these potential sources of bias, and declare any conflicts of interest. In qualitative research, clearly stating the position of the researcher within the work, termed "reflexivity," is a key aspect in judging the trustworthiness of the research report (Dodgson, 2019).

In healthcare research, sources of information may come from prospective trials, observational cohort studies, retrospective collection of patient outcome data, reviews of patient hospital records, or by collecting opinions in interviews or surveys. Patient outcome data may either be subjective (e.g., satisfaction with the last episode of healthcare); or objective, reflecting actual health outcomes, for instance blood sugar levels in diabetes, cardiac events in hypertension, waiting times, length of hospital stay or infection rates.

Data is most commonly acquired from surveys which can be linked to patient satisfaction or outcome data. Birkhäuer et al.'s (2017) meta-analysis includes data from 47 studies involving almost 35,000 participants in a variety of international settings. This study provides high-level evidence that trust in the healthcare professional positively impacts on subjective patient outcomes, with better patient satisfaction, compliance, symptom control, and quality of life. Although objective measures were not found to be significantly affected by trust, the authors indicated prospective studies would be warranted.

Whilst the vast majority of data on trust in healthcare has been survey-based, qualitative and mixed methods lend themselves well to examination of complex constructs like "trust."

Stakeholders and relationships in healthcare and healthcare professions' education

The researcher will need to determine the subjects, setting, and phenomena of interest. Who are the stakeholders and what is their relationship? At the basic therapeutic level, the participants in a clinical relationship include the patient and their treating clinician. With a wider lens, many others will be involved, all experiencing their own personal sets of risks and vulnerabilities. Family members, carers, healthcare team members, students, medical administrators, and other patients will all be impacted by each clinical decision. The complexity of healthcare relationships reaches its zenith in teaching hospitals, where a roll-call of stakeholders includes patients and their families, junior to senior doctors, nurses and allied healthcare workers, students, administrative and support staff, even before considering intersecting organizations such as community health providers, academic, professional, indemnity and accrediting bodies, and government.

Figure 15.1 identifies some of these stakeholders at interpersonal, organizational, and government levels. Although incomplete, this can be seen as a road map for trust researchers, identifying bidirectional relationships characterized by trust and risk.

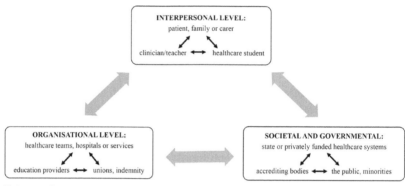

Note: Arrows represent bidirectional relationships
Source: Adapted from Damodaran, Shulruf, & Jones (2017)

Figure 15.1   A stakeholder relationship map for healthcare and healthcare education in teaching hospitals

Perspective and directionality are important. Patients' trust in doctors is different from doctors' trust in patients. Nurses will have a different perspective. The researcher will have to decide if they want to study many relationships that relate to a particular phenomenon or dive deeply into the viewpoint of one stakeholder in a trust relationship. In medicine, risk and context are also critical. What works for an emergency department may not be suitable for operating theaters or a palliative care setting.

In the following "perspectives" sections we elaborate on a selection of these. We look at the perspectives of the patient, the clinician, and the healthcare student or trainee in a teaching hospital setting. Within the limits of this chapter, sections are restricted to narrative highlights; however, we hope to pique the interest of potential trust researchers who may further explore one of these or another relationship.

Perspective of the patient

Patient's trust in their healthcare professional

Trust in one's doctor is an unsurprisingly perennial theme in the medical literature. Validated "trust in the physician" scales date back many decades (Anderson & Dedrick, 1990). In practice, "presence and connection" may be key ways in which physicians can project a sense of benevolence to the patient, particularly early in the therapeutic relationship (Zulman et al., 2020). Zulman et al. observed clinical interactions, interviewed professionals in relationship-centric fields including medicine, then ran a Delphi process to establish an expert consensus to identify trainable behaviors that facilitate this connection. Their top five identified behaviors included preparing for the interaction with that individual patient, listening intently and completely, agreeing with patients on their health priorities, connecting with the patient's story, and lastly exploring the patient's emotional cues. In an ethnographic study of patients new to an HIV clinic, behaviors that built trust in a new healthcare provider included providing reassurance, explaining test results, avoiding judgmental behaviors, and agreeing on treatment goals and preferences (Dang et al., 2017).

How then do we purposefully build trustworthy physicians? An important step is understanding the factors contributing to a perception of trustworthiness. As discussed in the first chapter of this book, the triad of benevolence, integrity, and ability (Mayer et al., 1995) has been well studied and is an attractive and parsimonious formulation (Mayer & Norman, 2004). In medical education other such formulations have been developed, such as integrity, competence, agency, reliability, and humility (Ten Cate & Chen, 2020).

Gupta et al. lists curricular inclusions purposefully designed to build public trust including "training in health equity, cultural humility and competence, shared decision-making, patient advocacy and safety and quality of care" (Gupta et al., 2020, p.981).

Public's trust in their healthcare organizations

Empirical research suggests that trust in one's doctor is a separate but complementary construct to trust in healthcare organizations (Zheng, Hui, & Yang, 2017). Public trust in healthcare, or "the degree of confidence that he or she will be adequately treated when requiring health care," is widely variable between countries but generally relates to healthcare spending (Zhao, Zhao, &

Cleary, 2019, p.132). Outliers to this relationship include the U.S.A. at the high end of expenditure per capita, and China and the Philippines at the low end.

International surveys demonstrate that trust in individual physicians or in healthcare systems can either align or diverge. The latter is increasingly evident in the U.S.A. where changing arrangements for healthcare financing (Mechanic & Schlesinger, 1996) have led to concerns about advertising, misinformation, leadership, transparency, consumerism, and affordability (Baker, 2020).

Trust in healthcare systems also varies for minorities. In the U.S.A., those from low-income families are significantly less trusting of physicians and are less satisfied with their medical care, a finding not necessarily seen in other countries (Blendon et al., 2014). Other survey studies corroborate that levels of trust in the healthcare provider differ by minority (Guffey & Yang, 2012), socioeconomic, gender, or age groups (Miller et al., 2015).

Evaluations of trust can be convincing to healthcare providers who can mobilize around increasing public trust, for instance ensuring that patients' trust in the organization is routinely measured and valued by leaders and boards, with concerns acted upon and patients having a role in designing solutions (Lee, McGlynn, & Safran, 2019).

Perspective of the clinician

Clinician's trust in their patients

Should physicians believe their patients? There is strong evidence that patients with chronic illnesses often fail to take prescribed medications over longer periods. Across the board one might expect about 50 percent of patients to drop off their prescribed treatment after a year. Indeed, rates of non-adherence range from 30 percent to 80 percent whether the chronic illness is hypertension, diabetes, HIV, gout, rheumatoid arthritis, or osteoporosis (Brown et al., 2016; Kelly et al., 2020).

Ironically, trust in the doctor may be the principal determinant of treatment compliance. Studies in different patient groups (Brown et al., 2016) demonstrate that compliance is complex and multifactorial with non-adherence so endemic it should perhaps be deemed human nature. Nevertheless, when deciding to comply with treatment, patients rank "trust in the doctor" an overwhelming first, ahead of the doctor's knowledge, or medication efficacy, side-effects, or cost (Kelly et al., 2020). The authors proposed that compliance could best be achieved by training doctors in trust.

Supervisors' trust in their trainee: trust as an assessment

A patient on the neurology ward needs to have a lumbar puncture performed. I could delegate this task to the intern, only a year out of medical school. She needs the experience; I am busy, but I am also responsible for the patient's care. So, do I trust her with this clinical task, with the risks this entails to the patient, the hospital, the intern, and to myself? This sort of loaded decision is a daily task of clinical teachers who need to balance patient care risks with developing their junior staff.

In 2005, Olle ten Cate proposed that "entrustment" to perform certain clinical tasks could be utilized as a workplace-based assessment (Ten Cate, 2006). He termed these "Entrustable Professional Activities" (EPAs), in the process adding the word "entrustment" to the medical education lexicon. EPAs have gone on to influence health education curricula around the world, for instance becoming the prescribed method of ensuring that all American medical students are able to carry out a selection of important clinical duties on grad-uation (AAMC, 2014).

A key to operationalizing trust as a workplace-based assessment has been the development of scales for levels of trust (Chen, Van Den Broek, & Ten Cate, 2015). Supervision scales have generally employed some version of the follow-ing: (1) only trusted to observe or practice in simulation; (2) trusted to perform task with direct supervision; (3) trusted to perform task with supervisor close by; (4) trusted to perform task with supervisor contactable if needed; and (5) trusted to perform task independently. Scales have been adapted for specific contexts such as undergraduate training (Chen et al., 2015).

To be trusted in the workplace presumes all the requisite competencies, and the ability to perform as needed in workplace conditions; but more than this, to be trusted is a judgment that the trainee's *future* unsupervised actions will be correct. Indeed, "trusted" can be argued to sit atop the hierarchy of possible workplace-based assessments (Ten Cate et al., 2021).

Perspective of the student/trainee

Trainees' trust in their supervisors

While not asking for help may endanger a patient, asking for help may entail risk to the trainee. Asking for help exposes deficits in knowledge or practice and exposes the student or trainee to potential criticism (Abruzzo, Sklar, & McMahon, 2019). As a student, if I ask for help, would I be criticized, or have further clinical learning opportunities limited? Kennedy et al. demonstrated that the decision for a trainee to reach out for clinical support was not just predicated on the clinical issue but modified by a perception of the supervisor's approachability and availability as well as a desire to maintain their own professional credibility (Kennedy et al., 2009).

The risks of not being trusted as a student/trainee

Furthermore, it appears that this apprehension is accurate. In an ethnographic study involving hundreds of hours watching interactions in a paediatric emergency department, Bannister et al. (2018) reported that medical and nursing staff limited a student's clinical experiences if the student was not trusted. Of course, student trustworthiness alone was not the only consideration: availability of supervision, judgment that the clinical circumstances were correct, physical constraints, and patient consent were among other factors identified.

Are there unintended consequences of relying on trust in medical education or other workplace teaching and training? The authors interviewed junior and senior doctors that participate in teaching, to identify some of the unintended consequences and potential pitfalls of relying on trust in clinical teaching and supervision (Damodaran et al., 2021). Trust was certainly valued by junior and senior doctors, bringing with it more clinical learning opportunities and better clinical team efficiency. Losing trust, on the other hand, created more work for other clinical team members and limited the student or trainee's opportunities for independent practice. Participants also noted an impact on well-being and sense of professional self-efficacy: feeling trusted improved motivation and performance, while not feeling trusted made it harder to feel confident and able. Furthermore, single breaches of trust, perhaps unrecognized by the learner, such as failing to perform a delegated task, withholding information, or leaving before the work was done, could have a profound and irreparable impact on trust.

Given these findings, we identified several potential pitfalls for the learner in clinical teaching environments. These included the potential for bias in trust decision-making, asymmetry of trust development and failure, and lastly what we referred to as sidelining. These pitfalls are consistent with phenomena described in other contexts. Unconscious bias is now well recognized to permeate the healthcare professions, leading to differences in hiring and promotion (Marcelin et al., 2019). The asymmetry of trust principle has also been well established, in that in undecided individuals, negative information is much more influencing than positive information (Poortinga & Pidgeon, 2004). Sidelining, pedagogically related to the phenomena of "learner neglect" (Buery-Joyner et al., 2019), occurs when a less-trusted student or trainee is not asked to perform clinical tasks and is therefore denied learning and development opportunities.

Trust and healthcare research directions, and cross-cutting interdisciplinary themes

Trust research directions within healthcare

There are many intriguing angles to explore and expand on in further research into trust and risk in healthcare education. Consideration of relationships between individuals and organizations, or between healthcare organizations (as suggested by Figure 15.1) may be productive.

While we have taken the perspectives of the patient, the clinician, and the learner to frame the discussion above, there are many other perspectives a researcher might take as their topic of interest within healthcare. One might start with a patient population of interest, particularly if there is a perception of inequity, for instance Guffey and Yang's (2012) study of African Americans' trust in doctors.

Alternatively, since many disciplines make up the healthcare team, looking at how trust and risk affect each discipline's workplace relationships would be another promising approach, as taken by Lundh et al. in Occupational Therapy (Lundh, Palmgren, & Stenfors, 2019) or Kong with Aboriginal health staff (Kong et al., 2020).

Addressing a phenomenon of interest would be another approach, for instance patients' non-adherence to prescribed medications, as examined by Kelly et al. (2020) or Rydenfält et al.'s (2012) analysis of trust between health professions in the operating theater.

In all of these settings, linking of trust interventions to patient outcomes will provide more robust data.

Trust research directions combining healthcare with other fields

In addition to relationships within healthcare, the exciting premise of this book is that interdisciplinary collisions may spark interesting and useful research trajectories. These intersections are innumerable, with many of the experts in this book presenting work where the intersections are overt, fascinating, and important. We briefly discuss three of these below.

Brewer et al. (Chapter 7) reflect on anticipatory thinking. Prospective decision-making rings true in the risk assessment a patient needs to make in order to trust a healthcare team to investigate their concerns or when a supervisor delegates a clinical task. How could a model of anticipatory thinking help us with help seeking or patient compliance? Anticipatory thinking is linked to the conceptualization of "trust" sitting atop Miller's pyramid of workplace-based assessment as proposed by Ten Cate et al. (2021), specifically because it is a judgment about future performance, rather than observation of current performance.

Wise et al. (Chapter 12) explore trust between the police and public, examining the reciprocal directions of the more visible trust relationship. Beyond adherence to therapy, can physicians trust their patients? Similarly, can organizations trust their staff in healthcare? In what ways can this trust be broken, and what are the consequences? Other professions may also benefit from the thinking and research that has gone into healthcare education in workplace-based assessments, in particular EPAs. We suspect EPAs may be a very useful way to train professionals in other fields with public-facing roles.

Lyons et al. (Chapter 10) note that intelligent machines are gaining in utility and autonomous capability, raising the prospect of human–autonomy teams. Humans may ultimately utilize an AI system as a valued addition to the healthcare team with potential to improve efficiency and clinical decision-making. This is consistent with Brewer et al.'s (Chapter 7) formulation of trust in that the trustor is human, but the subject of trust may be a human, or some combination of humans, animals, intelligent systems, or "abstract systems with fuzzy boundaries" such as government. What will be the characteristics of the healthcare team of the future, and how can we ensure their trustworthiness?

Conclusion

Healthcare and the healthcare profession's education take place in high-stakes clinical environments where trust is required by patients and all stakeholders to manage the risks and complexity. This chapter is intended to demonstrate that healthcare is an exciting and important environment in which to research trust, whether the researcher comes from within healthcare or can bring in perspectives from other fields.

References

AAMC (2014). Association of American Medical Colleges core entrustable professional activities for entering residency curriculum developers' guide. Retrieved from https:// members .aamc .org/ eweb/ upload/ Core %20EPA %20Curriculum %20Dev %20Guide.pdf

Abruzzo, D., Sklar, D., & McMahon, G. (2019). Improving trust between learners and teachers in medicine. *Academic Medicine, 94*(2), 147–150.

Anderson, L. A., & Dedrick, R. F. (1990). Development of the trust in physician scale: a measure to assess interpersonal trust in patient–physician relationships. *Psychological Reports, 67*(3_suppl), 1091–1100. https://doi.org/10.2466/pr0.1990.67 .3f.1091.

Baker, D. W. (2020). Trust in health care in the time of COVID-19. *JAMA: The Journal of the American Medical Association, 324*(23), 2373–2375. https://doi.org/10.1001/ jama.2020.23343.

Bannister, S. L., Dolson, M. S., Lingard, L., & Keegan, D. A. (2018). Not just trust: factors influencing learners' attempts to perform technical skills on real patients. *Medical Education, 52*(6), 605–619. https://doi.org/10.1111/medu.13522.

Birkhäuer, J., Gaab, J., Kossowsky, J., Hasler, S., Krummenacher, P., Werner, C., & Gerger, H. (2017). Trust in the health care professional and health outcome: a meta-analysis. *PLoS One, 12*(2), e0170988. https://doi.org/10.1371/journal.pone .0170988.

Blendon, R. J., Benson, J. M., & Hero, J. O. (2014). Public trust in physicians: U.S. medicine in international perspective. *New England Journal of Medicine, 371*(17), 1570–1572. https://doi.org/10.1056/NEJMp1407373.

Brown, M. T., Bussell, J., Dutta, S., Davis, K., Strong, S., & Mathew, S. (2016). Medication adherence: truth and consequences. *The American Journal of the Medical Sciences, 251*(4), 387–399. https://doi.org/10.1016/j.amjms.2016.01.010.

Buery-Joyner, S. D., Ryan, M. S., Santen, S. A., Borda, A., Webb, T., & Cheifetz, C. (2019). Beyond mistreatment: learner neglect in the clinical teaching environment. *Medical Teacher, 41*(8), 949–955. https://doi.org/10.1080/0142159X.2019.1602254.

Chen, H. C., Van Den Broek, W. E. S., & Ten Cate, O. (2015). The case for use of entrustable professional activities in undergraduate medical education. *Academic Medicine, 90*(4), 431–436. https://doi.org/10.1097/ACM.0000000000000586.

Damodaran, A. (2018). Time to say goodbye to learner-centredness? *Medical Education, 52*(1), 7–9. https://doi.org/10.1111/medu.13486.

Damodaran, A., Jones, P., & Shulruf, B. (2021). Trust and risk pitfalls in medical education: a qualitative study of clinical teachers. *Medical Teacher, 43*(11), 1309–1316.
https://doi.org/10.1080/0142159X.2021.1944613.

Damodaran, A., Shulruf, B., & Jones, P. (2017). Trust and risk: a model for medical
education. *Medical Education, 51*(9), 892–902. https://doi.org/10.1111/medu.13339.

Dang, B. N., Westbrook, R. A., Njue, S. M., & Giordano, T. P. (2017). Building trust
and rapport early in the new doctor–patient relationship: a longitudinal qualitative
study. *BMC Medical Education, 17*(1), article 32. https://doi.org/10.1186/s12909-017
-0868-5.

Dodgson, J. E. (2019). Reflexivity in qualitative research. *Journal of Human Lactation,
35*(2), 220–222. https://doi.org/10.1177/0890334419830990.

Guffey, T., & Yang, P. Q. (2012). Trust in doctors: are African Americans less likely to
trust their doctors than white Americans? *SAGE Open, 2*(4), 1–8. https://doi.org/10
.1177/2158244012466092.

Gupta, N., Thiele, C. M., Daum, J. I., Egbert, L. K., Chiang, J. S., Kilgore, A. E. J.,
& Johnson, C. D. (2020). Building patient–physician trust: a medical student
perspective. *Academic Medicine, 95*(7), 980–983. https:// doi .org/ 10 .1097/ acm
.0000000000003201.

Kelly, A., Tymms, K., Wit, M. d., Bartlett, S. J., Cross, M., Dawson, T., ... & Tong, A.
(2020). Patient and caregiver priorities for medication adherence in gout, osteoporosis, and rheumatoid arthritis: nominal group technique. *Arthritis Care and Research,
72*(10), 1410–1419. https://doi.org/10.1002/acr.24032.

Kennedy, T. J. T., Regehr, G., Baker, G. R., & Lingard, L. (2009). Preserving professional
credibility: grounded theory study of medical trainees' requests for clinical support.
British Medical Journal, 338, b128. https://doi.org/10.1136/bmj.b128.

Kong, A. C., Sousa, M. S., Ramjan, L., Dickson, M., Goulding, J., Gwynne, K., ... &
George, A. (2020). "Got to build that trust": the perspectives and experiences of
Aboriginal health staff on maternal oral health. *International Journal for Equity in
Health, 19*(1), article 187. https://doi.org/10.1186/s12939-020-01301-5.

Lee, T. H., McGlynn, E. A., & Safran, D. G. (2019). A framework for increasing trust
between patients and the organizations that care for them. *JAMA: The Journal of the
American Medical Association, 321*(6), 539–540. https://doi.org/10.1001/jama.2018
.19186.

Lundh, P., Palmgren, P. J., & Stenfors, T. (2019). Perceptions about trust: a phenom-
enographic study of clinical supervisors in occupational therapy. *BMC Medical
Education, 19*(1), article 404. https://doi.org/10.1186/s12909-019-1850-1.

Marcelin, J. R., Siraj, D. S., Victor, R., Kotadia, S., & Maldonado, Y. A. (2019). The
impact of unconscious bias in healthcare: how to recognize and mitigate it. *The
Journal of Infectious Diseases, 220*(Supplement_2), S62–S73. https://doi.org/10.1093/
infdis/jiz214.

Mayer, R. C., Davis, J. H., & Schoorman, F. D. (1995). An integration model of organizational trust. *Academy of Management Review, 20*(3), 709–734.

Mayer, R. C., & Norman, P. M. (2004). Exploring attributes of trustworthiness: a class-
room exercise. *Journal of Management Education, 28*, 224–249.

Mechanic, D., & Schlesinger, M. (1996). The impact of managed care on patients' trust
in medical care and their physicians. *JAMA: The Journal of the American Medical
Association, 275*(21), 1693–1697.

Miller, M. K., Ellis, K. L., Randell, K. A., & Lantos, J. (2015). Do adolescents trust
doctors? *Journal of Adolescent Health, 56*(2, Supplement 1), S71. https://doi.org/10
.1016/j.jadohealth.2014.10.142.

Poortinga, W., & Pidgeon, N. F. (2004). Trust, the asymmetry principle, and the role of prior beliefs. *Risk Analysis, 24*(6), 1475–1486. https://doi.org/10.1111/j.0272-4332 .2004.00543.x.

Rydenfält, C., Johansson, G., Larsson, P. A., Åkerman, K., & Odenrick, P. (2012). Social structures in the operating theatre: how contradicting rationalities and trust affect work. *Journal of Advanced Nursing, 68*(4), 783–795.

Schoorman, D. F., Mayer, R. C., & Davis, J. H. (2016). Empowerment in veterinary clinics: the role of trust in delegation. *Journal of Trust Research, 6*(1), 76–90. https:// doi.org/10.1080/21515581.2016.1153479.

Ten Cate, O. (2006). Trust, competence, and the supervisor's role in postgraduate training. *British Medical Journal, 333*(7571), 748–751. https://doi.org/10.1136/bmj .38938.407569.94.

Ten Cate, O., Carraccio, C., Damodaran, A., Gofton, W., Hamstra, S. J., Hart, D. E., ... & Schumacher, D. J. (2021). Entrustment decision making: extending Miller's pyramid. *Academic Medicine, 96*(2), 199–204. https://doi.org/10.1097/ACM .0000000000003800.

Ten Cate, O., & Chen, H. C. (2020). The ingredients of a rich entrustment decision. *Medical Teacher, 42*(12), 1413–1420. https://doi.org/10.1080/0142159X.2020 .1817348.

Zhao, D., Zhao, H., & Cleary, P. D. (2019). International variations in trust in health care systems. *International Journal of Health Planning and Management, 34*(1), 130–139. https://doi.org/10.1002/hpm.2597.

Zheng, S., Hui, S. F., & Yang, Z. (2017). Hospital trust or doctor trust? A fuzzy analysis of trust in the health care setting. *Journal of Business Research, 78*, 217–225. https:// doi.org/10.1016/j.jbusres.2016.12.017.

Zulman, D. M., Haverfield, M. C., Shaw, J. G., Brown-Johnson, C. G., Schwartz, R., Tierney, A. A., ... & Verghese, A. (2020). Practices to foster physician presence and connection with patients in the clinical encounter. *JAMA: The Journal of the American Medical Association, 323*(1), 70–81. https://doi.org/10.1001/jama.2019 .19003.

16 Religion and trust: basic theory and trust in organizations

Jasmine Cervantes, Alexandra S. Wormley, Jordan W. Moon, Sydney Tran, and Adam B. Cohen

Religion and trust: basic theory and trust in organizations

Within and outside of religious institutions, religion plays an important role in promoting trust, and these effects are likely to be complex and multifaceted. Religion could promote trust if people bond over shared religious beliefs and practices within the workplace. In contrast, opposing religions can create deep-seated mistrust, which can undermine trust within a given organization. Further, breaches of trust may be particularly damaging when perpetuated by religious organizations themselves, especially one's own religious organization.

Here, we discuss how religion can promote or diminish trust, and consider what happens when a major religious institution betrays the trust of its adherents. We do so in four main sections: situating religion within ideas about trust in organizations; reviewing basic theory and research about religion and trust; discussing the Catholic Church pedophilia scandal and effects on trust; and future directions.

Situating our contribution

Here, we argue that social context, such as religious diversity, has an impact on trust (Mayer et al., 2019). Perhaps more important than the actual religious diversity of the organization would be how employees treat each other, and how their organization cultivates trust or mistrust. Employees' trust is likely strongly affected by their organization's approach to religious diversity and inclusion. Accordingly, individual behavior and human resource practices that meaningfully respect religious diversity can build trust. Similarly, conflict management that is mindful of religious diversity and inclusion fosters trust in employees with religious affiliation. Broadly speaking, then, it is the goal of this chapter to raise attention to the effects of religious diversity on trust within organizations, stimulate thinking about research in this area, and raise research questions to offer concrete avenues of topics for scholars to take on this challenge.

While we think it is important for "human" reasons to respect religion, having nothing to do with profit per se, we also point out that there could be tangible benefits to taking religion seriously. Perceived organizational support, which reflects how benevolent an employee believes the employer is toward them, has been found to relate to employees' bonds to the organization in ways that are similar to trust (King & Williamson, 2005; Polley et al., 2005). Strikingly, companies that have more pro-diversity policies are more innovative than companies whose policies are less diversity-friendly (Mayer et al., 2018). We are confident this would occur in the context of religion, too, but more research is needed.

Certainly, religious diversity could have positive *and* negative effects on trust in organizations (Héliot et al., 2020). For one, an organization making allowances for religion (e.g., giving time off for holidays, accommodating religious diets) would have positive effects on trust and perceived organizational support. But what would happen if some accommodations were made, and others were not (sending the message "my holiday is important enough to accommodate, but yours is not")? Further, religion sometimes has far-reaching effects beyond the religious domain on how people act and communicate. There might be more subtle effects, such as in word choice, which could lead to tension within the group. Imagine a (Jewish) manager says one day during a meeting "Well folks I need to end a little early today because I have to go *daven minchah maariv* for my father's *yahrtzeit*." Does one offer congratulations or sympathy? Suddenly, people who understand Yiddish have bonded with the manager and solidified an ingroup, while outsiders now feel that they are not as connected to the manager or each other. Indeed, diversity within the workplace has been associated with negative effects in team performance (Horwitz & Horwitz, 2007; Kunze et al., 2013; Nielsen et al., 2018) without careful implementation and effective conflict management.

Though it is well recognized that employees are multicultural (e.g., country of origin, ethnicity), research on *religious cultural diversity*, especially the implications that it carries for trust in organizations, has lagged behind that of certain other areas. As one example, in the Academy of Management, the Spirituality and Religion interest group ranks as second smallest out of 25 divisions and interest groups with only 626 members (as of July 31, 2018: 3.1 percent). Similarly, the diversity recruitment websites of Fortune 500 mention religious diversity far less than other cultural identities, such as race or sexuality (Wormley & Cohen, n.d.). Though attitudes toward diversity seem to be increasingly positive, religion is not an apparent part of the broader definition of diversity yet.

In sum, when considering factors which play into trust within organizations, religious diversity is a critical, yet underappreciated, factor. Religious diversity can foster positive trust within organizations through increasing perceived organizational support of members. However, organizations should use caution when implementing these policies to minimize conflict and increase appreciation for religious differences.

Theory and research on religion and trust

Given how important religious identities are to people (Cohen, 2015), religious conflict in organizations may seem inevitable. How is employee trust affected for Jewish employees if the company cafeteria does not offer *kosher* meal options? Do Catholics feel isolated if on Fridays during Lent there are no appropriate meal choices? Might a woman wearing a *hijab* be less trusted by her colleagues? Surprisingly, the answers to these questions may be more complex—and optimistic—than intuition and current theory might suggest.

First, we review a major theory in psychology about why religion promotes trust (which it seems to do, at least sometimes; Tan & Vogel, 2008). "Big Gods" theory proposed that fear of supernatural punishment makes a person act in trustworthy ways, out of fear of divine retribution (Norenzayan et al., 2016). The notion here is that people who fear an all-knowing, morally concerned, punishing God will behave in more trustworthy ways, and that these kinds of fears enabled human societies to grow past the point at which individuals could reliably monitor each other's behavior directly. Consistent with this idea, people do seem to behave in more prosocial ways when the notion of supernatural punishment is made salient (Shariff & Norenzayan, 2007). Still, we note that there are other ways in which religion can promote trustworthy behavior: if people believe that God is benevolent, they might want to emulate God and in turn become more generous (Johnson et al., 2015).

The empirical picture about why religion promotes trustworthy behavior is somewhat mixed, and it is possible that either of those explanations (fear of God, emulation of nice God) might enhance perceived trustworthiness. Some experimental work has directly tested these hypotheses. Hall and colleagues (2015) presented participants with Facebook-like profiles that varied in whether the target person said they believed in a forgiving or punishing God; performed various costly acts related to religion (such as giving to religious charity or not, adhering to religious food restrictions or not); and shared a religion or differed in religious affiliation from the subjects (Muslim vs. Christian). To their surprise, Hall and colleagues found that the target's espoused beliefs (forgiving vs. punishing God) and religious affiliation (Christian vs. Muslim) made no difference in rated trustworthiness. Instead, participants trusted target people more if they performed costly behaviors consistent with their religion—regardless of which religion it was. Further work by Ellis et al. (2018) points to such results being driven by ascription of *integrity* on the part of people who do costly things to adhere to their religions, more so than ascriptions of benevolence or ability (Mayer et al., 1995). So, organizations can perhaps breathe a sigh of relief; if their policies seem to reflect integrity with regard to religion, that might increase perceived organizational support, and trust.

Another line of work has tried to examine what it is about religious people that makes them viewed as more trustworthy—is it their assumed belief, or do people make inferences about religious people's behavior? One important aspect of most religions is a preference for monogamous, high-investment relationships and opposition to sexual promiscuity (Moon et al., 2019; Weeden et al., 2008). Because such lifestyles are associated with less impulsive behavior, one possibility is that people perceive religious individuals as trustworthy partly because they are family oriented. Moon et al. (2018) tested this hypothesis in three studies. In one study, participants rated religious (vs. nonreligious) individuals as more trustworthy, and this effect was statistically mediated by their perceived "committed reproductive strategy" (i.e., their commitment to family and marriage). Another study experimentally manipulated both the targets' religion as well as "dating preferences" (i.e., whether they wanted to get married and have a family, or whether they preferred to stay uncommitted and "play the field"). When participants had access to targets' dating preferences, the target's religion no longer had a significant influence on ratings of trustworthiness. Instead, participants tended to see the committed (vs. uncommitted) targets as more trustworthy, regardless of whether they were religious.

This line of research suggests that, although religion can make a person be perceived as higher in trustworthiness, nonreligious individuals are not necessarily doomed to perpetual distrust by colleagues—to the extent that co-workers know something about their nonreligious colleagues' lifestyles, families, and so on. These factors might help override the distrust people often feel toward the nonreligious. Furthermore, the effects of religion on trust may be even more nuanced, as people sometimes express positive stereotypes about atheists, such as that they are more likely to be open-minded, scientific, or fun (Moon et al., 2021). In turn, it could be that people trust atheists in domains related to scientific rigor or rely on them to incorporate novel evidence into their opinions. These ideas remain to be directly tested in organizations.

A case study in religion and organizational betrayals of trust

What happens when religious organizations betray that trust? Clergy-perpetrated sexual abuse is an unfortunately common phenomena across religious groups; a 2008 survey of 3,559 individuals found that 3 percent of religious women had experienced sexual abuse at the hands of a minister, priest, rabbi, or other religious leader (Chaves & Garland, 2009). Here, we focus on sexual abuse within the Catholic Church, as a case study, and Cervantes' (2020) ongoing research on how this affects trust at different levels: trust in the priest, the Pope, and the Catholic Church, as well as the trust components of each: ability, benevolence, integrity (ABI).

An early study on trust in response to clergy-perpetrated sexual abuse found that survivors have decreased trust in their priest, the Catholic Church, and God (Rossetti, 1995). A later study by Easton et al. (2019) confirmed these findings with a larger sample. Oftentimes, the survivor's family also experiences a dramatic shift in worldview, leading them to doubt themselves, their faith, or even the victim (Wind et al., 2008). Even beyond those who were directly impacted by sexual abuse, non-abused Catholics felt hurt by the betrayal of church leaders in the crisis (Kline et al., 2008). Further, trust in the Catholic Church as an institution decreased in response to the ongoing sexual abuse scandal. Interestingly, increased media exposure was found to increase trust in the Catholic Church and its ability to prevent assault going forward (Mancini & Shields, 2014). Still, the hurt caused by sexual abuse within the Church has effects outside of the Church. Survivors report a decrease in trust not only in religious figures, but trust in men and trust in authority figures, including therapists (Pargament et al., 2008). Additionally, survivors may feel betrayed by those who they feel did not protect them from the abuse, such as parents or other congregation members (Finkelhor et al., 1986).

Not only are the victims subject to the authoritative power dynamic of the clerical position, the actions of the clergymen are viewed as a representation of God, which encourages secrecy and obedience (Fogler et al., 2008). Given that priests are seen as *alter Christus*, or another Christ, these betrayals call spiritual interactions into question (Guido, 2008). In sum, this suggests that the betrayal of religious figures and organizations carries additional weight.

While these studies demonstrate shifts in attitudes Catholics may have due to sexual abuse, little research has been conducted to examine attitudes Catholics have about different levels of the Catholic organization and its link to trust-based religious behavior, such as one's willingness to confess, in relation to perceptions of the sexual abuse scandal. Consequently, Cervantes (2020) investigated the trust dynamics that lead a Catholic to confess by looking at variables such as perception of the sex abuse within the Catholic Church, trust in the religious institution (Catholic Church), trust in religious individuals (priests and the Pope), and the perceptions of these figures' respective ABI.

As one can imagine, the concept of trust is much more complicated than it may seem as characteristics of the trustee can influence trust within a relationship. Previous literature has suggested that trust is reliant on a variety of character-istics; however, ability (influential skill and competency), benevolence (selfless goodwill toward the trustor, specifically), and integrity (strong moral princi-ples) are cited most often as playing a role in how people trust (Mayer et al., 1995; see also Mayer & Mayer, Chapter 1).

Furthermore, characteristics of the trustor, particularly one's propensity to trust, also influences trust within a relationship (Mayer et al., 1995). Propensity to trust is a relatively stable individual difference that describes the likelihood that one will trust across situations or contexts (Rotter, 1971). In other words, some people are naturally more likely to trust than others.

Ultimately, the goal of the Cervantes study was to determine whether Catholics' perceptions of the sexual abuse within the Church were related to their willing-ness to engage in confession. Confession is an act linked to trust as it requires a high degree of vulnerability from the confessant since they share confidential and personal information. The Cervantes study examined ratings of the ABI of the Catholic Church, the Pope, and one's priest, as predictors of willingness to confess. Analyses controlled for intrinsic religiosity, which is an approach to religion in which religion serves as its own incentive (Gorsuch & McPherson, 1989). Those with high intrinsic religiosity are more likely to engage in religious activities, such as confession, due to their desire to follow religious teachings and maintain a strong relationship with God.

This study of 117 Catholic undergraduates (F = 89, M = 28; 50 percent Latinx, 42 percent Caucasian, 4 percent Asian, 4 percent Other) found that there was no relation between trust in different levels of organization and a participant's willingness to confess. Issues related to the willingness to confess measurement may be responsible for the lack of connection between these two variables.

Although the original goal of this study did not come to fruition, other findings within this study had intriguing implications. Negative perceptions of sexual abuse within the Catholic Church predicted significantly lower perceived benevolence and integrity for the priest, Catholic Church, and Pope. On the contrary, there was a significant relationship between sexual abuse perception and ability for the Pope and priest, but not the Catholic Church. This could suggest that participants may make distinctions between an organization and an individual when considering one's ability in relation to their perception of sexual abuse within the Catholic Church.

Surprisingly, ability and benevolence significantly predicted trust in the priest and the Pope only. Trust in the Catholic Church, on the other hand, was significantly predicted by integrity and benevolence. This suggests that different facets of trustworthiness are considered when one chooses to trust an individual or an institution (see Schilke et al., Chapter 9).

While this study focused on one sexual abuse scandal in one religious community, it could provide an interesting model for future research on religion and trust. While we do not have extreme confidence in certain nuances of the findings, we see this study as a good model for research about the effects of religious betrayal on trust, and especially appreciate the notion that trust dynamics could differ at different levels of the organization (priest, Pope, the Church) (see Long & Sitkin, Chapter 6). Finally, it was a positive feature of this study that it examined a trust-based dependent variable that involved risk. Further research is needed to determine whether betrayal within a spiritual context carries more weight than that in a secular context.

Future directions for healing mistrust in organizations

The research on religious institutions and (dis)trust provide some clues as to how institutions can right their wrongs and restore trust. Selznick (1996) clarified the link between an institution and trust when he noted that two essential features of institutions were "character and competence." These two features possibly resemble Mayer et al.'s (1995) ability and integrity features of trustworthiness—thus providing insight about targets for restoring trust if perceptions of an institution's character or competence have been challenged. But there are other factors that trust/distrust research has identified that also help illuminate the underlying problems and point to potential practical solutions.

Regarding the Catholic Church scandal, survivors of sexual abuse seem to desire and benefit from therapy that directly addresses religion because of Catholicism's role in shaping a survivor's identity and the spiritual manipulation component involved in sexual abuse (Collins et al., 2014; Pargament et al., 2008). Pargament et al. (2008) suggest normalizing "spiritual dialogue" in therapy with survivors because it allows them to express another facet of the abuse, beyond the psychological, social, or physical aspects. On an institutional level, the Catholic Church attempted to restore trust with the public by replacing previously complicit leadership, implementing a code of conduct, and creating a culture of accountability (Senander, 2017). However, there may need to be a structural shift in the perception of the idea of anger and forgiveness in Catholic tradition to better serve the victims of sexual abuse. Unlike the idealized perspective that survivors should just forgive the perpetrator, building a community of restorative justice is important because it gives the actual victim a choice in their healing process, and encourages the perpetrator to truly realize the consequences of their actions (Pope & Geske, 2019).

Needed research on religion and trust in organizations

We close with some ideas about needed research. Here are some questions we are interested in and feel are important issues to promote research on trust within religious groups and organizations, an important and relatively neglected area:

- Are the organizational cultures of companies more aligned with the values, beliefs, and norms of some religions than others? If so, what are the implications of this for company performance and employee wellness?
- Which dimensions of religion (i.e., beliefs, behaviors) are particularly important for managers' focus?
- Which dimensions of religion do management's attention or inattention to have the greatest impact on employees' trust in the manager or in the company? How much does attention to these issues affect ability to recruit employees, or to retain employees?
- Do religious organizations differ from secular ones in the effects of their betrayal?

- Do experiences of sexual abuse vary across religious organizations? Is this a function of different organizational structures? Are such dynamics similar or different than in secular organizations, and why?

Finally, we recognize that the experience of religion within organizations is incredibly diverse. Monotheists will have different perspectives than polytheists; atheists will be different from theists; Southern Baptists will be different from Catholics. However, research to date has typically focused on a narrow set of religious experiences—typically that of white Protestants. Thus, to fully understand the role of religion in organizational trust, we must undertake the monumental task of understanding how the myriad of religious groups differently interact with organizations to promote trust.

In closing, religion is a critical area for work organizational trust, and though we think there has been some important research done, more research is needed to understand how to maximize perceived organizational support and interpersonal trust, cohesion, and employee well-being.

References

Cervantes, J. (2020). "Forgive Me Father": a look at trust engagement within Catholic confession [Honors Thesis]. Arizona State University.

Chaves, M., & Garland, D. (2009). The prevalence of clergy sexual advances toward adults in their congregations. *Journal for the Scientific Study of Religion*, 48(4), 817–824. https://doi.org/10.1111/j.1468-5906.2009.01482.x.

Cohen, A. B. (2015). Religion's profound influences on psychology: morality, intergroup relations, self-construal, and enculturation. *Current Directions in Psychological Science*, 24(1), 77–82. https://doi.org/10.1177/0963721414553265.

Collins, C. M., O'Neill-Arana, M. R., Fontes, L. A., & Ossege, J. M. (2014). Catholicism and childhood sexual abuse: women's coping and psychotherapy. *Journal of Child Sexual Abuse*, 23(5), 519–537. https://doi.org/10.1080/10538712.2014.918071.

Easton, S. D., Leone-Sheehan, D. M., & O'Leary, P. J. (2019). "I will never know the person who I could have become": perceived changes in self-identity among adult survivors of clergy-perpetrated sexual abuse. *Journal of Interpersonal Violence*, 34(6), 1139–1162. https://doi.org/10.1177/0886260516650966.

Ellis, D. M., Blais, C., Northover, S. B., Cohen, A. B., Mayer, R. C., Wingert, K., Corman, S. R., & Brewer, G. A. (2018). How religious (and nonreligious) behaviors influence trustworthiness: the role of integrity. Unpublished manuscript.

Finkelhor, D., Araji, S., Brown, L., Browne, A., Peters, S. D., & Wyatt, G. E. (1986). *A Sourcebook on Child Sexual Abuse*. Thousand Oaks, CA: Sage.

Fogler, J. M., Shipherd, J. C., Rowe, E., Jensen, J., & Clarke, S. (2008). A theoretical foundation for understanding clergy-perpetrated sexual abuse. *Journal of Child Sexual Abuse*, 17(3–4), 301–328. https://doi.org/10.1080/10538710802329874.

Gorsuch, R. L., & McPherson, S. E. (1989). Intrinsic/extrinsic measurement: I/E-revised and single-item scales. *Journal for the Scientific Study of Religion, 28*(3), 348–354.

Guido, J. J. (2008). A unique betrayal: clergy sexual abuse in the context of the Catholic religious tradition. *Journal of Child Sexual Abuse, 17*(3–4), 255–269. https://doi.org/10.1080/10538710802329775.

Hall, D. L., Cohen, A. B., Meyer, K. K., Varley, A. H., & Brewer, G. A. (2015). Costly signaling increases trust, even across religious affiliations. *Psychological Science, 26*(9), 1368–1376. https://doi.org/10.1177/0956797615576473.

Héliot, Y., Gleibs, I. H., Coyle, A., Rousseau, D. M., & Rojon, C. (2020). Religious identity in the workplace: a systematic review, research agenda, and practical implications. *Human Resource Management, 59*(2), 153–173.

Horwitz, S. K., & Horwitz, I. B. (2007). The effects of team diversity on team outcomes: a meta-analytic review of team demography. *Journal of Management, 33*(6), 987–1015. https://doi.org/10.1177/0149206307308587.

Johnson, K. A., Okun, M. A., & Cohen, A. B. (2015). The mind of the Lord: measuring authoritarian and benevolent God representations. *Psychology of Religion and Spirituality, 7*(3), 227–238.

King, J. E., & Williamson, I. O. (2005). Workplace religious expression, religiosity and job satisfaction: clarifying a relationship. *Journal of Management, Spirituality & Religion, 2*(2), 173–198.

Kline, P. M., McMackin, R., & Lezotte, E. (2008). The impact of the clergy abuse scandal on parish communities. *Journal of Child Sexual Abuse, 17*(3–4), 290–300. https://doi.org/10.1080/10538710802329817.

Kunze, F., Boehm, S., & Bruch, H. (2013). Organizational performance consequences of age diversity: inspecting the role of diversity-friendly HR policies and top managers' negative age stereotypes. *Journal of Management Studies, 50*(3), 413–442. https://doi.org/10.1111/joms.12016.

Mancini, C., & Shields, R. T. (2014). Notes on a (sex crime) scandal: the impact of media coverage of sexual abuse in the Catholic Church on public opinion. *Journal of Criminal Justice, 42*(2), 221–232. https://doi.org/10.1016/j.jcrimjus.2013.06.006.

Mayer, R. C., Cohen, A. B., & Barbour, J. E. (2019, August). Building organizational trust: towards understanding religious cultural diversity. In N. Gillespie (facilitator), Innovative Research Directions in Organizational Trust. Symposium presented at Academy of Management Conference, Boston.

Mayer, R. C., Davis, J. H., & Schoorman, F. D. (1995). An integrative model of organizational trust. *The Academy of Management Review, 20*(3), 709–734. https://doi.org/10.2307/258792.

Mayer, R. C., Warr, R. S., & Zhao, J. (2018). Do pro-diversity policies improve corporate innovation? *Financial Management, 47*(3), 617–650.

Moon, J. W., Krems, J. A., & Cohen, A. B. (2018). Religious people are trusted because they are viewed as slow life-history strategists. *Psychological Science, 29*(6), 947–960. https://doi.org/10.1177/0956797617753606.

Moon, J. W., Krems, J. A., & Cohen, A. B. (2021). Is there anything good about atheists? Exploring positive and negative stereotypes of the religious and nonreligious. *Social Psychological and Personality Science, 12*(8), 1505–1516.

Moon, J. W., Krems, J. A., Cohen, A. B., & Kenrick, D. T. (2019). Is nothing sacred? Religion, sex, and reproductive strategies. *Current Directions in Psychological Science, 28*(4), 361–365. https://doi.org/10.1177/0963721419838242.

Nielsen, M. W., Bloch, C. W., & Schiebinger, L. (2018). Making gender diversity work for scientific discovery and innovation. *Nature Human Behaviour, 2*(10), 726–734. https://doi.org/10.1038/s41562-018-0433-1.

Norenzayan, A., Shariff, A. F., Gervais, W. M., Willard, A. K., McNamara, R. A., Slingerland, E., & Henrich, J. (2016). The cultural evolution of prosocial religions. *Behavioral and Brain Sciences, 39*, e1. https://doi.org/10.1017/S0140525X14001356.

Pargament, K. I., Murray-Swank, N. A., & Mahoney, A. (2008). Problem and solution: the spiritual dimension of clergy sexual abuse and its impact on survivors. *Journal of Child Sexual Abuse, 17*(3–4), 397–420. https://doi.org/10.1080/10538710802330187.

Polley, D., Vora, J., & SubbaNarasimha, P. N. (2005). Paying the devil his due: limits and liabilities of workplace spirituality. *International Journal of Organizational Analysis, 13*(1), 50–62.

Pope, S. J., & Geske, J. P. (2019). Anger, forgiveness, and restorative justice in light of clerical sexual abuse and its cover-up. *Theological Studies, 80*(3), 611–631.

Rossetti, S. J. (1995). The impact of child sexual abuse on attitudes toward God and the Catholic Church. *Child Abuse & Neglect, 19*(12), 1469–1481. https://doi.org/10.1016/0145-2134(95)00100-1.

Rotter, J. B. (1971). Generalized expectancies for interpersonal trust. *American Psychologist, 26*(5), 443–452.

Selznick, P. (1996). Institutionalism "old" and "new". *Administrative Science Quarterly, 41*(2), 270–277.

Senander, A. (2017). Beyond scandal: creating a culture of accountability in the Catholic Church. *Journal of Business Ethics, 146*(4), 859–867.

Shariff, A. F., & Norenzayan, A. (2007). God is watching you: priming God concepts increases prosocial behavior in an anonymous economic game. *Psychological Science, 18*(9), 803–809. https://doi.org/10.1111/j.1467-9280.2007.01983.x.

Tan, J. H. W., & Vogel, C. (2008). Religion and trust: an experimental study. *Journal of Economic Psychology, 29*(6), 832–848. https://doi.org/10.1016/j.joep.2008.03.002.

Weeden, J., Cohen, A. B., & Kenrick, D. T. (2008). Religious attendance as reproductive support. *Evolution and Human Behavior, 29*(5), 327–334. https://doi.org/10.1016/j.evolhumbehav.2008.03.004.

Wind, L. H., Sullivan, J. M., & Levins, D. J. (2008). Survivors' perspectives on the impact of clergy sexual abuse on families of origin. *Journal of Child Sexual Abuse, 17*(3–4), 238–254.

Wormley, A. S., Rios, K., & Cohen, A. B. (n.d.). Conceptualizing diversity in the Fortune 500. Unpublished manuscript.

17 The complex social network web of entrepreneurial trust

James H. Davis

Risk is at the very core of entrepreneurship (Knight, 1921; Drucker, 1970). Everyone associated with a new venture risks losing something. Entrepreneurs risk personal savings, reputation, and employment stability; investors risk losing their investment in a deal; employees risk a return on their labor; customers risk purchasing a product or service that may not deliver the promised value for the price. Unfortunately, many of these parties will have poor returns on their investment in an entrepreneurial venture because the failure rate of entrepreneurs is incredibly high. The U.S. Small Business Administration reports that only half of new businesses survive at least five years.

Risk is also at the core of trust (Mayer, Davis, & Schoorman, 1995) and research on trust in entrepreneurship. The willingness of investors, employees, customers, suppliers, and others to be vulnerable to an entrepreneur and to take risk in the relationship is absolutely essential to the success of the venture. Given the incredibly high failure rate of entrepreneurs, why would any party make themselves vulnerable to—i.e., trust—an entrepreneur and his/her products? Yet, if the entrepreneur is unable to gain the trust of others the venture cannot succeed. Trust is arguably one of the most essential factors determining the success of the entrepreneur.

The purpose of this chapter is to examine trust and the entrepreneur. I begin with a discussion of trust in entrepreneurship and what makes it different than in other contexts. While a growing stream of research has emerged to investigate trust in entrepreneurship, a number of unanswered questions remain. This chapter aims to suggest promising questions for future research by examining critical areas of trust in a few relationships in an entrepreneur's social network. This is done by examining how different types of partnerships and the motivations of the entrepreneur may affect trust. Research examining "swift" trust is reviewed, as well as the complex decision social networks make when investing capital. By the close of this chapter, I hope that the reader will see avenues for future research on trust in entrepreneurship that may help risk management improve the probability of venture success.

Trust in entrepreneurship

Successful entrepreneurship requires a strong social network that provides resources the entrepreneur lacks (Pollack, Barr, & Hanson, 2017; Greve & Salaff, 2003). A failure to acquire labor, customers, capital, skills, mentoring, and so on will lead to the failure of the venture. Entrepreneurs must develop trust in a complex web of social relationships if the new venture has any chance of success. The successful acquisition of resources within a social network has been called a form of social capital in the literature (Burt, 1992; Gabbay & Leenders, 1999). Each party in the social network has the power and influence that their resources provide, and they risk losing that power and those resources in a social exchange with an entrepreneur. The integration of the literatures of trust and social capital in entrepreneurship has not been done and would be an interesting avenue of future research.

In many cases, the level of experience with the entrepreneur that those from whom the entrepreneur needs trust is quite limited. Given the dearth of experience they have, any information a trustor can gain about the entrepreneur's trustworthiness dimensions is likely to loom large. As a consequence, small and seemingly unrelated matters can undermine the development of their trust in the entrepreneur. While this is true in any trust relationship, what differentiates this challenge for the entrepreneur is that the entrepreneur must garner a great deal of trust quickly, so there can be no room for missteps on the entrepreneur's part.

Government regulation, laws, and rules may help mitigate some risk in an entrepreneurial relationship and make risk-taking in the relationship easier; however, trust is still necessary. Research has shown that legalistic remedies for trust are not effective (Sitkin & Roth, 1993). The relationship between exogenous control and trust will be demonstrated throughout this chapter as another avenue for potential scholarly investigation.

The risk that players within a social network who are dealing with an entrepreneurial venture take depends upon the stage of the deal and their tacit knowledge in the venture. The deal and the entrepreneur bring intellectual property, sweat equity, and personal investment to the venture. Owners of resources within the social network risk wealth and reputation within the investment community. The vulnerability and the risk entrepreneurs and investors take in the relationship is managed in part by the valuation of the venture determined through negotiation between the two parties. The outcome of negotiations between owners of resources and the entrepreneur evolves with the venture and reflects how trust develops within entrepreneurial relationships. Very little research has been done to examine the dynamics of trust within this negotiation, and how it affects the relationship going forward with the deal. What are the best practices from the negotiations literature that can be applied to trust development in entrepreneurship?

A description of trust between the entrepreneur and two critical social network stakeholders, along with potential avenues of research involving them, follows. I will begin with a discussion of employees and describe how trust is established and managed with them. The types and stages of investment are then examined to show how the drivers, risk, and nature of trust evolve with the venture.

Employees

The ability of an entrepreneur to attract employees to his/her venture has become a measure of performance (Brush & Vanderwerf, 1992). To be successful an entrepreneur must attract employees who can add real value to the venture. In the very early stages of an entrepreneurial venture, the deal may be judged by others in the social network by the quality of employees attracted to the deal. The perceived ability of the entrepreneur and the venture increases with the addition of high-quality employees. If ability, benevolence, and/or integrity are in doubt within the network, bringing employees into the deal who have strong reputations in the industry may increase social network perceptions of the entrepreneur.

In the early stages of a deal based upon tacit technology, how does an unknown entrepreneur gain the trust necessary to attract employees that will bring real value to the venture? A recent theoretical study by Moser, Tumasjan, and Welpe (2017) employed psychological contract theory and legitimacy theory and argued that the employee's entrepreneurial-mindedness explained their motivation. In essence, entrepreneurs attract entrepreneurially oriented employees. They also argued the venture and entrepreneur's attractiveness, identity, and legitimacy in terms of trustworthiness, credibility, and reliability are critical to recruiting high-quality employees. While their study and others (e.g., Ryan, 2012) describe trust as essential to hiring talent, they do not explicitly explain *how* perceptions of trust and its antecedents are formed by potential employees when no real relationship exists.

As will be described in the investors section below, potential employees may build their perceptions of trust based on signals from other parties in the entrepreneur's social network who are engaged in the venture (Williamson, 2000). Moser et al. (2017) argued that such signaling can increase start-up legitimacy (Navis & Glynn, 2011). Regarding trust, if a potential employee has knowledge of other employees, investors, or companies and executives who have engaged with the entrepreneur and the new venture whom he/she trusts, they are more likely to trust the entrepreneur they do not really know. In short, if party A trusts party B, and party B trusts party C, then party A will also trust party C. An interesting avenue for future research in employee trust is determining how this signaling of values works. What antecedents of trust can be communicated most effectively through others' evaluation?

If second-order trust is not possible and there are no market signals, the risk new employee faces may be very high. The terms of employment and trust, the balance between risk and reward, must be negotiated to the satisfaction of both the entrepreneur and the employee to achieve the correct balance for employee risk-taking in a relationship with the entrepreneur. The only power the entrepreneur has in this case is ownership. To mitigate the risk the employee candidate faces, the entrepreneur must share ownership in the form of equity with the employee: the higher the risk, the greater the equity that must be shared. Entrepreneurially minded employees (Moser et al., 2017) are more willing to accept this form of risk management. If the entrepreneur is greedy or does not trust the employee's ability, benevolence, or integrity, he/she will not risk equity and will not successfully hire the talent. As with any negotiation, as described above, research is needed to understand how this works. Which of the three factors is most important? How does this change as the venture ages and grows? More research is needed to determine how the terms of employment change as a result of employee perceptions of ability, benevolence, and integrity.

Investors

To successfully grow their venture, entrepreneurs must garner trust from investors or the venture will not reach its full potential. A number of studies have shown that investor trust in the entrepreneur is among the top investment criteria for their investment decision (Bammens & Collewaert, 2014; Sudeck, 2006; Van Osnabrugge & Robinson, 2000). While this research points to the importance of angel investor trust, it fails to capture the evolution of how trust and the relative importance of its antecedents change as ventures move through the various stages and types of investment.

Procuring outside funding is very difficult for entrepreneurs when they and their offering are unknown to the market, the investment community, and the industry. Securing investment becomes essential as the venture outgrows the ability of the entrepreneur to fund venture development and growth. Later investment stage entrepreneurs are better known, and the risks with them better understood. In later stages not only is the ability of the entrepreneur much more certain, but perceptions of integrity and benevolence have had time to develop. Future research must investigate how investors within the entrepreneur's social network approach risk and trust, and how they morph as the venture moves through the investment stages: pre-seed, seed, series A, B, and C. A brief description of how trust differs in each of these stages follows.

Pre-seed funding

Pre-seed funding is the earliest form of finance for a new venture. At this stage the entrepreneur has a feel for what they would like to do, but the business model may not be fully formed, the technology may still need development, and the idea needs market vetting. At pre-seed stage there may not even be paying customers. This stage is much too risky for most investors in the typical entrepreneur's network. They will not trust the entrepreneur at this stage because they are often unknown, and they lack start-up experience. Still, they are in desperate need of resources for their venture's launch. Seed funding is arguably the most difficult capital to raise. At this stage, entrepreneurs typically depend upon the generosity of family and friends, as well as their own financial resources. Even though friends and family may not be familiar with the deal, they know the entrepreneur and are willing to invest funds based upon their relationship and their perception of the entrepreneur's benevolence and integrity. Their perceptions of the entrepreneur's ability in this particular deal may grow, but very early on their investment appears to often be based upon their knowledge/perception that the entrepreneur would never do anything to purposefully hurt them (benevolence) and they will adhere to values they find mutually acceptable (integrity). This form of funding may keep the venture alive, but it is typically not enough to grow the deal. Research is needed to test the trust antecedent perceptions. Do benevolence and integrity drive pre-seed funding? Does the relative importance of ability, benevolence, and integrity evolve as suggested here?

As mentioned in Mayer and Mayer (Chapter 1), the trusting party's propensity to trust can carry their risk-taking in the relationship with the entrepreneur to a degree where perceptions of the entrepreneur's ability, benevolence, and integrity have yet to develop. It is interesting to find that there are geographic pockets of high entrepreneurial activity. It is plausible that propensity to trust is higher in some geographic areas than in others. This is another area where research is needed.

Seed round funding

Seed round funding typically involves venture equity and investors from outside the entrepreneur's social network. By this stage the initial business model (seed) is formed and ready to launch. Seed funds are needed to get the venture off the ground. Investment helps the entrepreneur go to market and develop the product. Angels and very select venture funds are common at this stage of investment. While research has demonstrated, as described above, the importance of trust at this stage, more is needed to understand how it is formed. The venture is still young, and investors may lack reliable knowledge of the deal and the trustworthiness of the entrepreneur. They may perform due diligence on the entrepreneur, the venture, and its market potential, but there is still a great deal of uncertainty and risk.

For the entrepreneur, relationships within his/her social network develop painfully slowly. Suppliers are too slow providing the materials needed for production. Investors take too long making the investment in the venture. Distributors take too long deciding to distribute their products. It can be argued that the time delays are due to the fact that members of the social network have little or no interpersonal history on which to build trust and engage in commerce. How can trust develop more quickly without necessary collaboration so that the venture can move forward?

Meyerson, Weick and Kramer (1996) developed the concept of "swift trust" to explain how trust emerges in uncertain situations where parties don't know each other well. Swift trust is based upon roles played, categories, trusting pre-dispositions, shadow of the past and shadow of the future, active engagement, and "as if" behavior (Kroeger, Racko, & Burchell, 2020). In each of these situations the trusting party extends trust to the particular entrepreneur based on their propensity to trust and upon similar situations, companies, and people. Swift trust in essence is learned behavior based more upon the trusting party's experience than upon their perceptions of the entrepreneur. As they engage with the entrepreneur trustworthiness perceptions will develop, but initially they must make a judgment based upon previous experience and propensity to trust (Long & Sitkin, Chapter 6). The trust may not be in the entrepreneur seeking the funds per se, but is because of the history, opinion, and background of the investor and/or his/her advisors. If the entrepreneur/venture compares favorably with the investor's positive experiences and history they will be trusted, and investment will be made. If the comparison is unfavorable the investment will not occur. Still, the venture is very risky, and a large equity stake may be expected in exchange for investment.

Swift trust depends more upon the trusting party's prior experience, correctly or incorrectly applied to the entrepreneur. The predisposition makes it so the investor is slow or refuses to engage with entrepreneurs with particular backgrounds, characteristics, or ideas, regardless of the current deal. Alternatively, it could make it so that the deal is worthy of resources simply because the entrepreneur has a particular characteristic or comes from a certain geographical area. The trusting party generalizes from their background and trusts based on the presumption that all entrepreneurs who attended that school have ability and from that region integrity. Swift trust can unfairly bias the social network in favor of or against a deal.

Much more research is needed on how swift trust is related to the antecedents of trust in an entrepreneurial context. Which of the antecedents is most affected by previous experience? If an investor experienced broken trust as a result of an integrity or benevolence violation, does that affect other "swift" venture trusts more than an ability violation? Is swift trust simply a form of propensity to trust from the Mayer et al. (1995) model? How the idea of swift trust fits into literature would be a major contribution.

Series A, B, C funding, and beyond

Series A and beyond funds are needed to grow the venture by increasing the market share and growing revenue. The seed/venture has taken root by this juncture and a market presence has been established. This and later rounds (series A, B, C) of investment rely upon an established track record based upon venture performance and returns in earlier rounds. It is more likely that investors can have perceptions of the entrepreneur/venture's ability, benevolence, and integrity based upon the company's track record. The entrepreneur/venture team has or has not demonstrated their ability. If perceptions of the entrepreneur's ability are low, investment will occur with a change in venture leadership. If the deal can be done by a single investor, they use their perceptions of the entrepreneur/venture, negotiate an acceptable level of equity to balance the risks that will be taken in the relationship, and make a decision whether to invest in the venture.

In most situations the money needed for series A funding can be substantial, running into the millions of dollars for a technology deal. The capital needed for series A financing often requires investment from several venture capital firms—a syndicate. The role of the lead investor in an investment syndicate is critical to a venture. The entrepreneur may soon learn that not all money is good money. He/she must carefully choose a firm that is respected and trusted within the social network. Other firms may not know the entrepreneur or the deal but may know the lead venture capitalist. Trust from other firms may be in the lead investor and their judgment, more than in the entrepreneur and the deal. The selection of lead investor by the entrepreneur is critical because other investors are attracted to a deal in which a trusted lead investor with a strong history of trustworthiness to other venture capitalists is involved. In this case the trust is more in the lead investor than the entrepreneur and the venture. Other firms trust the entrepreneur simply because of the level of trust the lead venture capitalist places in him/her. *This creates a complex web of trust based upon the relationships outside of those with the entrepreneur.* This is trust based upon the trust of the judgments of other investors. Research is needed to understand how trust works within a syndicate. Since venture capitalists represent a group of fund investors, the performance of investments is critical. To that end, is trust based mainly upon ability the only factor that matters? Venture capitalists are often called "vulture capitalists" because they lack benevolence and integrity. How does trust work among venture capitalists who are driven for performance and returns?

A study by Sorenson and Stuart (2008) examined syndicate partnerships in venture capital networks and argued that trust is essential because of the "distant" ties between investment partners and the entrepreneur/target company. They argued that the perceptions venture capitalists have from their own experience and/or perceptions reported from *trusted* affiliates affect both the selection of partners and the investment in the venture. Sorenson and Stuart (2008) found that the probability of forming a distant relationship increases in settings where trust already exists with other investors. What is needed is research that explains how the factors that drive trust develop in distant, risky relationships where trust is not as strong. As argued above, one could hypothesize that ability initially drives the deal, and perceptions of benevolence and integrity may take longer to develop.

The lead investor of a venture capitalist syndicate often requires the entrepreneur and venture to be geographically close, and s/he engages regularly in the day-to-day operations of the company and decisions of the entrepreneur. As a result, other investors' trust in the lead investor in the syndicate is critical. Sorenson and Stuart (2001) argued that a trusted investment syndicate within a geographically and industry-diverse market allows investment in attractive, non-local opportunities. Each venture capitalist represents a pool of investors, and perceptions of *their* ability, benevolence, and integrity of members of that pool is at risk. Too much is at stake for their own trustworthiness to fail in a risky deal. One could easily argue that the important trust here is between investors and the lead venture capitalist who manages the entrepreneur and the deal. Research is needed to explain the complex web of trust and its relative importance, lead investor relationship with the venture/entrepreneur, members of the investment syndicate and the lead investor, and syndicate members and the entrepreneur.

A great deal of research discusses the importance of reciprocation and repeated exchange for building trust (e.g., Blau, 1964; Sorenson & Stuart, 2008), but more is needed in the entrepreneurial context. At this stage of the venture a new element is required in the venture business plan: milestones. Milestones form a critical way in which unacquainted partners (lead investor, syndicate members, and entrepreneur) can initiate substantial exchanges to build trust. In each round of funding beginning with series A, the entrepreneur lays out the track record of the deal and how each round of funding has achieved milestones to advance the valuation of the company. Achieving performance milestones is critically important for the development of trust. The ability (capability to meet milestone) and integrity (honesty of the investment) of the entrepreneur and lead investor is judged with every milestone. Venture capitalist syndicate members hold the entrepreneur and lead investor to these targets; their trust and future engagement in this and future deals is at stake. If the entrepreneur and lead investor cannot meet milestones their trustworthiness is questioned, it may result in the replacement of the leader of the entrepreneurial venture by the lead investor. How do the perceptions of risk and the trust antecedents develop with milestones? Do all investors need a sense of all three trustworthiness factors? Are the perceptions different for the lead investor and the entrepreneur? Research using social exchange theory (Blau, 1964), particularized trust (Schilke et al., Chapter 9), and effectuation (Sarasvathy, 2008) may help explain how trust and its antecedents develop in this context.

Ventures seeking investment for later rounds (series B, C, and beyond) have typically moved beyond the tipping point, and are seeking mass market success (Sinek, 2011). Investments in these latter stages are used for talent acquisition, logistical development, sales, and support. The average capital needed for later rounds may run into the tens of millions of dollars. By the later stages the venture depends upon a management team, and venture capitalists have typically replaced the founding entrepreneur with professional management (Ewens & Marx, 2018). Trust by these stages is between investors in the social network as described above and the professional leadership of the venture itself. Later round trust is based upon the investor's perceptions of the ability, benevolence, and integrity of professional management. By this stage the company typically has an established record of success, the investment risk is lower, and as a result, the company must give up much less equity for the investments made. By round C very risk-averse investors like investment banks, private equity firms, and hedge funds begin to provide financing for the company. The pool of investors knows that a liquidity event such as an initial public offering or acquisition is close. When that happens, investors realize the return on their investments. It can be argued that trust becomes less and less necessary as, from pre-seed to series C and beyond, perceptions are replaced by knowledge and more certainty. Research is also needed to determine if there is a point at which investor perceptions of ability, benevolence, and integrity are no longer needed in a deal. Finally, research must determine how trust and investment in a deal change when investors install their own professional management in place of entrepreneurs.

Throughout the investment process, trust evolves as risk and experience change. Research is needed to examine both the evolution and the complex web of players involved in investment relationships. Research must examine the tradeoffs with equity dispersion and how lead investor and strength of *trust within the syndicate* mitigate the uncertainty in perceptions of the entrepreneur's ability, benevolence, and integrity. Those tradeoffs incentivize investors in the social network to take risks in the relationship and trust the entrepreneur.

Conclusion

Trust is arguably one of the most essential factors in entrepreneurship. While the stream of research examining trust in the entrepreneurial context is growing, there is much left to do. I hope that the discussion in this chapter will serve as a call for additional research focused on understanding trust within this web of relationships.

References

Bammens, Y., & Collewaert, V. (2014). Trust between entrepreneurs and angel investors: exploring positive and negative implications for venture performance assessments. *Journal of Management*, 40(7), 1980–2008.

Blau, P. (1964) *Exchange and Power in Social Life*. New York: Wiley.

Brush, C. G., & Vanderwerf, P. A. (1992). A comparison of methods and sources for obtaining estimates of new venture performance. *Journal of Business Venturing*, 7(2), 157–170.

Burt, R. S. (1992). *Structural Holes: The Social Structure of Competition*. Cambridge, MA: Harvard University Press.

Drucker, P. (1970). Entrepreneurship in business enterprise. *Journal of Business Policy*, *1*(1), 3–12.

Ewens, M., & Marx, M. (2018). Founder replacement and startup performance.*The Review of Financial Studies*, *31*(4), 1532–1565.

Gabbay, S. M., & Leenders, R. Th. A. J. (1999). CSC: the structure of advantage and disadvantage. In R. Th. A. J. Leenders & S. M. Gabbay (eds), *Corporate Social Capital and Liability* (pp. 1–14). Boston, MA: Kluwer Academic Press.

Greve, A., & Salaff, J. W. (2003). Social networks and entrepreneurship. *Entrepreneurship Theory and Practice*, *28*(1), 1–22.

Knight, F. H. (1921). *Risk, Uncertainty, and Profit*. New York: August M. Kelley.

Kroeger, F., Racko, G., & Burchell, B. (2020). How to create trust quickly: a comparative empirical investigation of the bases of swift trust. *Cambridge Journal of Economics*, *45*(1), 129–50.

Mayer, R. C., Davis, J. H., & Schoorman, F. D. (1995). An integrative model of organizational trust. *Academy of Management Review*, *20*(3), 709–734.

Meyerson, D., Weick, K. E., & Kramer, R. M. (1996). Swift trust and temporary groups. In R. M. Kramer & T. R. Tyler (eds), *Trust in Organizations: Frontiers of Theory and Research* (pp. 166–195). London: Sage.

Moser, K. J., Tumasjan, A., & Welpe, I. M. (2017). Small but attractive: dimensions of new venture employer attractiveness and the moderating role of applicant's entrepreneurial behaviors. *Journal of Business Venturing*, *32*, 588–610.

Navis, C., & Glynn, M. A. (2011). Legitimate distinctiveness and the entrepreneurial identity: influence on investor judgments of new venture plausibility. *Academy of Management Review*, *36*, 479–499.

Pollack, J. M., Barr, S., & Hanson, S. (2017). New venture creation as establishing stakeholder relationships: a trust-based perspective. *Journal of Business Venturing*, *7*, 15–20.

Ryan, A. M. (2012). Applicant–organization relationship and employee–organization relationship: what is the connection? In L. M. Shore, J. A.-M. Coyle-Shapiro, & L. E. Tetrick (eds), *The Employee-Organization Relationship* (pp. 363–389). New York: Routledge.

Sarasvathy, S. (2008). *Effectuation: Elements Of Entrepreneurial Expertise*. Cheltenham, UK and Northampton, MA, USA: Edward Elgar Publishing.

Sinek, S. (2011). *Start with Why: How Great Leaders Inspire Everyone to Take Action*. London: Penguin Books.

Sitkin, S. B., & Roth, N. L. (1993). Explaining the limited effectiveness of legalistic "remedies" for trust/distrust. *Organization Science*, *4*(3), 367–392.

Sorenson, O., & Stuart, T. E. (2001). Syndication networks and the spatial distribution of venture capital investments. *American Journal of Sociology*, *106*, 1546–1588.

Sorenson, O., & Stuart, T. E. (2008). Bringing the context back in: settings and the search for syndicate partners in venture capital investment networks. *Administrative Science Quarterly*, *53*, 266–294.

Sudeck, R. (2006). Angel investment criteria. *Journal of Small Business*, *17*(2), 89–103.

Van Osnabrugge, M., & Robinson, R. J. (2000). *Angel Investing: Matching Start-up Funds with Start-up Companies: The Guide for Entrepreneurs, Individual Investors, and Venture Capitalists*. San Francisco, CA: Jossey-Bass.

Williamson, I. O. (2000). Employer legitimacy and recruitment success in small businesses. *Entrepreneurship Theory & Practice*, *25*, 27–43.

Index